M000205034

Responding to Human Trafficking

PENNSYLVANIA STUDIES IN HUMAN RIGHTS

Bert B. Lockwood, Jr., Series Editor

Responding to Human Trafficking

Sex, Gender, and Culture in the Law

Alicia W. Peters

PENN

UNIVERSITY OF PENNSYLVANIA PRESS

PHILADELPHIA

Copyright © 2015 University of Pennsylvania Press

All rights reserved. Except for brief quotations used for purposes of review or scholarly citation, none of this book may be reproduced in any form by any means without written permission from the publisher.

Published by
University of Pennsylvania Press
Philadelphia, Pennsylvania 19104-4112
www.upenn.edu/pennpress

Printed in the United States of America
on acid-free paper

10 9 8 7 6 5 4 3 2 1

A Cataloging-in-Publication record is available from the Library of Congress
ISBN 978-0-8122-4733-6

To Tara and Kleio, my love and my light

Contents

List of Abbreviations   ix

Preface   xi

Introduction   1

PART I. TRAFFICKING ON THE BOOKS

Chapter 1. A Dichotomy Emerges   43

PART II. THINKING, ENVISIONING, AND INTERPRETING TRAFFICKING

Chapter 2. The Experts Make Sense of the Law   73

Chapter 3. "Things That Involve Sex Are Just Different"   90

Chapter 4. Defining Trafficking Through Survivor Experience   127

PART III. THE LAW IN ACTION

Chapter 5. Intersections on the Ground   151

Chapter 6. Moving the Antitrafficking Response Forward   191

Appendix A. Data Archiving Requirements and Threats
to Confidentiality   205

Appendix B. Interviewees Quoted in the Text   207

Notes   209

Bibliography   225

Index   237

Acknowledgments   243

Abbreviations

AUSA   Assistant United States Attorney

BJA   Bureau of Justice Assistance

CEOS   Child Exploitation and Obscenity Section

CP   Continued Presence

DHS   Department of Homeland Security

DOJ   Department of Justice

DOL   Department of Labor

DOS   Department of State

EAD   Employment Authorization Document

ECPAT   End Child Prostitution and Trafficking

ESL   English as a Second Language

FBI   Federal Bureau of Investigation

GED   General Equivalency Diploma

G/TIP   Office to Monitor and Combat Trafficking in Persons

HHS   Health and Human Services

HRW   Human Rights Watch

HTPU   Human Trafficking Prosecution Unit

ICE   Immigration and Customs Enforcement

IJM   International Justice Mission

NGO	Nongovernmental Organization
NOW	National Organization for Women
ORR	Office of Refugee Resettlement
OVC	Office for Victims of Crime
PICW	President's Interagency Council on Women
PRM	Bureau of Population, Refugees, and Migration
PITF	President's Interagency Task Force to Monitor and Combat Trafficking in Persons
SIJS	Special Immigrant Juvenile Status
SPOG	Senior Policy Operating Group
TIP Report	Trafficking in Persons Report
TVPA	Trafficking Victims Protection Act
USCIS	United States Citizenship and Immigration Services
VAWA	Violence Against Women Act
VSFT	Victim of a Severe Form of Trafficking

Preface

The inspiration for this research came to me as I was traveling around Italy during the summer of 2003 researching the movement and migration of Albanian women into sex-related labor in Italy. As it turned out, the migration of Albanian women to Italy, which had been increasing throughout the late 1990s and early 2000s, dramatically dropped off in the year leading up to my fieldwork there. A number of factors were responsible for this shift, including a recently signed bilateral agreement between the two nations, increasing awareness by Albanian women of Italy as a destination site for "trafficking," and growing opportunities for cheap labor in other parts of Europe. However, the point that struck me most as I spoke to service providers and government bureaucrats about their work with these women (particularly those who qualified for social services as trafficking victims) was the prominence of Italy's new antitrafficking law, known as Article 18, in forming their understanding of "trafficking" and responses to it. I quickly realized that although my planned study was not going to evolve as I intended it to, a more interesting question had formed in my mind: how does the formation, interpretation, and application of law and policy contribute to the social construction of a socially, morally, and legally loaded issue such as trafficking, and vice versa?

The U.S. Congress had recently passed antitrafficking legislation of its own, the Trafficking Victims Protection Act of 2000, and similar issues were arising in cities throughout the U.S. as service providers, prosecutors, law enforcement agents, and government bureaucrats struggled to understand the significance of the law. My research quickly changed course, and I set out to learn all I could about the law and those involved in its implementation, as well as advocacy efforts around the issue of "trafficking." As a result,

I developed the questions driving the research that ultimately became this book and conducted fieldwork between May 2006 and November 2008.

The issue of trafficking is an ideological minefield, and my intention is not to engage in the ideological debates around it. Rather, my goal is to illustrate the ways in which ideology and other cultural and symbolic frameworks are incorporated into the cultural text of the law, through its drafting, interpretation, and implementation. It would be easy to take an ideological stand on the issue, but I believe the more important insights that I offer highlight how the various actors involved conceptualize and talk about the issue, the factors that contribute to their understandings, and the effects on implementation of U.S. antitrafficking law and policy. My goal from the beginning of this research has been to fairly represent *all* of my informants, not to say which of them is right.

Introduction

Everyone up here [on Capitol Hill] knows that trafficking is
something that is bad and that trafficking is modern-day slavery and
therefore horrible, but [they] don't really know what trafficking is,
and so you can totally mischaracterize it in so many different ways if
you're inclined to do so.

—Victor, congressional staffer

A lot of it has to do with how we define trafficking, and even though
we have a federal definition I don't think there's true agreement as to
what trafficking is, as can be seen between all the advocates and all
the law enforcement agents.

—Audra, immigration attorney

In July 1997, four deaf and mute Mexican immigrants—three men and one
woman—entered a police station in New York City and reported via sign language and written notes that they were indentured laborers. Their captors,
Jose Paoletti Moreda and his son Renato Paoletti Lemus, oversaw a ring that
smuggled fifty-seven men, women, and children into the United States. The
fifty-seven individuals were forced to work eighteen hours a day, seven days
a week, selling key chains and other trinkets on subways and in airports
and then turning over their earnings to an "enforcer." When they went out to
peddle their wares, they were told not to return until they had $100 each and
were beaten or sexually abused if they returned with insufficient funds
or tried to escape. Living in two extremely crowded apartments in Queens,
they had freedom of movement, but their "bosses" had confiscated their
personal documents upon arrival in New York City and used them as a means

of control.[1] The novelty of the crime presented a challenge to local officials: the case had elements of extortion but also resembled indentured servitude. The social services needed for this large a group of people were considerable because the disabled migrants were undocumented and had a double language barrier. Public sympathy for the victims and the fact that many New Yorkers had encountered these very individuals in their daily commutes prompted the city to offer an enormous amount of public resources to the victims—providing housing, counseling, monetary assistance, interpreters, job training, and education. However, although the case was highly successful from a victim services point of view, the generous response was not a sustainable model, especially because during the 1990s several similar cases emerged, involving forced agricultural work and forced commercial sex. Existing legislation did not address many of these issues, which authorities handled on an ad hoc basis. The needs of immigrant victims were particularly underserved by existing policies, and as more and more cases involving physical or psychological control and forced labor emerged, so did the need for additional tools for prosecution and victim services.

Signed into federal law in October 2000, the Trafficking Victims Protection Act, or TVPA,[2] was designed to systematically address offenses like those committed in the Paoletti case by criminalizing the forced or deceptive movement of people into exploitative conditions of labor and by providing protections for the immigrant victims of those offenses. Although the law was written to protect anyone subjected to forced labor, six years later as I began fieldwork on the TVPA's implementation I found that a particular form of trafficking—involuntary commercial sex work—was dominating the process. "In my opinion it's worse than murdering someone, to continuously degrade someone like that," Jim, a federal law enforcement agent and the head of a human trafficking unit, told me. "I think about my sisters, my wife, my daughters, what I would do."[3] Despite being charged with enforcing a law that criminalizes both forced commercial sex and other forms of compelled labor, Jim perceived forced prostitution as the most morally objectionable and serious offense under the trafficking umbrella, and he took it as the primary focus of his work. Like many of the individuals I interviewed over the course of two and a half years of fieldwork in New York City and Washington, D.C., Jim assigned victims of so-called sex trafficking a special place in his conception of the issue.[4] Associating a unique type of vulnerability and harm with this form of trafficking and inserting a particular vision of morality into efforts to counter it became a consistent theme over the course of my research.[5] Beyond its recurrence, what became clear was that people held widely varied understandings of trafficking, despite the federal definition established in law. While some still maintained the broad notion of trafficking as forced or coerced labor, many others were relying on much more specific definitions focused solely on commercial sex or cases involving extreme violence. What happened over the course of the decade between the Paoletti case and my fieldwork to cause such divergent conceptions of trafficking?

An ethnography of the U.S. human trafficking response, this book examines beliefs about sex, gender, victimization, crime, and vulnerability as they intersect the drafting, interpretation, and implementation of the Trafficking Victims Protection Act. What has led to trafficking's narrow construction as an issue predominantly about sex? And, more important, how does that affect victims of trafficking? These are two of the central questions with which this book grapples. More broadly, the book aims to uncover the distinct *meanings* that people assign to trafficking and to the elements of the TVPA. Indeed, the law holds changing valences and has different consequences for government bureaucrats, criminal justice authorities, NGO (nongovernmental organization) service providers, and victims of trafficking[6]—and even within these groups the views are not static. The multiple ways in which trafficking is understood reflect professional and political struggles over meaning and the range of language, symbols, and motivations that have become associated with the term. Although the lens of gender and sexuality has most profoundly shaped views on trafficking, it is not the only possible approach, and assumptions about violence, crime, and victimization also frame how the phenomenon is commonly understood.

I make three main arguments throughout the book. First, I argue that the meaning of trafficking is widely contested and not as established as codified law would suggest. Construals of trafficking are informed by a series of complex cultural beliefs and values. Building on this first contention, norms regarding sex and gender, for instance, influence the implementation of law and policy and have real consequences for trafficked persons in terms of their access to benefits and services and the attention given to different kinds of cases. Finally, I argue that victim narratives contest the notion that sexual harm is the most severe form of suffering: victims may even attribute their suffering to a set of circumstances (e.g., isolation, deceit, and threats to their families) entirely different from what various implementers of policy imagine.

The book is the result of two and a half years of multi-sited ethnographic fieldwork conducted between May 2006 and November 2008 in New York

City and Washington, D.C. The majority of my time in the field was spent conducting participant observation at one of the largest and most respected NGOs providing services to trafficking survivors, as well as at law enforcement trainings, court proceedings and prosecutions, congressional hearings, and trafficking-related events. A connection to the NGO service-providing agency served as my entry point into this research and granted me the legitimacy to conduct research on this highly sensitive and politicized topic. Supplementally, I interviewed service providers, law enforcement personnel, government officials, and trafficked persons. Combined with policy analysis, these interviews weave a fabric of simultaneous narratives and discourses on trafficking: the official and dominant discourse produced via federal policy, reports, and speeches; the interpretations of federal and local officials; the accounts produced by NGO service providers serving as advocates, mediators, and liaisons between trafficked persons and the state; and the experiential narratives of trafficking survivors. Drawing on this ethnographic evidence, the book interlaces the perspectives of state agents, service providers, and formerly trafficked persons to present a multidimensional account of the TVPA's spotty and tendentious implementation.

Many have noted the need for in-depth research on human trafficking and its construction. Sociologist Liz Kelly asserts, "How service providers and state agents define trafficking, especially the extent to which they introduce additional requirements which do not appear in the [law] in order to construct a category of 'deserving' victims or ration scarce resources, is seldom studied in any depth."[7] This book fills that gap by examining from an ethnographic perspective the implementation of the TVPA and the complexity of issues arising around this process. Empirical research on trafficking is extremely limited, and ethnography is a particularly strong tool for deciphering struggles over meaning and uncovering the motivations, values, and symbols informing social and legal discourse. It provides an unparalleled ability to capture the complexity of an issue that is too often oversimplified, much as the ramifications of trafficking response are. Trafficking has become an increasingly contested sphere since the passage of the TVPA, and this book stands alone in its examination of the ways that contestation enters the implementation process and affects victims.

Law and policy are enacted by officials with diverse folk knowledges and interpretive systems related to sexuality, gender, and victimization. Due to their varying roles, priorities, and interaction with victims, implementers with distinct relationships to the law often conceive of trafficking in markedly different terms—while law enforcement think in terms of prosecutable cases and may prioritize cases involving forced commercial sex, the service providers I encountered viewed the conditions of work as more defining than the type of work to which victims were subjected. These varied conceptions significantly affect how victims are identified and how they access the protections granted to them under the law. For instance, although NGO providers endeavored to access benefits and protections for anyone they deemed to have been forced, coerced, or defrauded into an exploitative labor situation, criminal justice authorities were sometimes hesitant to take on cases (and provide endorsements for victim benefits) if survivors did not fit their expectations of how trafficking should manifest.

While there is nearly unanimous agreement that human trafficking is a serious and despicable crime, there has been far less consensus on what trafficking actually is and how to approach the problem. Precisely because so many constituencies have a hand in the shape of trafficking policy, the drafting of the TVPA was marred by debates over how to define the crime and who should be considered a victim. The resulting law reflects this discord: ultimately, the law defined trafficking broadly to cover men and women forced into all labor sectors but symbolically privileged exploitation for forced commercial sex in a number of ways. The charge of this book is, therefore, to trace the cultural and symbolic frameworks regarding sex, gender, and victimization as they were incorporated into the drafting of antitrafficking legislation and have been replicated through the interpretation and implementation of the law.

As a function of the multiple individuals, agencies, and agendas involved in antitrafficking work, a cacophony of voices and narratives emerges to circumscribe the idea of trafficking, the value of different types of victims—if we can even speak of such divisions—and the goals of the law itself. Although all are at work on trafficking writ large and guided by the legal text of the TVPA, the bureaucratic process of identifying the phenomenon is tremendously subjective. We learn much when we consider those profound gaps in understanding that pervade implementation as service providers and criminal justice authorities strive to collaborate and perform their duties.

How do the complex social, cultural, and political concerns, anxieties, and norms held by various professionals conspire with legal definitions of trafficking to be translated into practice? And how do the different priorities and institutional cultures of federal agencies and NGOs influence diverse understandings of trafficking and the law? These questions are central to discussions about how to effectively address trafficking in the United States and who is included in or excluded from the response. Despite the fact that the TVPA proffers a definition, there is still much debate—confusion, actually—about what human trafficking is and who counts as its victim.

The views of the federal law enforcement agent Jim are, in fact, aligned with dominant media discourse, which is skewed toward sensationalized stories of "sex trafficking" and informs most of the American public's perceptions of trafficking in general. Indeed, when I ask students in my undergraduate classes whether they know what human trafficking is, I am greeted by a sea of nodding heads followed by some form of the question, "Isn't that, like, sexual slavery?" Although this response, not to mention the media portrayals that reinforce it, is not wholly inaccurate, it reflects a partial and fractured understanding that is highly problematic.[8] The American public is aware of the problem of human trafficking, but the common view of the issue is shaped by superficial pop-cultural treatments based on questionable data and lacking the complexity characteristic of the phenomenon of human trafficking itself. More problematic still is that this skewed perception of trafficking as only "sex trafficking" permeates the United States' response to the issue, particularly in the realm of law enforcement, despite a legal framework that recognizes all forms of forced labor (whether in agricultural settings, factories, restaurants, nail salons, the domestic sphere, commercial sex, or elsewhere) as trafficking and evidence that suggests that upwards of 50 percent of individuals trafficked in the United States have been pushed into sectors other than commercial sex.[9]

In addition to being inaccurate, framing trafficking as an issue of involuntary prostitution has real repercussions for real people. Many media representations of trafficking misinform the public by virtue of being incomplete, but when these misinterpretations infiltrate the criminal justice system, the consequences are dire. When Jim and other law enforcement agents direct their attention to identifying cases of trafficking involving forced prostitution, and when they make a point of signing off on paperwork for those particular victims so they can quickly access benefits and protections, it means that other victims are being overlooked. Despite the equal protections granted under the law to all victims of trafficking, the moral outrage over so-called sex trafficking has resulted in a stratified response. Few are actively searching for additional Paoletti cases, but investigations of sex trafficking are commonplace.

To better appreciate that distortion, this book traces the path of the TVPA over the course of nearly a decade, from its genesis to eight years following its passage, and takes a threefold approach. First, it historicizes and situates the TVPA as a law emanating from a particular social context that continues to reverberate as the law is put into practice. The current conflict over meaning can only fully be understood in the context of a drafting process marred by disputes over the role of prostitution in defining trafficking. Second, the book explores precisely how trafficking is understood by various implementers and the factors that influence these varying interpretations. Despite a broad definition that encompasses trafficking of men and women into all labor sectors, the same dualities that informed the drafting process continue to determine how various implementers conceptualize trafficking, usually through a gendered lens focused on commercial sex. Finally, it analyzes the law's implementation trajectory and its effect on victims, many of whom, I argue, are missing out on the law's promised protections as a result of law enforcement investigators' distorted interpretations of what counts as trafficking. Through this multitiered approach, the book uncovers distinctions between the "law on the books," the "law in their minds," and the "law in action."[10] Because deep-seated beliefs about sex, gender, and victimization situate trafficking for forced prostitution and trafficking in general as significant policy issues, my goal is to illuminate the ways in which these views intersect the drafting, interpretation, and implementation of antitrafficking law and policy.

The narratives I draw on illuminate the gulfs in meaning between the varied groups involved, but these stories also highlight the diversity of beliefs held by individuals within those groups.[11] I have embraced George Marcus's notion that the anthropologist can say more by letting others say it,[12] and the resulting volume is composed of multiple voices and perspectives that augment description of the law's implementation. Individual interpretations of the TVPA, conceptions of trafficking, and application of the law are highly nuanced and not easily characterized based solely on the belief holders' professional roles. In particular, survivor narratives add a type of voice that is often absent from policy debates; they highlight the multiplicity of trafficking experiences lost in the narrative portrait of the "typical" trafficking victim.

By weaving together multiple and simultaneous narratives, it becomes possible to create a more holistic understanding of how trafficking's conceptualization has real-world implications. I analyze how the various actors involved talk about trafficking and sex and the value they attribute to different categories of "victims." Norms regarding sex and gender influence the implementation of law and policy and have significant effects for trafficked persons, which becomes quite serious when we realize that the law has created the conditions for investigators to become arbiters of victim benefits, while service providers and survivors are compelled to plead their cases and present evidence of "victimhood."

My work builds on that of a growing number of feminist scholars and social scientists who have begun to critically explore trafficking through analysis of the TVPA's legislative history,[13] the conflation of sex work and trafficking,[14] the U.S. government's disproportionate focus on trafficking for forced commercial sex,[15] and specific issues surrounding implementation of the law.[16] Scholars have described the pervasive morality and ideology evident in antitrafficking policy and discourse[17] and the symbolic function that the law performs in communicating moral messages.[18] Seeking to uncover the complexities that emerge as a result of the implementation process, this book builds on the work of anthropologists and sociologists who have begun to explore trafficking and the discourses surrounding it through ethnography.[19] Denise Brennan's recently published chronicle of the lived experiences of survivors post-trafficking, *Life Interrupted: Trafficking into Forced Labor in the United States*, is particularly relevant in its poignant and honest analysis of real people's lives, struggles, and successes. Brennan presents an account of the migratory policies that put people at risk for trafficking, the conditions under which trafficked persons (and many other migrants who never earn that classification) labor, and the systems and challenges that formerly trafficked persons navigate as they attempt to move forward with their lives after trafficking. Brennan's ethnographic encounters with survivors and assistance-givers "introduce readers to real people, not mythologized versions of 'trafficked persons.'"[20]

Guided by an interpretive anthropological approach, I have been inspired by work that leverages ethnographic methods to capture the complexity and nuances of varied subject matter.[21] Most closely linked to implementation, Alison Mountz's ethnography of the Canadian immigration system combines the perspectives of bureaucratic actors and those affected by policy implementation in order to demystify state practices. I have embraced her contention that the practices and beliefs of civil servants can be captured with ethnographic research to reveal the taken-for-granted assumptions guiding public policy.[22] In what follows, I look specifically at the ways an ethnographic approach helps to decipher and unravel the meanings and assumptions embedded within U.S. antitrafficking law and policy.

The TVPA as Cultural Text

To make sense of the contested political nature of trafficking, it will be essential to uncover the cultural assumptions embedded within antitrafficking law and policy. Legal and policy institutions order social life, constructing cultural meaning and shaping group and individual identities. Anthropologists Chris Shore and Susan Wright propose that policies be analyzed as freighted cultural texts, calling the issues that laws and policies aim to address "crowded spaces already filled with moral values and preconceptions."[23] Before and after the TVPA, trafficking has been an area of charged values, taboos, and morals, particularly with regard to so-called sex trafficking. By examining the ways in which U.S. antitrafficking law (and related policy) incorporates the social and political context in which it was created, we shall see that the subtle incorporation of cultural norms and assumptions, particularly about sex, into the legal text of the law has further inserted these issues into public discourse and magnified their power and meaning. The greater social meaning attached to (sex) trafficking influences the implementation of law and policy with significant effects for trafficked persons, including decreased access to the law's protections for those who do not meet the cultural stereotype.

Without first probing the law's origins, it is impossible to understand fully why the TVPA's implementation is so focused on forced commercial sex and its consequent effects on victims. Excavating the TVPA's drafting and analyzing its implementation trajectory allows for an explanation of the process that has imbued trafficking with such powerful cultural resonance. Foundational scholarship on law and society establishes that there is always a gap between the "law on the books" and the "law in action," so I take that cue and parse discrepancies between the law as formally prescribed in text and as actually implemented.[24] Since the 1990s, the concept of "legal consciousness" has been used to draw out the ways in which everyday actors experience and understand the law.[25] Juxtaposing the narratives of local and federal officials, trafficked persons, and NGO service providers is key to appreciating those varying levels of legal consciousness.

"Law in their minds," a category proposed by legal scholar Peter Schuck to denote a specific form of legal consciousness,[26] is especially useful for making sense of the implementation process because it is the law in the mind—or the law as it is imagined and interpreted by implementers of the law and those invested in its goals—that helps elucidate the relationship between the law on the books and the law in action. In the case of the TVPA, the way in which trafficking is understood varies depending on who is doing the interpreting, that actor's role in implementation, and his or her personal worldview. Here, the *their* in "law in their minds" refers to the wide range of implementers active in the U.S. antitrafficking response. Schuck notes that groups of actors will identify different aspects of the system or see the same aspects differently.[27] I suggest that in the case of the TVPA, the "law in their minds" is especially important precisely because of the cultural values about sex, victimization, and human rights that were incorporated into the legal text, allowing for manifold interpretations across sectors and by individual implementers.

The painstaking negotiations of language that occurred during the TVPA's drafting ground our conceptions of trafficking today. While all laws are subject to interpretation regarding meaning and application, the TVPA contains an especially complicated and layered definition of trafficking, due largely to the fact that the act was a carefully negotiated compromise emerging out of extensive debates regarding the law's goals and the problem it was meant to address. With incredibly diverse constituencies involved in the negotiations—antiprostitution feminists, evangelical Christians, and human rights practitioners, among others—the resulting law embodies the wide range of values, beliefs, and anxieties held by the parties active in the drafting effort. The TVPA's convoluted and layered definition of trafficking can be interpreted in numerous ways, reflecting the complex legal contours of trafficking as preimagined by various stakeholders and campaigners during the drafting process.[28]

Of particular significance is that the act's definition conceives of trafficking broadly, in all labor sectors, and is gender neutral; however, the law emphasizes sex trafficking (by force, fraud, or coercion) by marking it as a special category distinct from other forms of forced labor. On paper, "sex" and what I refer to as "non-sex" (often referred to as "labor") trafficking appear equal; however, the public imagination perceives the law as targeting the trafficking of women and children for sexual exploitation.[29] Implementation reproduces this codified "gender regime."[30] In practice, the marked category of sex trafficking is privileged in terms of law enforcement identification and victim protection, while the unmarked category of non-sex trafficking serves as a category of exclusion, with its victims often assigned a lower priority in the eyes of law enforcement. Just as anthropologist David Valentine explains the expansion and contraction of the term *transgender* happening contextually,[31] *trafficking*, too, takes on more or less expansive meanings depending on who is utilizing the term. Although the legal definition is broad enough to include men, women, and children whether they are working as nannies, agricultural laborers, or sex workers, in practice investigators like Jim may taper the classification in such a way to exclude a broad portion of those who fall under the legal category. A particular vision of trafficking (forced prostitution) and a specific type of victim (women forced into prostitution) are privileged in complicated ways that divert attention from trafficking into other labor sectors (e.g., agriculture, factory labor, domestic work, and nude dancing) and from men altogether. At stake are differing conceptions not only of *trafficking* but also of authentic victims (and overlooked victims) and of prosecution-worthy cases (and those that are disregarded).

Although the law statutorily defines trafficking, complex interpretive frameworks shape the ways in which varied implementers understand the law and define the phenomenon for themselves. As Audra, an immigration attorney, put it, trafficking "is seen as a non-controversial idea. It's not like abortion or something. Everyone agrees no one should be trafficked, but it comes down to what trafficking is. That's where it all falls apart." Given the complicated history, the law is applied inconsistently, ultimately delivering uneven outcomes for survivors, depending on the sector into which they were trafficked. Although certain victims, usually those trafficked into forced prostitution and those who attract law enforcement attention, easily access benefits, others (in many cases victims of "labor trafficking," and especially men) are obliged to overcome additional hurdles to receive the same protections.

The antitrafficking response is not neutral or objective because what we see upon careful inspection is that the law itself is not neutral or objective. Indeed, when I asked Jim, the federal agent, how he defined trafficking, he quickly responded, "By the statute," implying the statutory criminal definition of trafficking that covers forced labor and forced commercial sex. Yet it became clear that only the sex trafficking portion of the definition held any meaning for him, and Jim's beliefs and investigative efforts mirrored the TVPA's symbolic privileging of sex trafficking. The law applied "in action," as Patricia Ewick and Susan Silbey suggest, "reproduces norms, activities, and relationships that exist independent of the law,"[32] such as the belief that certain victims of trafficking are more worthy than others. While no law is entirely objective and all laws allow for multiple interpretations, the incorporation of sexually infused values into the TVPA creates an extreme set of circumstances and a considerable amount of leeway for those charged with determining what counts as trafficking. Even those working under the auspices of the law assign widely divergent, and often contradictory, meanings to trafficking. Creating a category for sex trafficking within the broader definition has contributed to this confusion and to a sex-dominated discourse on the issue.

Tracing the ways in which the sex/labor split has manifested in U.S. antitrafficking law and policy, I ultimately conclude that this distinction has been counterproductive to the U.S. antitrafficking response. The legal definition of trafficking is comprehensive but breeds exclusivity as a result of its structure and language. By creating two categories of trafficking—"sex" and "non-sex"—the law effectively canonizes a hierarchal approach that is harmful to survivors. As I make clear in the book's conclusion, this imbalance needs to be remedied either by amending the definition or making significant adjustments to implementation policy. My findings make abundantly clear that sex has been disproportionately used to frame the issue, but this book also takes the opportunity to identify some of the specific areas in which policy change is needed. The research is not fully realized until it effects some change.

Putting Trafficking in Cultural Context

Although it harks back to late nineteenth- and early twentieth-century concerns over the "traffic in women," the term *trafficking* is a relatively recent addition to the American cultural vocabulary and only became part of the mainstream vernacular following the passage of the TVPA and consequent media coverage on the issue.[33] Trafficking, in the public imagination, is based on oversimplified and sensationalized narratives of the "sex trafficking" of women and girls that dominated the period during and following the TVPA's drafting. Those stories justifiably attracted lawmakers' and the public's sympathy. Much like the nineteenth-century panic around "white slavery" and the "traffic in women," these early twenty-first-century framings drew on anxieties surrounding the decency, virtue, and purity of women and children, qualities called into question by the trafficking phenomenon. The moral outrage reinforces societal ideals around virginity and monogamy. As I will discuss in Chapter 1, there was a significant contingent of advocates and government officials pushing for a broader conception of trafficking, and there were certainly counternarratives in circulation during the drafting process. Nonetheless, alarmism about the dangers of so-called sex trafficking resonated most with the media, the public, and many lawmakers.

Drawing on Jyoti Sanghera,[34] Elżbieta Goździak and Micah Bump note that "the dominant antitrafficking discourse is not evidence-based but grounded in the construction of a particular mythology of trafficking," which among other things constructs the issue as solely involving prostitution.[35] Yet focusing on trafficking of women specifically into forced prostitution privileges one gender-specific group of victims and conflates trafficking with movement into prostitution. When, within the trafficking paradigm, normative representations of gender and sexuality are used to frame the problem and its solution, other approaches are discounted. Eithne Luibhéid contends that through the process of describing certain identities (e.g., "lesbian" or "prostitute"), the state contributes to constructing the very sexual categories and identities through which policies are then applied; the categories themselves (used to label [in]appropriate sexuality and behavior) take on meaning through the implementation of border policy.[36] In the same way, U.S. antitrafficking law and policy, when combined with normative conceptions of gender and sexuality during the implementation process, influence the construction of victims as women forced into prostitution.

Although the stereotypical trafficking victim is most often portrayed as an innocent young girl who has been lured into the sex industry against her will,[37] few trafficking victims fit this description. First, survivors are men and women, adults and children, and foreign nationals and U.S. citizens who have been compelled into countless types of labor, including work in agriculture, factories, restaurants, nail salons, topless bars, and domestic situations and being made to peddle on subways. Even in cases of forced commercial sex, the majority of women are aware that they will be working in prostitution but are deceived about the conditions or are later exploited.[38] The association of trafficking only with the most extreme cases of victimization and with prostitution sustains the view that there is only one type of victim. State-sponsored policies and reports, as well as media coverage and documentaries, often rely on uncritical representations of victims because they rouse political support, encourage public sympathy, and appeal to socially concerned audiences. As much as the public wants a dramatic story so that its intervention can complete a fairy-tale-like rescue, there is no perfect, morally unimpeachable victim prior to maltreatment. There are, however, perfectly human individuals targeted for exploitation at the hands of the unscrupulous.

Criminologist Nils Christie has noted the paradox between how ideal victims are constructed and the experience of actual victims, describing the ideal victim as "a person or category of individual who—when hit by crime—most readily are given the complete and legitimate status of being a victim."[39] Ideal victims are weak, vulnerable, defenseless, blameless, and worthy of sympathy and compassion. According to sociologist Sandra Walklate, ideal victims are vulnerable, both physically and economically, and they must be identified as *innocent*.[40] The construction of a trafficking victim who appeals to the public and policymakers must be sexually blameless, and antitrafficking policies continue to be based on the notion of the innocent, unwilling victim who is in need of rescue—that is, who was brought to the United States to engage in prostitution against her will. Sexual harm is itself a key component of antitrafficking campaigns, adding emotional intensity to both policy and advocacy efforts. The iconic sex trafficking victim who passively waits for rescue by law enforcement is often viewed in contrast to "undeserving victims" who fit the "illegal alien" stereotype of male migrants who knowingly violate the law to enter the United States and work.[41] This framing is part of what criminologist Chris Greer describes as a hierarchy of victimization that is reflected and reinforced in the media and official discourses: "At one extreme, those who acquire the status of 'ideal victim' may attract mass levels of media attention, generate collective mourning on a near global scale, and drive significant change to social and criminal justice policy and practice (Greer 2004; Valier 2004). At the other extreme, those crime victims who never acquire legitimate victim status or, still worse, are perceived as 'undeserving victims' may receive little, if any, media attention, and pass virtually unnoticed in the wider social world."[42]

Funding follows heartstrings. Victims' stories become a type of currency, the symbolic capital needed to exchange for material resources. This process reduces complicated stories, based in real events, to what anthropologists Arthur Kleinman and Joan Kleinman describe as "a core cultural image of *victimization*."[43] Since the nineteenth century, the somatization of deviance, as Jennifer Terry and Jacqueline Urla call it, has been part of a larger effort to organize social relations according to categories denoting normality versus aberration, health versus pathology, and national security versus social danger. Scientific and popular modes of representing bodies are never purely objective but always tied to larger systems of knowledge production and to social and material inequality.[44] Through norms and representations, the state and its institutions define appropriate and inappropriate forms of sexuality, which only add to the power of law.[45] By attaching notions of crime and violation to trafficked female bodies, the state adjudicates between victims worthy of sympathy and assistance and those that are not.

Current concerns over trafficking, which incorporate narratives of criminality and sexual victimization, have transformed into a full-fledged moral panic that displaces anxieties about female sexuality onto trafficking victims. Sociologist Stanley Cohen defines a moral panic as "A condition, episode, person or group of persons emerges to become defined as a threat to societal values and interests; its nature presented in a stylized and stereotypical fashion by the mass media; the moral barricades are manned by editors, bishops, politicians, and other right-thinking people; socially accredited experts pronounce their diagnoses and solutions; ways of coping are evolved or (more often) resorted to; the condition then disappears, submerges, or deteriorates and becomes more visible."[46] To call the phenomenon a moral panic does not imply that it is not real; rather, it is fully operational as a collective belief that simplifies and distorts reality.[47] In the misleading light of panic, trafficking looks like an issue of purely *sexual* violation instead of forced or coerced labor and service of all stripes. As we all can attest, contemporary conflicts over sexual values acquire immense symbolic weight: trafficking is no exception. Anthropologist Gayle Rubin emphasizes that sexual morality can become a receptacle for other concerns, even unrelated ones: "Disputes over sexual behavior often become the vehicles for displacing social anxieties, and discharging their attendant emotional intensity. Consequently, sexuality should be treated with special respect in times of great social stress."[48] When examined, the discourses around so-called sex trafficking demonstrate that the trafficking issue has been utilized to make larger claims about sex more generally.

Numbers and the Power of Exclusion

Along with tales of sexual horror, shocking estimates of the scope of trafficking further the moral panic surrounding the phenomenon. Because of the covert nature of trafficking, accurate statistics on its prevalence are necessarily difficult to establish. Nonetheless, agencies, advocacy organizations, and media outlets routinely circulate estimates, speculating not only that vast numbers of women and children (usually less emphasis is placed on men) are being trafficked on daily, weekly, and yearly bases but also that the number is actually increasing with every minute that passes. In truth, no accurate estimates of the scope of trafficking exist.[49] As anthropologist David Feingold admits, "The trafficking field is best characterized as one of numerical certainty and statistical doubt. Trafficking numbers provide the false precision of quantification, while lacking any of the supports of statistical rigor."[50]

Estimates gain acceptance through repetition even when their sources are questionable, suggests Feingold's analysis of the origins of trafficking numbers.[51] For example, prior to the passage of the TVPA, a CIA report estimated that 50,000 individuals were trafficked into the United States each year.[52] Although the *Trafficking in Persons Report* downgraded the estimate to 18,000–20,000 individuals in 2003 and again to 14,500–17,500 in 2004, the 50,000 number continued to surface for years after these newer approximations emerged. The shifting estimates themselves raise doubts about the credibility of the methods used to generate them. In fact, a 2006 report, issued by the Government Accountability Office, questioned the reliability of federal government estimates of trafficking to the United States and internationally:

> The U.S. government estimates that 600,000 to 800,000 persons are trafficked across international borders annually. However, such estimates of global human trafficking are questionable. The accuracy of the estimates is in doubt because of methodological weaknesses, gaps in data, and numerical discrepancies. For example, the U.S. government's estimate was developed by one person who did not document all his work, so the estimate may not be replicable, casting doubt on its reliability. Moreover, country data are not available, reliable, or comparable. There is also a considerable discrepancy between the numbers of observed and estimated victims of human trafficking. The U.S. government has not yet established an effective mechanism for estimating the number of victims or for conducting ongoing analysis of trafficking-related data that resides within government entities.[53]

Despite these criticisms, the State Department has yet to reveal details of the methodology used to generate the statistics or update the estimates themselves.

Stories of trafficking tend to be so horrifying that emotion outweighs critical reflection on the veracity of statistics. Although circulating hefty estimates is an effective advocacy and fundraising tool, these numbers rarely reflect the reality of trafficking. Certainly if one person is trafficked, it is one too many, so what could be the harm in relying on large numbers to bring attention to the issue? For one thing, there are massive gaps between the number of estimated victims and the number of victims who are actually identified and benefit from promised protections each year. Relying on the most conservative U.S. government estimates, one would conclude that between the 2000 passage of the TVPA and 2011, the year for which the most recent statistics are available, upwards of 150,000 individuals were trafficked into the United States. Yet, as of the end of fiscal year 2011, only 3,181 individuals (2 percent of the estimated total) were certified by the U.S. government as victims of trafficking.[54] Either the U.S. government is doing a very poor job of identifying victims of trafficking (a question I will explore throughout the book) or the estimates are hugely inflated and inaccurate. Both prospects may be contributing to the problem.

If the estimates do not reflect the total number of trafficked person in the United States, then what do they show? Methodologically, determining how many people are at risk for trafficking versus how many people are actually trafficked is a challenging proposition,[55] and various estimates rely on differing definitions of trafficking, many of which conflate it with prostitution or certain types of migration. Despite estimates that incorporate large numbers of people who are not actually trafficked, in the eyes of the state one is either trafficked or not. Those who fit the criteria are entitled to benefits and protections, and those who fall outside of determined boundaries are excluded. Even relying on the broadest reading of the federal definition, trafficking as a category excludes many others who fall along the spectrum of exploitation. The system prioritizes protecting the most severely exploited but not preventing the conditions that make people vulnerable to trafficking in the first place.[56] Those not meeting the definitional guidelines for having been trafficked may be viewed as criminals and labeled illegal migrants or prostitutes, although as I discuss in Chapter 2, determining whether someone fulfills the criteria for having been trafficked is much more ambiguous a process than it might seem. Rather than providing resources to assist street-involved youth or undocumented domestic workers and agricultural laborers to reduce their vulnerability to exploitation, the policy categorically excludes those individuals until they cross the definitional threshold. Although few would question that intervention once a runaway living on the street has been recruited and abused by a pimp is the right thing to do, there is more reluctance to provide housing or fund job-training programs that would help to prevent that eventual outcome. The U.S. approach to trafficking tends to be driven by a criminal justice focus on prosecution rather than programs designed to prevent trafficking. Helping those at risk does not have the same emotional appeal as rescuing victims *after* they have been trafficked.

The U.S. Antitrafficking Apparatus

Miriam is a 29-year-old mother of two from Mexico. She was smuggled into the United States and brought to New York City by a network of her "boyfriend's" family members. Having seized her documents, her boyfriend-turned-captor repeatedly coerces her into prostitution using threats to harm her children, who are under the care of his mother back in Mexico. He forces her to turn over all of her earnings to him and insists she not speak to anyone beyond the group of women with whom she shares a small apartment. Following a tip from a family member and an extended period of surveillance, Immigration and Customs Enforcement (ICE) agents and local police officers raid the premises. Based on evidence gathered at the scene and interviews with Miriam and the other women, investigators believe Miriam to be a victim of trafficking. ICE refers her to the Empower Trafficking Services Program, an NGO social service support provider.[57] Miriam is assigned a case manager, Laura, who gains her admission to a shelter for victims of domestic violence and begins the process of helping Miriam to secure the benefits she is entitled to under the TVPA.

At this stage, Miriam is pre-certified, meaning she has been identified as a potential victim of trafficking but has not yet been officially classified by the federal government as such. Because Empower receives funding from the Department of Justice's (DOJ) Office for Victims of Crime (OVC) to provide comprehensive case management, Laura must document all of the services she provides or assists Miriam in accessing (intensive case management, food, clothing, shelter, medical and dental care, mental health treatment, translation and interpretation services, immigration legal assistance, and more) and submit regular reports to the OVC administrator in Washington, D.C. Because victims of trafficking interact with multiple domains and agencies—including law enforcement agents, prosecutors, immigration attorneys, health providers, mental health professionals, shelter staff, public benefits administrators, employers, and landlords—having a central case manager is critical to coordinating communication and services.

The criminal investigation of the case is ongoing, so Laura and Empower's immigration attorney, Vanessa, act as liaisons between Miriam, local and federal investigators, and prosecutors. They accompany Miriam to meetings with the Assistant United States Attorney (AUSA) to assess whether she is prepared to offer testimony in the case against her trafficker. Because this is an especially complex case, attorneys from the DOJ Human Trafficking Prosecution Unit (HTPU) in Washington, D.C. are also involved. As Miriam shares information about her time being held against her will, prosecutors work with ICE and local investigators to gather additional evidence in the case.

As the case progresses, Laura advocates on Miriam's behalf, requesting that the lead ICE agent file paperwork asserting that Miriam is, indeed, a victim of trafficking and that she has complied with requests for assistance in the investigation and prosecution of her trafficker. Once the agent completes the form, Laura and Vanessa assist Miriam in compiling the lengthy application materials for the T visa (a nonimmigrant status that allows a foreign victim of trafficking to remain in the United States for up to four years and to obtain an Employment Authorization Document, or EAD, allowing the victim to work legally in the States). After her bona fide application for a T visa is submitted to the Department of Homeland Security's (DHS) Vermont Service Center for processing, the Department of Health and Human Services (HHS) Office of Refugee Resettlement (ORR) issues Miriam a certification letter, which entitles her as a foreign national victim of trafficking to receive benefits and services to the same extent offered to a refugee.

Laura continues to help Miriam access needed services, documenting eligible expenses for reimbursement by HHS. Over the next year, Laura meets with Miriam regularly to evaluate her needs. She helps Miriam find an apartment, accompanies her to file for Social Security, takes her for eye exams, and refers her to counseling. She also helps Miriam enroll in ESL classes, provides job search support, and teaches her about the American banking system and New York City subway navigation. As the court case against her trafficker progresses, Laura supports Miriam through the transitional and rehabilitation process.

Miriam is an amalgam of several of the survivors I came to know and of clients receiving services at Empower, but this vignette illustrates the complex and layered implementation of the TVPA domestically. As a result of the law's passage, numerous professionals, many of them previously unfamiliar with the issue of trafficking, are now investigating the crime, providing services to victims, and assuming various roles in law and policy implementation.

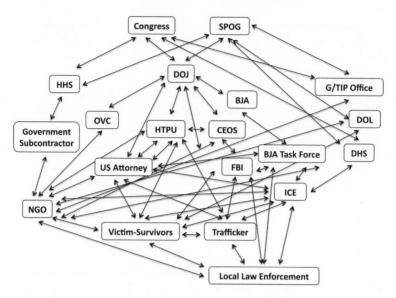

Figure 1. U.S. antitrafficking apparatus. Arrows represent a relationship between agencies/actors.

The government is overseeing funding streams, developing policies and regulations, expanding bureaucracy, and forming task forces to address human trafficking. Multiple actors inside and outside government, with a variety of worldviews and beliefs about trafficking, are now working on the issue with varying degrees of influence within the U.S. antitrafficking apparatus (see Figure 1 and Table 1). The newness of the issue, the vastness of the bureaucracy, and the diversity of institutions and individuals involved with implementation result in numerous possibilities for interpretation and reinterpretation of the law. Although Miriam's story appears relatively straightforward, few cases follow such a clear-cut trajectory, and most, as I will describe in the chapters that follow, are in fact quite tangled and messy as a result of the numerous parties involved. The U.S. domestic response to trafficking includes high-level policy development and oversight, multiple layers of bureaucracy, investigation and prosecution, and service provision. The web-like complexity of the implementation structure and the sheer number of institutions and individuals involved produces opportunities for multiple and conflicting interpretations of the law and of trafficking's meaning

Table 1. Organizational Components of the Antitrafficking Apparatus

Entity	Responsibilities
Federal Government	
Congress	o Drafted and passed TVPA of 2000 o Amends and/or reauthorizes the TVPA every 4 years o Holds committee hearings on relevant issues
The President's Interagency Task Force to Monitor and Combat Trafficking in Persons (PITF)	o Coordinates federal efforts to combat trafficking in persons at the cabinet level o Meets annually and is chaired by the Secretary of State
Senior Policy Operating Group (SPOG)	o Coordinates interagency policy, grants, research, and planning issues involving international trafficking in persons and the implementation of the TVPA
Department of State (DOS)	
▪ Office to Monitor and Combat Trafficking in Persons (G/TIP)	o Funds international antitrafficking programs o Produces the annual *Trafficking in Persons Report*
▪ Bureau of Population, Refugees, and Migration (PRM)	o Funds the Return, Reintegration, and Family Reunification Program for Victims of Trafficking
Department of Justice (DOJ)	
▪ Human Trafficking Prosecution Unit (HTPU) (housed within the Criminal Section of the Civil Rights Division)	o Holds primary responsibility for the forced labor, sex trafficking, involuntary servitude, and peonage statutes o Oversees prosecution of highly complex cases, primarily involving adults o Assists and advises U.S. Attorney's Offices on the prosecution of human trafficking cases
▪ Child Exploitation and Obscenity Section (CEOS)	o Holds primary responsibility for prosecution of cases of domestic minor sex trafficking
▪ Bureau of Justice Assistance (BJA)	o Funds local antitrafficking task forces

(*continued*)

Table 1 (*continued*)

Entity	Responsibilities
▪ Office for Victims of Crime (OVC)	o Provides funding for pre-certified survivors of trafficking
▪ FBI	o Responsible primarily for investigation of cases involving domestic minor sex trafficking or other U.S. citizens
▪ U.S. Attorney's Offices	o Responsible for prosecution at the district level
Department of Homeland Security (DHS)	
▪ Immigration and Customs Enforcement (ICE)	o Responsible for investigating cases of human trafficking domestically and abroad o Provides training and support to international and domestic law enforcement
▪ United States Citizenship and Immigration Services (USCIS)	o Awards T visas and coordinates with ICE's Parole and Humanitarian Assistance Office on awarding continued presence status
Department of Health and Human Services (HHS)	
▪ Office of Refugee Resettlement (ORR)	o Provides certification for foreign victims of human trafficking to confer eligibility for benefits and services under any federal or state program to the same extent as a refugee o Provides funding for case management and victim assistance, public awareness, and identification of foreign and internally trafficked victims in the United States. HHS funds the Rescue & Restore public awareness campaign and the National Human Trafficking Resource Center
Department of Labor (DOL)	
▪ Wage and Hour Division	o Investigates complaints of labor law violation that may lead to the identification of trafficking
Local	
State and local police departments	o Cooperate with federal authorities in the investigation of human trafficking

Table 1 (*continued*)

Entity	Responsibilities
Nongovernmental Organizations (NGOs)	o Provide intensive case management (including shelter and housing referrals, supportive counseling, assistance with material needs, facilitation of access to public benefits, legal assistance, and criminal justice advocacy) and immigration assistance to survivors. Coordinate with law enforcement and other service-providing agencies
	o Deliver training and technical assistance

and significance more generally. I interviewed policymakers, bureaucrats, and implementers at all of these levels; incorporating their diverse views makes for a rich, textured picture of the machinery working to address trafficking.

Multiple federal departments and agencies, including the Departments of Justice, State, Labor, Health and Human Services, and Homeland Security, administer layers upon layers of bureaucracy to address the problem. Within these departments, manifold programs and offices are now devoted to trafficking policy, program implementation, grants administration, investigation, prosecution, victim services, and so forth. Within the Justice Department, the Human Trafficking Prosecution Unit in the Civil Rights Division shares responsibility with the Child Exploitation and Obscenity Section (CEOS) for prosecuting human trafficking crimes and depends on the cooperation of U.S. Attorneys in districts around the country.[58]

On the investigative side, the Federal Bureau of Investigation (FBI) and ICE have human trafficking programs at headquarters in Washington, D.C. as well as regional investigative units. Federal law enforcement agents often work in conjunction with state and local police departments, in many cases serving on Bureau of Justice Assistance (BJA)–funded task forces together with federal prosecutors and local service providers.

Through contracts and subcontracts to a number of NGOs, HHS funds comprehensive services for victims of trafficking. OVC provides additional funding for services; grantees include organizations with varying focuses, such as human trafficking, victim services, refugee resettlement, immigrant issues, violence against women, and the commercial sexual exploitation of children, as well as faith-based groups.

NGOs have traditionally stepped in where governments fail to or are unable to take initiative and are well suited to work with trafficked persons who, due to their undocumented or illegal status, may fear and distrust state-based organizations.[59] When providing services to trafficking survivors, NGOs act as mediators between them and the state, delivering direct services and comprehensive case management to survivors as well as coordinating access to shelter, general health and mental health care, legal services, job skills training, educational services, and cultural support. In many ways, state actors serve as gatekeepers to benefits, while NGOs act as buffers, advocates, and mediators. Because the law complicates interactions between trafficking survivors, service providers, and various criminal justice authorities, NGOs offer a unique vantage point from which to explore victims' experiences.

For all of these players working in these diverse capacities, defining trafficking and establishing "what counts" is crucial to implementing their individual pieces of the TVPA. Yet what counts may vary depending on who is making the interpretation and on the purpose for which they are using the law. As Dvora Yanow cautions, "All language, objects, and acts are potential carriers of meaning, open to interpretation by legislators, implementers, clients or policy 'targets,' concerned publics, and other stakeholders. At the same time, they are tools for the recreation of those meanings and for the creation of new meanings."[60]

"Studying Through" the Antitrafficking Apparatus

Clearly, the U.S. government's response to trafficking is highly complex, involving multiple and intersecting layers of bureaucracy, investigation and prosecution, and service provision. Despite hours spent poring over government reports and scanning agency websites, prior to initiating my fieldwork I could assemble nothing beyond a surface-level picture of the work being done. Much as Alison Mountz found during her ethnography of the Canadian immigration system, I realized that "the policies of the state are enacted amid tension and difference, but higher-level bureaucrats and communications employees construct coherent narratives for the public, which tend to provide relatively little insight into what actually took place."[61] Although

I had read the glossy-covered reports and understood that the United States was responding to trafficking by investigating the crime and funding services to victims, it was not clear *how* exactly the process worked. Ethnography, the process of careful listening and systematic observation as a means of un-covering taken-for-granted meanings and beliefs, became an especially useful tool for deciphering the precise responsibilities and mapping the complex connections between the myriad governmental and nongovernmental agen-cies involved in the antitrafficking apparatus. Working ethnographically—that is, in a way that privileges people (*ethno-*) over or in combination with text and other types of data—allowed for uncovering the contradictions be-tween policy as written and policy as imagined and operationalized. One of the advantages of ethnography, as anthropologist Steve Herbert asserts in his study of community policing, "is that it enables social meanings and pro-cesses to be rendered understandable through the actual words of residents and the actual practices of important actors like the police."[62] Although the U.S. government's "Three Ps" framework of prosecution, protection, and prevention provides a superficial sketch of the goals of TVPA implementation, the words and actions of real-life implementers are what actually reveal the underlying meanings and their regeneration as policy unfolds. Long-term research engagement enables the ethnographer, more than other kinds of re-searchers, to establish relationships based on trust and rapport. The in-depth quality of the research creates the conditions for decoding what Clifford Geertz described as "a multiplicity of complex conceptual structures, many of them superimposed upon or knotted into one another, which are at once strange, irregular, and inexplicit."[63] The web-like complexity of the antitraf-ficking apparatus begs for this rich, embedded type of investigation.

Since the late 1990s, scholarship on trafficking has expanded exponen-tially. While the topic was once confined to the realm of journalism and NGO reports, there is now growing interest within academe. However, the major-ity of writing on trafficking is not buttressed by empirical research but rather by legal analysis, social commentary, or reviews of the literature.[64] Empiri-cal research on trafficking has been limited due to its time-consuming demands, the clandestine aspects of the phenomenon, and the inherent challenges of accessing survivors and institutional actors involved in anti-trafficking work.[65] The present study outright avoided some of these obsta-cles (by focusing on implementation of the law rather than trafficking per se) and surmounted others, including dedicating more than two years to field-work and simultaneously earning the trust of hard-to-reach and hesitant research populations. While the bulk of research on trafficking focuses on one particular group (e.g., NGOs, law enforcement, or survivors[66]), my goal was to look at the connections between all of these groups by interacting with and observing them directly.

Anthropology has evolved significantly since Laura Nader's original plea for "studying up,"[67] and ethnographers have moved from solely studying the "managed" to also researching the "managers" and deciphering complex bureaucracies. Because policy involves the governed as well as the governors,[68] this book investigates the messy linkages between the two. Anthropology's ground-up approach offers an important counterpoint both to the top-down approaches usually applied to policy issues and to the oversimplified and sensationalist accounts that dominate media coverage of trafficking.[69] Because of the myriad methodological challenges that exist in conducting research on trafficking, I will elaborate on my research strategy in some depth. Although it is typical to limit such discussion to dissertations or to relegate them to appendices, the lack of data and politicized nature of the field necessitates situating the research and explicit description of method to distinguish it from simple commentary as well as from literature driven by ideology and sensationalism.

Delineating the Field for Participant Observation

The implementation of the TVPA occurs at many levels in multiple locations across the country, but research centered primarily on New York City. I looked at the metro region as a case of trafficking implementation at the micro level, with additional fieldwork focused on macro-level policy in the nation's capital. This diversified research strategy allowed me to explore connections between policy implementation from the bottom up and the top down. The New York metro area is a major entry point for migrant workers from around the globe: the city sustains high demand for cheap labor and boasts a thriving market for commercial sex. New York is home to multiple organizations providing services to trafficked persons and has one of the country's largest concentrations of individuals receiving that vital certification as victims of severe forms of trafficking. During my fieldwork, at least six NGOs were providing legal and case-management services to trafficked persons. In addition, there are often connections between antitrafficking efforts in New York City and those on Long Island and in New Jersey. This made it an ideal setting for exploring the implications of U.S. trafficking law and policy.

Since the late 1980s, anthropologists have problematized the notion of "the field"—as the isolated, bounded third-world village of traditional anthropological research—and proposed broadening the sites of anthropological inquiry.[70] George Marcus, for instance, advocates multi-sited ethnography, suggesting that the anthropologist can say more "by juxtaposing multiple levels and styles of analysis."[71] This ethnography takes that possibility seriously and relies on multiple narratives and sources of information to provide a complex and holistic view of the implementation of U.S. antitrafficking law and policy. Anthropologists Shore and Wright note, "The sheer complexity of the various meanings and sites of policy suggests they cannot be studied by participant observation in one face-to-face locality. The key is to grasp the interactions (and disjunctions) between different sites or levels in policy processes. Thus, 'studying through' entails multi-site ethnographies which trace policy connections between different organizational and everyday worlds, even where actors in different sites do not know each other or share a moral universe."[72] While I spent a year observing one NGO that easily could have been the entire subject of the ethnography, my field site went far beyond that locale, as my true focus was on the process of implementation and the social and political space surrounding it. Studying the process of implementation meant that "the field" for me was actually many field sites, which I describe below, as I became immersed as a participant observer in New York City's antitrafficking community.

In addition to these diverse sites of observation, I also expanded "the field" to include various legal records, policy documents, and archival materials, treating these documents as valuable sources of ethnographic data and analyzing them as cultural texts. Over the course of my fieldwork, I complemented participant observation and interviews with archival research on the drafting of the TVPA and reviewed key legislative and policy developments related to trafficking in the United States—this included studying the congressional records and the legislative history of the TVPA and its reauthorizations, reviewing government and nongovernment websites and reports, and tracking media accounts of trafficking. I also tracked indictments, trial briefs, and other legal documents.

Entering the Field: Accessing the Antitrafficking Apparatus

Gaining access to the antitrafficking community was initially challenging. Knowing that as a researcher I would be met with hesitation and skepticism,

I spent my first year of fieldwork familiarizing myself with the local topography of antitrafficking work and making myself a familiar name and face within the milieu by attending trafficking-related events and meetings that were open to the public, sending explanatory e-mails to various organizations, and gradually making connections. At first I found that antitrafficking insiders held anyone labeled a researcher at arm's length. Although there was a notable dearth of empirical research on the topic when I began my fieldwork, professionals were nonetheless hesitant to participate in research studies; the issues are so highly politicized, and they understandably feared misrepresentations and negative depiction. Service providers staunchly protect their clients, who are vulnerable to exploitation by the media and researchers who swoop in to collect career-making data and never look back. These were concerns I shared, and I made every effort to demonstrate my dedication to protecting research participants and my desire that the research would ultimately be used to inform and improve future policy.

I was lucky to establish a connection early on with one of the key figures in New York City's NGO community. While a mutual acquaintance had vouched for my credibility and I had provided a lengthy written description of my research plan, the palpable turning point when I made real headway in earning her trust occurred when I described declining a sizable research grant from the National Institute of Justice because it would require me to compromise the confidentiality protections I had built into my study (see Appendix A for a detailed discussion of the incident and how ethical and safety concerns conflicted with research funding requirements).[73] Once our mutual commitment to protecting privacy was established, she started introducing me to other key service providers. Gaining the endorsement of a trusted member of the antitrafficking community made all the difference in moving the project forward: although others were still hesitant to speak with me, the referral helped me get in the door to make a case for my research and explain that I was hoping to provide a holistic account of how all the pieces of the implementation process fit together. People soon recognized that I was not out to villainize their work or make my career and leave for the next project. My results would ultimately have practical value for them.

As I gradually became acquainted with the various actors composing the antitrafficking community, I contacted organizations receiving federal trafficking funds, reached out to individuals at network meetings, and sought out referrals from my existing contacts. I also gained credibility through the connection to my NGO field site, which was pivotal to securing interviews with the program's law enforcement and government contacts in both New York and Washington, D.C. This combination of targeted and snowball sampling methods proved to be very effective. Through a series of sixty in-depth interviews I was able to collect accounts from individuals from all corners of the U.S.'s domestic antitrafficking response, including twenty-one NGO service providers (case managers; social workers; client advocates; administrators; and immigration attorneys representing organizations devoted to immigrant rights, victim services, refugee resettlement, sex workers' rights, and combating commercial sexual exploitation of children) from twelve organizations; thirteen law enforcement officials (including federal and local agents, victim witness coordinators, and federal prosecutors) from seven agencies or offices; six government bureaucrats from four agencies; and eight congressional staffers involved in the drafting and/or reauthorization of the TVPA. (See Appendix B for a table of interviewees and their roles.) Although I faced some obstacles in penetrating bureaucracies—for example, waiting nearly six months for Empower's Institutional Review Board to approve my application for research and negotiating with one law enforcement officer for another six months until he finally approved my research request and then promptly retired, leaving me to start the process over with a new officer—in almost all cases my requests for interviews were granted. My commitment to confidentiality meant that interviewees were generally willing to be very open about their thoughts and frustrations regarding the TVPA implementation process.

Once my fieldwork was in full swing, I became entrenched in the daily activities of antitrafficking work across the city, while also extending my reach to chronicle the history and bureaucracy of antitrafficking implementation in Washington, D.C. During a typical week I might arrive at my main NGO field site, Empower, on Monday morning for a staff meeting followed by an afternoon of reviewing client charts and attending a financial literacy seminar for clients. The next day I would travel to D.C. for a hearing of the House Judiciary Committee on the reauthorization of the TVPA followed by two days of interviews with congressional staffers and a smattering of federal administrators. Back in New York, I would spend another day immersed in the routine activities of Empower, ending the week by attending a training designed to help members of the local police department identify trafficking. In addition, I became a regular attendee and participant observer of meetings for a city-wide antitrafficking service provider network and of national conferences, where I noted how staff members from separate organizations talked about forced labor and the specific issues that continually resurfaced as areas of negotiation and contestation. I also attended other public events, such as city council hearings, public roundtables, and awareness events hosted by NGOs, advocacy groups, and universities. On the government side, I went to trainings and conferences hosted by and geared toward law enforcement and a variety of court proceedings (including sentencing hearings for several high profile cases). Because the antitrafficking community in New York is relatively small and most members tend to be deeply invested in the issue, I often saw many of the same people at events held across the city and spoke to attendees with varying roles—shelter advocates, court employees, and state trafficking specialists, for example. My primary NGO field site requires more explanation due to the extended amount of time I spent there and the level to which I became immersed in it.

During my second year of fieldwork, I spent approximately three-and-a-half days per week, over the course of twelve months, conducting participant observation at a large NGO providing services to trafficking survivors in New York City. Over time, I was incorporated into the Empower team as an honorary member. Program staff assigned me a cubicle in an area with two case managers. I attended weekly staff meetings, sat in on client meetings and workshops, helped organize files, reviewed documents, and chatted casually with staff regarding case updates. I was included as a member of the team on group e-mails and attended social events with program staff. When my scheduled year of fieldwork with Empower came to an end, I continued to attend weekly staff meetings for several months in order to maintain a link to the antitrafficking world.

My connection with the organization allowed me to directly observe implementation of the law from the service provider's side and to witness the ways in which social service activities intersected with the criminal justice sector. Speaking with providers and observing their activities on an almost daily basis, I was able to observe the impact of law and policy on their and their clients' interactions with law enforcement, collaborations with other NGOs, and the process of securing funding for the organization and its clients. Empower also provided a critical link to survivors of trafficking, without whose voices this project would not be complete.

Interviewing Survivors

Six survivors of trafficking, who had received or were currently receiving services from Empower, granted me interviews, and these conversations in particular warrant elaboration because talking with crime victims presents some distinct methodological challenges. Although there are ethical considerations involved in conducting research with all human subjects, survivors of trafficking are an especially vulnerable group, making sensitivity to their safety and careful planning vital to the research process.[74] Protecting the identities of crime victims is paramount in preventing retaliation from traffickers, stigmatization by coethnics (for bad judgment and poor decision making), and intrusions by the press. Conducting research with a vulnerable population requires balancing the safety and well-being of participants with the political need to bring attention to the issue. There is always the risk that researchers may misrepresent trafficking survivors when they "speak" for them;[75] however, I have done my best to accurately represent the stories of the survivors I met, relying on their own words to describe relevant experiences when possible and being cognizant of the potential impact of sharing their accounts with a broad audience of readers.[76]

When it came to recruiting survivors to participate in my research, I viewed my NGO service provider contacts-cum-colleagues as important intermediaries in the process. While the act of retelling the trafficking story can be cathartic for some, it can be retraumatizing for others. Though my intention was not to ask specific questions about the trafficking experience, it was important to ensure that the participants were emotionally stable and comfortable speaking about their experiences even generally. Many survivors experience a deep loss of trust as a result of being trafficked, so it was crucial to work with case managers who had already formed trusting relationships with survivors and were able to convey initial information about the study and my credibility. I deliberately waited until I had established firm associations with the case managers at Empower before attempting to initiate interviews with survivors so that the providers felt comfortable introducing me to their clients.

My goal was to capture the meanings these survivors assigned to their own lives, not only in terms of trafficking but also more generally. I avoided inquiring about survivors' trafficking experiences, instead asking about growing up in their home countries, their career aspirations, how they left their trafficking situations, and their experiences working with NGOs and law enforcement. However, given the open-ended structure of the interviews, most survivors chose to elaborate on their trafficking situations, citing a hope to assist in research on trafficking and to "help other people" in similar situations. I kept in touch with several of the survivors, speaking by phone, e-mail, and in person at NGO-sponsored events. Most survivors also gave me permission to review their case management charts, which provided contextual information about their trafficking experiences, any criminal prosecutions related to their cases, and access to federal benefits. Along with the six life history interviews, I spoke informally with a number of additional survivors at empowerment groups and other events; I also joined several survivors and their case managers in meetings, going to medical appointments, conducting shopping trips to Target, and making calls to law enforcement and other agencies, and I draw on their experiences in my analysis as well.

There are two potential and related limitations with this group of survivors—the small sample size and the fact that I included only those referred by service providers. (I was interviewing a total of sixty individuals and conducting participant observation at the same time, so it was time prohibitive to interview a large number of individuals from any one group.) The small sample size is the result of those time constraints and an inherent ceiling on the number of survivors who were emotionally ready and willing to participate in the research project. The sample of survivors is small, but the triangulation that occurred through interviewing service providers and observing the daily activities at Empower allowed me to confirm that the survivors I did interview were not outliers or categorically distinct from other survivors enrolled in the program in any significant way. While I conducted formal interviews with six survivors, I was actively involved in discussions surrounding all of the more than thirty clients enrolled at Empower during the course of my fieldwork, and many of the issues that came up in the survivor interviews also came up in discussions with providers—from Empower and other NGO programs—describing other clients.

The majority of research on trafficking in the United States has focused on survivors who have officially been recognized as victims of severe forms of trafficking.[77] Brunovskis and Surtees note that there are likely systematic differences between assisted and unassisted victims and that it is important to recognize which victims are included and omitted from studies.[78] Because the goal of my research was to examine the implementation of the law, the choice to focus on survivors receiving services from NGOs was deliberate. Although my findings cannot speak to the experiences of those survivors who never access services, my fieldwork did allow me to observe how the current system works for some survivors and harms others. As I will discuss in Chapter 5, my work highlights some of the specific ways in which law enforcement overlooks certain survivors who subsequently have difficulty accessing benefits legally afforded them.

As with all ethnographies, this one is a product of the historical moment in which it was conducted. As a result, this book focuses primarily on the implementation of the TVPA as it relates to *women*. Although almost all of the NGOs that I worked with and most law enforcement agents had encountered male trafficking victims (sometimes many of them) in the past, during the time of my fieldwork there were very few active cases involving men in the New York City area. I did encounter male survivors from time to time, but my interaction with them was limited due to language barriers, the victims' ages (under eighteen), and their stages of recovery. All of the survivors I interviewed were women in their twenties and thirties, but they emigrated from three continents with a range of backgrounds. One woman had a fourth-grade education, while another had completed college prior to being trafficked and was attending law school at the time I was writing this manuscript. The women had been forced into various sectors, including domestic labor, sex work, nude dancing, and retail.

The Trafficking Taboo

The sensitive political nature of trafficking complicated the methodology. Given the relatively small size of the antitrafficking community, almost everyone is familiar with the other professionals working in the field. Some informants were hesitant to be interviewed because of the volatile political climate during the second Bush administration, which coincided with my fieldwork. For example, Fran, who was overseeing a federal grant program, initially expressed concern when I asked whether I could record her interview. "Well, you've seen the headlines," she remarked as explanation for her worry about being quoted saying anything potentially not in line with the Bush administration's focus on sex trafficking. Her fears were not unfounded, as I will discuss in later chapters. Although some individuals self-censored, in other cases I encountered official efforts to uphold approved talking points. During an interview I conducted with representatives from one federal agency, not one but two public affairs representatives sat in to monitor the interview. While this made it exceptionally difficult to elicit much beyond the agency's official message, thankfully this type of oversight was the exception rather than the rule. Others asked to review any of the direct quotes that I used and wanted to be assured they would not be identified by name or job title—even those no longer working in the antitrafficking apparatus. Some informants asked me to turn off the recorder when answering certain questions.

Despite concerns that participants would not be open about their experiences, I found most antitrafficking professionals to be extremely supportive of my research. When I attended one annual conference for the second year in a row, I was astounded by how many people from other regions of the country approached me to give updates on their work, have lunch, or discuss matters casually. Some long-term informants expressed genuine disappointment when I could not attend the third year due to financial constraints and writing commitments. Similarly, as I made contacts with law enforcement and government professionals, I began to receive phone calls and e-mails inviting me to upcoming trainings and events. Survivors with whom I became acquainted through my time at Empower would chat with me in the hall or stop and embrace me en route to meet with their case managers. Over and over, people commented about the dearth of research on trafficking in the U.S. and their enthusiasm to read my findings.

Because of the sensitive and politically charged nature of my research, I have tried to obscure the identities of my informants as much as possible while still contextualizing their perspectives. All names are pseudonyms, with the exception of those individuals speaking at public events. The descriptions of informants' job titles are purposely vague. To preserve confidentiality, I changed the job titles of certain individuals and gave some more than one pseudonym. While I interviewed federal prosecutors from both the DOJ HTPU in Washington, D.C. and at the district level in New York, I do not attach this information to content that the prosecutors shared. I have provided especially limited biographical information on survivors, in some cases withholding even country of origin. Any case details I have disclosed are available in public court documents or media accounts.

The Limits of Ethnography

While multi-sited ethnography has expanded the ethnographer's ability to explore complex topics and cross boundaries, the research scope nonetheless requires a high degree of focus. Ethnography's greatest strength is its level of depth and detail, often delivered at the expense of generalizability. Many of my findings could easily apply to the implementation of antitrafficking law and policy in cities across the country, but others are uniquely tied to New York, the site particular to this research. Because of the volume and long history of cases in New York, criminal justice officials there often held very fine-tuned understandings of the issue that might not be evident in other geographic areas. The level of experience held by NGO service providers and prosecutors in the area is notable. Several of the organizations I observed had worked on trafficking cases prior to the passage of the law and consequent appropriation of funds for services. As a result, their dedication to the issue was driven by long-standing values as opposed to a desire to follow government funding streams. In her work on institutional responses to sex trafficking in three countries, Dewey notes that many NGOs enter antitrafficking work because of competition for donor funding rather than a commitment to assisting survivors;[79] however, I did not find this to be the case with the NGOs I observed.

As is to be expected in any ethnography, some of these site-specific particularities prevent broader generalization. Nonetheless, the experiences and beliefs of the investigators, providers, and survivors that I came to know illuminate the meanings that trafficking takes on within the broader context of implementation. Because the field was more dispersed than in most traditional ethnographies, I was able to speak with individuals from multiple sectors and even multiple organizations within sectors, allowing for observation and analysis of wider patterns. For example, I observed the TVPA sex/labor split's impact on implementation in the New York City context, but by talking with providers at national conferences and bureaucrats in Washington, D.C., I was able to determine that this divide was part of a larger pattern and not an isolated response. Certainly further research is needed to illuminate the diverse ways this phenomenon is playing out in cities across the United States and the specific consequences for survivors.

Although this study illuminates many of the challenges to the U.S. government's domestic implementation strategy, it does not address the international scope of the TVPA and the foreign policy implications of the law. Under the TVPA, the U.S. government actually established standards for other countries in terms of prevention of human trafficking, prosecution of traffickers, and protection of victims. The Trafficking in Persons (TIP) Report is the U.S. government's principal tool for monitoring and ranking foreign governments on their progress, and the Department of State (DOS) places each country annually onto one of three tiers based on the extent of its government's efforts to comply with the "minimum standards for the elimination of trafficking" found in Section 108 of the TVPA. Several authors[80] have analyzed the ramifications of the United States acting as what Janie Chuang terms "Global Sheriff," granting itself the authority to rank other nations on their efforts to combat trafficking. In-depth ethnographic studies of how those rules affect lived experiences in diverse locales are also greatly needed.

Structure of the Book

The book is organized into three parts, reflecting the framework of the law "on the books," "in the mind," and "in action." Part I of the book is composed entirely of Chapter 1 and presents the historical foundation on which the remainder of the book is based. In its development and drafting, the TVPA emerged as a cultural text grounded in a series of heated social and political debates around prostitution, victimization, and human rights. It is this backdrop that contextualized the resulting law and from which many implementation issues stem. Although the TVPA definition of trafficking gives the illusion of fairness by covering male and female victims forced into any labor sector, several compromise elements of the definition skew interpretation and application of the law toward trafficking of women into forced prostitution. Through this excavation of the TVPA's underpinnings and of the social and political context in which the drafting occurred, it becomes possible in subsequent chapters to make sense of the complex ways in which trafficking is conceptualized by those implementing the law.

To explicate the law "in the mind," Part II, "Thinking, Envisioning, and Interpreting Trafficking," explores how various individuals involved in or affected by TVPA implementation understand trafficking and make sense of the law. Chapter 2 focuses on NGO service providers, immigration attorneys, law enforcement agents, and prosecutors. Compromise elements in the law created the space for implementers to incorporate additional factors (e.g., cultural and moral frameworks about sex, professional biases, and past experiences with trafficking) into their understandings as they translate the legal definition into meaningful action. While the law on the books appears relatively fair, it is at this interpretive stage that a narrower, more exclusionary vision of trafficking starts to emerge. Even those most intimately connected to the law have difficulty defining exactly what trafficking is.

Chapter 3 explores how interpretive frameworks about sex, gender, and victimization operate for implementers across the antitrafficking apparatus. The chapter begins by introducing four individuals involved in implementation—two from the criminal justice sector and two with expertise in victim services—and their diverse perspectives on the significance of sex to trafficking. The narratives highlight the "special" status assigned to so-called sex trafficking, particularly among law enforcement, and the ways that service providers call into question this distinctive treatment. The heated negotiations over the meaning of trafficking and the goals of the law continually resurface in the conceptions of trafficking held by those implementing the TVPA. The chapter describes how many of the most common misunderstandings revolve around the special status assigned to sex and sex trafficking, including the conflation of trafficking and prostitution, the reduction of all trafficking to forced commercial sex, and the prioritization of sex over non-sex trafficking.

Chapter 4 opens with five life histories of trafficking survivors—those whom the TVPA was designed to protect. We then follow the issues that the survivors themselves chose to emphasize, including their lives prior to trafficking, memories of being trafficked, the meanings they ascribe to their experiences, how they escaped, interactions with law enforcement and service providers, and efforts to rebuild their lives after trafficking. The second part of the chapter argues that the experiences of trafficked persons challenge the ways in which trafficking is most commonly imagined. Drawing on the language of NGO service providers, the chapter highlights the ways these individuals express agency and transition from victims to survivors. The chapter delves into the meanings that trafficked persons assign to their own experiences. Interviews and observation with survivors and service providers, along with case analysis, illustrate that trafficking survivors and the situations they endure are not easily characterized.

Part III takes as its core the intersecting legal and conceptual understandings in the law's application. In providing services, identifying victims, prosecuting traffickers, and accessing resources, the meanings that involved professionals assign to trafficking influence the work they do. Chapter 5 explores how the law as written combines with the law as imagined, ultimately resulting in a highly uneven implementation. I contend that the combination of inconsistencies in the law and the discretionary powers of law enforcement agents as "street-level bureaucrats"[81] results in huge meaning gaps in terms of what counts as trafficking, and in particular who counts as a victim. While protection for all victims could be read from the letter of the law, its execution privileges criminal prosecution of sex trafficking instead. The chapter describes the complex implications for trafficking survivors, who often experience long delays in accessing the protections promised them under the law.

The book concludes with the discussion of one particular case that was especially successful from law enforcement, service provider, and victim perspectives. Although the case reveals a model for successful NGO–law enforcement cooperation, it is also limited to a very particular set of conditions that are not present in most cases. I argue that the factors that made this particular case successful—sympathetic victims forced into commercial sex, law enforcement's role in identifying the case, and agreement between law enforcement and service providers on how to respond to victims—make it an exception rather than the norm and point to some of the interpretive struggles that overshadow cases not meeting these criteria. The case's ideal conditions raise questions of how to successfully respond to less than ideal cases. In the latter part of the chapter, I describe the ways that the TVPA and its implementation have succeeded and the areas where improvement is most needed. Hopeful that the ethnography will inform institutional change, I present policy recommendations based on the evidence I collected over the course of my fieldwork.

A Solution or a New Problem?

Despite being part of the inspiration for the passage of the TVPA, the case involving the Mexican immigrants forced to peddle trinkets mentioned in the opening pages remains one of the few instances involving forced labor to grab headlines or serious law enforcement attention in the New York area. As I wrapped up my fieldwork in 2008, a newspaper headline read, "4-foot-10 Mexican 'mini-madam' facing slave trial,"[82] reflecting the sensationalized spotlight on so-called sex trafficking but also the law enforcement focus on the issue, since many of the trafficking stories reported are drawn from the prosecutorial record. The one newsworthy "non-sex" case at the time involved a Long Island couple who had enslaved two Indonesian women as domestic workers in their home. The case captured headlines and the interest of law enforcement when one of the women walked into a Dunkin Donuts bruised and wearing only pants and a towel. One article reported that the women "spoke of starvation, beatings, and torture. Their compensation of $100 a month for working 17-hour days with no days off amounted to a wage of roughly 20 cents an hour."[83] Although the women had not been trafficked for commercial sex, the abuse they experienced was so obvious that it was impossible for law enforcement to overlook. The exploiting couple was convicted on numerous charges, including forced labor, and the survivors were awarded special visas reserved for trafficking victims.

Yet the cases of numerous other trafficking survivors identified during this same period of time never made headlines, their traffickers were never prosecuted, and in many cases the victims did not receive in a timely manner the benefits or immigration status they were entitled to under the law—all because the details of their cases did not fit into the dominant cultural narrative of trafficking that governed the decision-making practices of law enforcement agents. As I will document, many of the survivors I encountered, especially those trafficked for involuntary "non-sex" labor, faced significant obstacles in obtaining protections promised to them under the TVPA because their experiences were not "horrific enough" or they did not appear "vulnerable enough" or they simply didn't make "good victims" for a number of other reasons. When we look at the factors that have led to this situation, it becomes clear that although the Trafficking Victims Protection Act provided a solution to the service and immigration needs faced by the immigrant victims of the Paoletti case, that solution has resulted in new problems of interpreting the meaning of trafficking.

PART I

Trafficking on the Books

C h a p t e r 1

A Dichotomy Emerges

There is no single, correct solution to a policy problem any more
than there is a single correct perception of what that problem is.
—Dvora Yanow, *How Does a Policy Mean?*

Angela, a former federal policy advisor who was actively involved in discussions about defining and addressing human trafficking during the drafting and early implementation of the TVPA, reflected during our conversation on the ease with which I used the language of the act: "It's interesting to hear you talk about 'force, fraud and coercion' . . . that phrase might not necessarily have rolled off the tongue 10 years ago, because we were still trying to figure out what words [to use] . . . You're just like, 'force, fraud and coercion,' but . . . when you think about it . . . how do you identify what the harm is and then reduce that to words in a statute? And a lot of thought went into that." Identifying and agreeing on the harm of trafficking was a highly contentious process. And though no law can be understood outside its social and political context,[1] background is especially critical to understanding the TVPA and its implementation. Without knowledge of this context, we risk blaming issues of execution on the professionals themselves as opposed to a law embedded with a deeply divided history. In the pages that follow, I culturally excavate and reconstruct the TVPA's drafting, drawing on transcripts of congressional hearings and the accounts of congressional staffers and federal employees who were active in the effort and thus hold unique insight into the process.

The intricacy of the "law on the books" is due largely to the fact that the TVPA was a carefully negotiated compromise emerging out of extensive debates regarding the goals of the law and the meaning of trafficking. The effort to draft the law was dichotomous due to divergent visions of trafficking, and the definition being used today is simultaneously ambiguous, if not paradoxical (in that some activities with no legal consequences, e.g., movement into prostitution, are labeled "trafficking"), and overly specific (in that trafficking into forced prostitution is marked as a special category). This definitional complexity contributes to extensive confusion and mystification of related policy, resulting in uneven implementation of the law and contributing to the invisibility of certain victims. Ambiguity results in uneven treatment. The TVPA definition of trafficking gives the illusion of fairness by covering male and female victims trafficked into any labor sector; however, several compromise elements in the law, resulting from debates over how to define trafficking, skew interpretation and application of the law toward trafficking of women into forced prostitution.

The TVPA is a highly bifurcated law. It has two main goals: prosecuting traffickers and protecting victims. As a result, there are two levels of definitions—one for victims of trafficking and another for the crime of trafficking—and two competing groups of professionals trying to implement the law—NGO service providers and criminal justice authorities. In addition, the law distinguishes between "severe" and "nonsevere" forms of trafficking, that is, those forms of trafficking that have legal consequences and benefits for survivors subjected to them and those that do not, and in reality do not constitute trafficking at all. The term "severe" became a way to differentiate forced, coerced, or defrauded labor or sex from voluntary movement into prostitution, which antiprostitution advocates maintained should also be called trafficking. On top of these bifurcations, there is another that has created more problems than any other: the definitional distinction between severe forms of "sex" and what I label "non-sex" (the catch-all for everything except sex trafficking) trafficking.

The Roots of the Law: Toward a Definition of Trafficking

While notions of trafficking first arose nearly a century prior to the TVPA, and cases of involuntary labor and forced prostitution had surfaced in the United States throughout the last two decades of the twentieth century, renewed interest in "trafficking"[2] emerged in the late 1990s and was rooted in anxieties over globalization, migration, organized crime, and women's sexuality. Jeffrey Weeks notes, "The political moment—that period when moral attitudes are transformed into formally political action—can be of key importance in nuancing the regulation of sexuality, and at crucial times a moral schema has been of prime significance in political propaganda."[3] In the two decades preceding the political moment when the TVPA drafting was taking place, feminist activism around issues including rape, domestic violence, sexual harassment, and child sexual abuse had been especially successful. A particular strand of feminism grounded in notions of sexual victimization, as opposed to the possibilities afforded by increased agency, prevailed in the media and popular culture.[4] As a result of the emphasis on addressing violence against women at the Fourth World Conference on Women in Beijing, China, trafficking entered the global political spotlight, framed as a gendered issue and a violation of women's human rights.[5]

The first step toward an official U.S. policy on trafficking occurred in March 1998, when President William Jefferson Clinton issued an executive memo on trafficking in which he referred to "the problem of trafficking in women and girls" as "an insidious form of violence." The president declared, "Here in the United States, we have seen cases of trafficking for the purposes of forced prostitution, sweatshop labor, and exploitative domestic servitude. The victims in these cases often believe they will be entering our country to secure a decent job. Instead, they are virtual prisoners, with no resources, little recourse, and no protection against violations of their human rights."[6] The memo continued by laying out what would become the administration's antitrafficking strategy of prevention, protection, and prosecution—"the Three Ps"—and went on to charge the President's Interagency Council on Women (PICW) with coordinating the U.S. government's domestic and international policy on trafficking. Along with the Council on Women, Clinton tasked the secretary of state and attorney general with examining current treatment of victims, reviewing existing criminal laws, developing strategies to protect and assist victims, aiding the international community, raising awareness, and generating strategies to combat trafficking.[7]

From the beginning, the Clinton administration's stance on trafficking was multidimensional in that it addressed trafficking into all labor sectors, and it quickly grew to include not only "women and girls" but also men and boys. Following the issuance of the executive memo, interagency working groups quickly formed to assess the situation of trafficking both domestically and internationally. From the administration's point of view, there was a crime to be addressed (forced and coerced prostitution or labor) and victims to protect (through prevention and the provision of services). Angela, the former federal policy advisor mentioned earlier, told me about the importance these interagency groups placed on defining the problem of trafficking: "People really hoped that if we just keep working hard at trying to define what trafficking is in a way that we think is fair and honest and reflects what the problem is, it will give us the tools we need to address trafficking in all its forms." As part of the government team assigned to the issue, Angela believed it was imperative to come up with a "fair" and broad definition of trafficking and not to define it too narrowly. This issue of definition was key because in 1998 there was no agreed-upon concept of trafficking. Governments and organizations were still trying to understand and document the problem.

Within the U.S. government, the phenomenon was being conceptualized as modern-day slavery,[8] a term distinguishing the "modern" methods of coercion used to control victims from the physical and legal means used during chattel slavery—and existing laws were viewed as insufficient to address the ways in which it was occurring. The post–Civil War slavery and peonage statutes covered certain elements of this more "modern" phenomenon but were lacking in areas such as psychological coercion and protections for the "new" types of victims being harmed. Victim protections became paramount as cases emerged of men and women being lured to the United States by promises of well-paying jobs, forced into servitude, threatened and mistreated, eventually freed by law enforcement, and then deported to their home countries because of their undocumented status. The idea of formulating a new law to address these inadequacies grew.

Concurrent with the government's interagency effort, Congress started acting on the trafficking issue. Although a number of congressmen and congresswomen were active in drafting antitrafficking legislation, two men led the effort: the late Democratic senator Paul Wellstone of Minnesota and Republican representative Chris Smith of New Jersey. Senator Wellstone became interested in the issue when he encountered trafficking victims while traveling overseas with his wife, Sheila. He and his colleague Senator Sam Brownback (R-Kansas), who came to understand trafficking through the lens of slavery in the Sudan, both viewed the issue as encompassing trafficking into any forced or coercive labor.[9] In 1998, Senator Wellstone introduced a resolution of concern on the worldwide trafficking of persons,[10] and he followed up in March of the following year by introducing the International Trafficking of Women and Children Victim Protection Act of 1999.[11] Although the bill's title emphasized trafficking of women and children, its definition of trafficking was gender neutral and covered trafficking into all labor sectors.

Republican representative Chris Smith of New Jersey, meanwhile, introduced the Freedom from Sexual Trafficking Act of 1999 to the House in March of that same year.[12] Prior to the trafficking issue, Smith was best known for championing the rights of religious minorities and as cochair of the House's Pro-Life Caucus.[13] Chuck Colson, the evangelical activist, and Michael Horowitz, senior fellow at conservative think tank the Hudson Institute, introduced Smith to the issue of sex trafficking.[14] As a result, Smith's initial bill was limited to trafficking as forced commercial sex acts.

Neither of these bills made it out of committee, but both Wellstone and Smith were dedicated to the issue, introducing new bills in November 1999. Wellstone introduced the Comprehensive Antitrafficking in Persons Act of 1999,[15] which maintained that trafficking was broad in scope; Sam Gejdenson (D-Connecticut) sponsored the companion bill in the House.[16] Chris Smith introduced the Trafficking Victims Protection Act of 1999,[17] a compromise bill combining his and Sam Gejdenson's (and thereby Senator Wellstone's) earlier bills. The bill ultimately became the template for the Trafficking Victims Protection Act of 2000 and reflected the divergent views held by its odd-bedfellow sponsors Smith and Wellstone. This bill was broader than Smith's previously introduced legislation in that it covered both sexual and nonsexual forms of compelled service, but it specifically delineated forced prostitution as separate from trafficking into other sectors. Additionally, the bill included a definition of "sex trafficking," which as conceived of in the bill did not require any elements of force, fraud, or coercion; the legislation therefore covered *any* movement into prostitution. Hoping to move legislation forward, Paul Wellstone and Sam Brownback introduced similar bills in the Senate.[18]

Although all parties ultimately agreed upon a bill, the path to compromise was a long one, with its twists and turns reflected in the ambiguity of the final law. As these bills made their way through the House and Senate, negotiations took place on many interconnecting fronts: several congressional committees addressed trafficking in hearings, the government formed working groups, and various NGOs and think tanks initiated lobbying efforts.[19] On the government side, the Departments of Justice, State, Labor, and Health and Human Services, as well as the President's Interagency Council on Women, were all actively involved in discussions of what the bills should include. A number of contentious points were debated, including sanctions against countries not making significant efforts to address trafficking, labor protections, victim benefits, and immigration remedies, but the most controversial was so-called sex trafficking. Core concerns revolved around whether the new law should focus solely on forced prostitution or cover trafficking into all work sectors and whether consent was relevant to involuntary sex work; that is, could someone freely choose to work in prostitution, or is all prostitution inherently coercive and therefore all prostitution should be considered trafficking?

While one group of supporters viewed the specific marking of "sex trafficking" a distraction to the overall purpose of the legislation, the other believed it should be the centerpiece of the law. Representative Chris Smith adamantly believed that a U.S. antitrafficking law should solely address trafficking into forced prostitution as a uniquely horrific act, and he became the chief proponent in Congress of this perspective. Because most Democrats viewed trafficking more broadly and believed Smith's focus was too narrow, the role of sex trafficking in the law became a key sticking point. During review of the Freedom from Sexual Trafficking Act of 1999 in the Subcommittee on International Operations and Human Rights of the House International Relations Committee, Representative Cynthia McKinney (D-Georgia) remarked, "As important as sexual trafficking is, it is only one reason why people sell other people. People are also sold into bonded sweatshop labor and into domestic servitude and this is not just a labor issue. These are all slavery-like conditions often involving sexual exploitation by the employer as well. We ought to look for a way to deal with all of these conditions at once."[20] She noted elements common to all forms of trafficking and endorsed the approach taken by Senator Wellstone and Representative Gejdenson in their companion trafficking bills.

In response to the criticism of his narrow view, Chris Smith proclaimed "sexual trafficking" a singularly abhorrent act. "The evil we address in the Freedom from Sexual Trafficking Act is uniquely vile, uniquely brutal, and cries out for its own comprehensive solution."[21] The next month, at another hearing on Trafficking of Women and Children in the International Sex Trade, Smith acknowledged that trafficking was far-reaching in scope but reemphasized his commitment to sex trafficking as a unique harm:

> Our bill explicitly recognizes that international sexual trafficking is not the only form of traffic in persons. Innocent people are lured, pressured, and lied to every day all over the world in all kinds of situa-

tions, and I take second place to no one in my commitment to ending all labor practices that are coercive, deceptive, or otherwise improper, or even when they involve labor that is not in and of itself inherently degrading. The problem with addressing all of these evils in one bill, the idea that one size fits all, is that they involve [a] wide range of different situations which may call for an equally broad range of solutions. So we decided to start by attacking the most brutal form of trafficking, I believe, the use of force and deception in the systematic degradation of millions of women and children, and singling it out for swift and certain punishment.[22]

Smith's comments about "the most brutal form of trafficking" reveal entrenched beliefs about the "inherently degrading" nature of prostitution and highlight a fundamental discomfort with the exchange of sex for money. Indeed, the sexual component of trafficking, rather than its coercive nature, was what attracted Smith and other conservatives to the issue. The notion of *women* being coerced into *commercial sex* was viewed as indisputably more horrific and "evil" than any abuse (including noncommercial sexual abuse) experienced by women coerced into other labor sectors (e.g., domestic work or agriculture) and more appalling than any harm potentially experienced by men. For Smith and others, trafficking was an issue of moral purity confined to women and children, and this perception of forced commercial sex as the worst form of trafficking has persisted into the implementation process, as I will describe in Chapter 3.

NGOs, Advocates, and Lobbyists Seek to Define the Issue

Within Congress, the disagreement regarding trafficking into forced commercial sex versus trafficking into all sectors was split primarily along party lines, with Republicans favoring a bill focused solely on sex-related trafficking and Democrats pushing for a law covering trafficking into all labor sectors.[23] Outside of Congress, views crossed traditional right/left boundaries in complicated ways. Because the drafting of the TVPA was happening simultaneously with the drafting of the optional UN Protocol to Prevent, Suppress, and Punish Trafficking in Persons, Especially Women and Children, discussions regarding definitions for the two instruments became intertwined.[24] Much of the public debate on the issue occurred around the drafting of the UN Protocol, while most lobbying around the

TVPA took place behind the scenes. The protocol defined trafficking broadly to encompass all forms of labor and services, but the drafters endlessly debated the role that force, fraud, and coercion would play within that definition when it came to commercial sex.[25] These questions were quickly incorporated into the TVPA negotiations, and in this context, the subject of the debate and lobbying efforts on the issue shifted to how sex trafficking would be defined.

As Barbara Stolz explains, the enactment of the TVPA "is, at least in part, a story of interest groups educating policymakers about a shocking and heinous social problem and defining a 'new crime' with global dimensions and corresponding societal responses. In so doing, the groups set the criminal justice policy agenda."[26] Special interests included religious conservatives, antiprostitution feminists, and human rights advocates, among others. Representatives from the Florida Immigrant Advocacy Center, the Global Survival Network, Human Rights Watch (HRW), the International Justice Mission (IJM), the Protection Project, the Southern Baptist Convention, the Women's Commission for Refugee Women and Children, and other agencies testified at congressional hearings on the issue.[27] Stolz notes that the groups constituted two spheres of interest—what she refers to as the "antiprostitution sphere" and the "human trafficking sphere," each composed of diverse clusters of organizations and individuals.[28] The antiprostitution sphere (sometimes referred to as "the abolitionists") focuses primarily on trafficking into prostitution and includes conservative, faith-based, and some radical feminist organizations. The groups in this sphere generally believe that sex trafficking is more serious than other forms of forced labor, they conflate prostitution and trafficking, and they seek to end the demand for prostitution. Alternatively, various human rights, public health, labor, and migration organizations constitute the human trafficking sphere. These groups and individuals advocate for construing "human trafficking" to include forced movement into all work sectors, including involuntary prostitution and compulsory labor. They take the position that trafficking can happen to anyone in any sector as long as force, coercion, or deception is present or the individual is under eighteen years of age.[29] These two opposing spheres symbolized the disjunction and lack of agreement regarding the meaning of trafficking and how "it" should best be addressed.

During negotiations for both the TVPA and UN Protocol, discussions became particularly tense regarding the relevance of consent and the presence of force, fraud, and coercion in trafficking for prostitution. Lobbying groups such as the Human Rights Caucus (a coalition of human rights organizations advocating for a broad definition of trafficking) argued for a definition that recognized women's agency: "Obviously, no one consents to abduction or forced labour, but an adult woman is able to consent to engage in an illicit activity (such as prostitution, where this is illegal or illegal for migrants)."[30] A roundtable made up of human rights activists, scholars, and professionals and devoted to the "Meaning of 'Trafficking in Persons'" concluded, "With respect to the *definition* of trafficking, the nature of the work or relationship is not the key. The crucial elements of trafficking are the exploitative or servile conditions of the work or relationship and whether or not those conditions are consented to through the exercise of free will."[31]

The Clinton administration took a position generally in line with the "human trafficking sphere" groups that including force and deception in the definition was necessary in order to distinguish between trafficking and prostitution and to recognize variations in the legal status of prostitution across nations.[32] During his testimony to the Senate Foreign Relations Committee, Harold Koh, Assistant Secretary of State for Democracy, Human Rights, and Labor, specified the need for force, fraud, and coercion as defining elements of the crime of trafficking. He emphasized that the *conditions* of work or services, as opposed to the *type* of work or service performed, were the core of any trafficking offense and noted the many iterations trafficking could take. In response, Senator Wellstone asked Koh to specifically address the prostitution issue that rested at the heart of the debate: "Can I just ask you to speak to . . . whether or not we are talking about voluntary prostitution versus forced prostitution, this whole key question . . . I see more division around this question than any other, and I would like to get your testimony on this." Koh responded by referring to the UN Protocol definition and making a clear delineation between prostitution and trafficking: "Our position is very clear that prostitution is a practice we would like to eliminate. We abhor it, and we certainly do not want in any way to endorse it, or to help it. The issue arises in important part in the [UN] Protocol that is being negotiated . . . and trafficking is described therein as basically trafficking across borders by reason of force or deception or coercion, and does not include voluntary acts."[33]

In contrast, antiprostitution groups argued that trafficking should include all forms of recruitment and transportation for sex work, regardless of the presence of force or deception.[34] A diverse range of groups supported this argument, but the language was generated by the feminist abolitionist movement, which equates all prostitution with sex trafficking (or sexual slavery) and sees sex-trafficking victims as in need of rescue.[35] Adherents to this position view all prostitution as sexual violence and exploitation, which victimizes all women, reducing them to sexual objects. If there can be no distinction between forced and voluntary prostitution, then prostitution cannot truly be consented to because it "reduces women to commodities for market exchange."[36] Antiprostitution activists saw the trafficking issue as a lever they could use to make headway on their prior commitment to eradicate sex work across the board.

In response to the Clinton administration's position, conservative Christians and antiprostitution feminist groups—two poles of the "antiprostitution sphere"—launched a barrage of attacks. For conservative Christians and evangelicals, the issue of trafficking, and sex trafficking in particular, was an example of depraved moral behavior that violated the principle that sex should be reserved for marriage between a man and a woman.[37] As Jacqueline Berman notes, "The mere existence of prostitution is antithetical to their moral system. Thus, constructing human trafficking as sex trafficking allows the Christian right to reiterate and reinvigorate their other ideological positions, ultimately equating loose sexuality with criminality."[38] Debates around the TVPA became a way for conservatives to engage in "human rights" work and put a moral spin on trafficking that reinforced a particular conception of sexuality.

Conservatives William Bennett and Chuck Colson wrote an opinion piece in the *Wall Street Journal*, "The Clintons Shrug at Sex Trafficking," decrying the administration's efforts to distinguish between forced and voluntary prostitution in both the TVPA and the UN Protocol:

"In defining the term sexual exploitation, the administration has supported using the phrase forced prostitution rather than simply prostitution. In this instance the adjective forced makes all the difference. If the administration's position is accepted, the focus of attention would shift from the profiteers who traffic in women to the supposed state of mind of the victimized women." They continued, "Even if it were practical to distinguish between consent and force in such cases, the administration's position would still contradict common sense and decency. Prostitution and pornography inevitably exploit women, whether they consent to it or not."[39] Not only do words such as *decency* highlight the moral tone of the article, but the title of the piece itself raises another issue: the lack of agreement on demarcating trafficking allowed groups and individuals on either side of the debate to ascribe meaning to the phenomenon in any way they wished. Although it may have been more accurate to title the piece "The Clintons Shrug at Prostitution" (and this would be itself an oversimplified claim), Bennett and Colson exploited the ambiguity of language so that the reader might surmise from the headline that the Clintons shrug at *forced* prostitution. Bennett and Colson argued there was no difference between prostitution and forced prostitution, but their choice of language helped normalize this hotly debated claim.

Exploring the seemingly perplexing alliance between Christian groups and radical feminists around the issue of "sex trafficking," Berman suggests,

> Shared views of sexuality, prostitution, the role of morality in public life, and universalist constructions of women have combined to produce a conflation of trafficking in women and prostitution that has made possible the alliance between conservative Christians and radical feminists in the fight against human trafficking. This conflation reduces all human trafficking to sex trafficking, which in turn is reduced to prostitution. However, their particular vision of prostitution is one in which all women in the sex industry are seen as exploited victims without any specific agency of their own. For both of these groups, there is no debate about whether this is the correct view or understanding of prostitution. Rather, it is this shared view of, and focus on, prostitution that creates the bond between two such seemingly disparate groups.[40]

Antiprostitution feminists responded with views similar to those of conservative Christians on defining human trafficking in U.S. antitrafficking legislation. A coalition of feminist organizations sent a letter to Senator Wellstone regarding his International Trafficking of Women and Children Victim Protection Act,[41] which construed trafficking broadly. The letter (signed by Jessica Neuwirth of Equality Now, Gloria Feldt of Planned Parenthood Federation of America, Patricia Ireland of the National Organization of Women, Dorchen Leidholdt of the Coalition Against Trafficking in Women, Eleanor Smeal of the Feminist Majority, Gloria Steinem, and others) urged altering the definition of trafficking "to reflect the international consensus that the transport of human beings for the purpose of sexual exploitation constitutes trafficking, regardless of whether or not such persons have 'consented' to their exploitation."[42] The letter requested dividing the definition into two parts—sex trafficking and labor trafficking—with the requirement of force, fraud, and coercion limited solely to the latter. Citing a rarely used 1949 UN Convention concept of trafficking, the signatories argued, "Exploitation, rather than coercion, is the operative concept."[43] However, their application of this concept was limited to commercial sex, so the definition they proposed encompassed an uneven conception of trafficking that left the language of "force, fraud, and coercion" attached to labor exploitation only but categorized all movement into prostitution as trafficking.

Linking "Trafficking" to "White Slavery"

The rejection of the distinction between forced and voluntary prostitution and the reference to an "international consensus" by abolitionist feminists in the letter cited above alluded to a half-century-old international treaty with roots going back another half century to the "white slavery" campaigns taking place at the turn of the twentieth century. The term *trafficking in women* first emerged as part of the campaigns against white slavery that erupted in the late nineteenth and early twentieth centuries; they depicted young and naïve, innocent women lured by evil traffickers into horrendous and inescapable circumstances.[44] Much like trafficking, the term *white slavery* meant different things to different people, ranging from all prostitution, to crossing international borders for the purpose of prostitution, to the forceful abduction and transport of women for prostitution.[45] Not unlike current concerns about "sexual slavery" and "sex trafficking," outrage about white slavery was powered by evangelicals and female abolitionist reformers. A necessary objective of these white slavery abolitionists was to gain public sympathy for prostitute-victims. Thus, the white slave image broke down the separation between voluntary and involuntary prostitutes, constructing all prostitutes as victims and appealing to the sympathies of the middle-class reformers. Doezema argues that so-called white slavery was largely mythical and very few actual cases were reported; rather, stories of white slavery were triggered by actual increases of women, including prostitutes, migrating from Europe to find work in the U.S. So narratives about both white slavery and trafficking in women express deeper fears and anxieties about women's sexuality and independence, the breakdown of the family, migration, and racial and national purity.[46] As Gayle Rubin has noted, anxieties over social questions are often transformed into sexual ones.[47]

In response to the issue of so-called white slavery, a series of international treaties and federal statutes emerged to address the "traffic in women." A 1904 international agreement required signatories to collect information regarding the procurement of women abroad for "immoral purposes."[48] The 1910 International Convention for the Suppression of the White Slave Traffic went further by criminalizing anyone who "in order to gratify the passions of another person, has procured, enticed, or led away, even with her consent, a woman or a girl under age, for immoral purposes" across borders.[49] As the term *traffic* implies, these early conventions were limited to the process of recruitment and transportation and did not require nations to criminalize prostitution, forced or otherwise.[50] In 1910, the U.S. Congress also passed the White-Slave Traffic Act (more commonly known as the Mann Act), which prohibited interstate transportation of women for "immoral purposes."[51] Following several decades and the authorization of numerous other international conventions, the United Nations passed the Convention for the Suppression of the Traffic in Persons and of the Exploitation of the Prostitution of Others (the "1949 Convention") to consolidate the earlier treaties on trafficking. While the 1949 Convention does not explicitly define trafficking, it penalizes procurement, regardless of consent, in international and domestic trafficking for prostitution.[52] Its extension into domestic policies on prostitution prompted only a few member states to sign on to the 1949 Convention (the U.S. did not ratify it); nevertheless, it is this notion of trafficking that antiprostitution feminists and conservative Christian groups supported during the drafting of the UN Protocol and the TVPA. It is widely believed that the 1949 Convention defines prostitution as trafficking. However, legal scholar Janie Chuang suggests that a UN report issued pursuant to the convention reveals that the drafters did not intend to regulate or prohibit prostitution but rather wanted to work toward the abolition of the "exploitation of prostitution."[53] While abolitionist groups advocated keeping the spirit of the 1949 definition (which applied regardless of consent), others argued that it was precisely because of this limited and inadequate definition that it was necessary to establish a broader, updated definition of trafficking.[54]

Reclaiming and Redefining "Trafficking"

Over the course of the 1990s, the term *trafficking* took on increasingly greater legal significance. The U.S. government had been tackling a number of crimes falling under the umbrella of trafficking (including peonage and involuntary servitude) since the ratification of the Thirteenth Amendment in 1865, so the issue was not entirely new. However, as various interest groups adopted the word *trafficking* to describe particular issues, the term absorbed manifold meanings. *Trafficking* resonated with various groups because it was descriptive of the cross-border movement common in many forced labor cases and because it recalled the image of "traffic in women" that abolitionist feminists hoped to restore. As Mark, a federal prosecutor, told me, incorporating the term *trafficking* was not a straightforward process.

> The story of slavery and trafficking . . . over the last fifteen years can . . . be described as people come in with whatever their pet issue is, try to say that that's what this is, and then [we have] to push back and force people to look at the thing more broadly with the focus being on the underlying denial of freedom as opposed to the type of work, or the type of slave, or type of services that are involved. Because first it's . . . let's have a sweatshop working group. Well no, it's gotta be bigger than that. Then, of course, everybody's like, let's do something about trafficking of women and children as a result of the First Lady's participation in the Beijing conference, and kind of suddenly you get this importation of the term *trafficking* into what had been a perfectly good involuntary servitude and slavery program.

Trafficking becomes everything to everyone, a convenient but vague container for axes needing grinding. Mark continued by discussing the repercussions of this change in terminology: "Eventually then it starts being called 'trafficking' as opposed to 'involuntary servitude' and 'slavery' . . . So the 90s were kind of a grudgingly accepting the term *trafficking* to be imposed upon [our] pre-existing work." For Mark and other members of the federal government, *trafficking* became a new way to describe crimes previously conceptualized as involuntary servitude, peonage, and slavery; however, the change of terminology had broader consequences than merely renaming the U.S. government's involuntary servitude program. The new attention to prostitution and the reclaiming of the term *trafficking* redefined the issue. "The problem with *trafficking* the term, of course, is that trafficking is understood by most people since 1880 to mean moving women for prostitution," Mark emphasized. As a result, taking on trafficking meant taking on all of the thorniness and complexity tied to any issue involving sex.

Part of the role of the TVPA was transformational in nature—an old crime was taking on new meaning and significance. A number of my infor-

mants who were involved with the drafting talked about what it meant to create a federal crime of trafficking. Paul, a federal policy advisor, noted, "Just
about everything that has been prosecuted under the TVPA probably could
have been prosecuted under other statutes. . . . But even though we could have
prosecuted those things under the existing law, I think it was very important from the United States' perspective to be seen as a leader in the area and
pass a statute that had a crime called 'trafficking' because we were encourag-
ing everybody else in the world to do it, and other countries did not have the
tools that we already had." Although the government had a variety of criminal statutes to use to prosecute cases, the types of cases that emerged during
the 1990s highlighted criminal law's insufficiency as a solution to the problem. Over the second half of the twentieth century, prosecutors utilized Civil
War–era peonage and involuntary servitude statutes[55]—combined with extortion, kidnapping, and alien smuggling statutes, as well as Mann Act
charges—to address trafficking-like crimes; in the 1990s it became clear that
a new approach was needed, including service provision for immigrant victims. Two cases created what Mark, the federal prosecutor mentioned above,
described as a "perfect storm" effect, leading the Clinton administration to
focus on issues of worker exploitation: the El Monte sweatshop case and the
Miguel Flores case. In 1995, police discovered seventy-two Thai garment
workers being held in a guarded factory in El Monte, California. The opera-
tor of the factory had lured the workers to the United States with promises
of employment, but upon their arrival she forced them to work up to twenty-
two hours a day under threats and with physical violence. They were paid
less than a dollar an hour. The Los Angeles U.S. Attorney's office charged the
factory operators with involuntary servitude, criminal conspiracy, kidnapping, and smuggling and harboring aliens.[56] Two years later, in 1997, Miguel
Flores and Sebastian Gomez were charged with involuntary servitude, extortion, and firearms violations as well as harboring aliens, among other
charges. Flores and Gomez forced more than 400 men and women, mostly
indigenous Mexicans and Guatemalans, to work ten- to twelve-hour days, six
days per week, harvesting vegetables and citrus under the watch of armed
guards for as little as $20 per week.[57]

The Flores case, as it has become known, in particular created a blue-
print for tackling trafficking cases. Due to the large number of forced laborers,
federal authorities were forced to collaborate with service organizations to
meet victim needs. This model of working with NGOs to provide services to
victims was incorporated into the TVPA along with the provision of federal

benefits and immigration relief. Although some members of Congress argued that undocumented immigrants would falsely claim they were trafficking victims in order to gain immigration status, it was ultimately decided that these benefits were needed to gain victim cooperation in trafficking prosecutions. As I will describe in Chapter 5, the process of obtaining victim benefits and immigration relief is so cumbersome and complex that even authentic victims are often unable to successfully access these entitlements. Concerns over others cheating the system have proven to be misplaced.

Two additional cases significantly informed the bill: the Paoletti case in New York and the Cadena case in Florida. Combined with the El Monte and Flores cases, these cases revealed the rise in large-scale forced labor involving undocumented immigrants, the need for a legal conception of psychological coercion, and necessity of specialized social services for victims. The 1997 Paoletti case mentioned in the opening chapter, also known as the "Deaf Mexican" case, was one. The defendants ultimately pleaded guilty to conspiracy to commit extortion and alien smuggling charges.[58] The second case, *United States v. Cadena*, involved, according to a DOJ press release, "Mexican women and girls as young as 14 years of age [who] were brought to the United States with promises of good jobs as waitresses and landscapers, only to be held as slaves in a high-volume prostitution operation. The Cadena family would hold the women in their service by shooting into the ground at their feet, threatening their families, beating them, and raping them as punishment if they tried to run away. The ringleader and six other men were convicted in 1999 of involuntary servitude."[59]

All of these cases influenced the broad conception of trafficking codified in the TVPA and bolstered the move away from a sex trafficking only approach. Paul, the federal policy advisor quoted previously, explained how the experience of working on these cases informed the government's perspective: "In the U.S. a very significant part of the trafficking is not for sex; it's for forced work in sweatshops and so forth. And we knew that from the start. We already had cases where there were fifty or seventy-five people working inside barbed wire fences and never allowed to leave. . . . So from the start those of us who understood the problem always favored covering other types of labor, not just prostitution." Paul's reference to "those of us who understood the problem" underscores that people understood the problem of trafficking in different ways and also that the Clinton administration was committed to responding to the issue based on its history of actual cases. Paul and others working in government recognized similarities in the types of abuse and coercion being used to hold people in exploitative situations. Individuals working in government had seen cases—some involving prostitution and others involving factory work or agriculture—but the common thread was foreign victims being forced, coerced, and deceived into servitude, and this was the crime in the eyes of various government practitioners. Although migration is not a precondition for trafficking, cases involving foreign-born victims raised particular concern due to the lack of legal protections for undocumented survivors.

In addition to increased penalties and attention to the issue, government officials involved with the drafting concluded that additional tools could be introduced to fill gaps in the existing criminal law, especially in the area of psychological coercion. A number of my informants perceived this as a defining element of trafficking—something they had observed in cases over the years: a multitude of methods could be used (beyond physical violence) to hold someone in servitude and create a climate of fear, including threats to the person's family in their home country or threatening to report the victim to immigration officials.

The notion of including psychological coercion in the statute emerged in response to a series of somewhat schizophrenic interpretations of involuntary servitude in the courts.[60] Most recently, in the 1984 Mussry case, the Ninth Circuit Court of Appeals offered a broad interpretation of the statute, recognizing that forms of coercion beyond the physical could result in involuntary servitude. Nonetheless, in 1988 the Supreme Court's decision in *United States v. Kozminski* interpreted the existing involuntary servitude statute (18 U.S.C. § 1584) to require the use of physical or legal coercion. The case involved a defendant charged for holding two developmentally disabled men in involuntary servitude. The government provided evidence that the two men worked on the defendant's farm seven days a week, often seventeen hours a day, at first for $15 per week and eventually for no pay. In addition to actual or threatened physical abuse and a threat to reinstitutionalize one of the men if he did not do as he was told, the defendant used various forms of psychological coercion to keep the men on the farm. The Supreme Court ruled, "For purposes of criminal prosecution under 241 or 1584, the term 'involuntary servitude' necessarily means a condition of servitude in which the victim is forced to work for the defendant by the use or threat of physical restraint or physical injury or by the use or threat of coercion through law or the legal process. This definition encompasses cases in which the defendant holds the victim in servitude by placing him or her in fear of such physical restraint or injury or legal coercion."[61] From the government's perspective, one of the primary goals of drafting new trafficking legislation was a return to the pre-*Kozminski* standard of involuntary servitude. Mark, a federal prosecutor, told me, "It was a kind of a restoration, as it were." According to Mark, adding a new statute that fixed what *Kozminski* had taken away was long in the making: "Congresspeople like Chris Smith and others were convinced that they had invented trafficking, that they had invented . . . the legal standards and all this other stuff. You know, that's fine, we can let them continue to believe that, but really what it was was . . . a return to . . . the Ninth Circuit standard in the *Mussry* case and others that the Supreme Court had overturned."

Individuals who had been active in the drafting effort noted that the initial bill introduced by Representative Chris Smith and backed by abolitionist feminists and conservatives effectively restated the Mann Act (outlawing interstate commerce for "immoral purposes") and did not provide additional tools, other than perhaps more focused attention on the issue of sex trafficking. Smith's bill had very little in the way of trafficking into forced labor. The notion that a bill focusing solely on trafficking into forced prostitution would set the U.S. antitrafficking agenda was troubling to many who perceived Smith's bill as a misguided attempt to redefine the government's approach to trafficking and slavery. Victor, a congressional staffer, told me that Smith's bill "had nothing to do with slavery." He continued, "Senator Wellstone and Congressman Gejdenson, they understood what the [Justice Department] approach was on it and that it was much more focused on Thirteenth Amendment slavery . . . as opposed to being just a rehashing of the Mann Act." "It became a kind of war of the bills," Megan, a former congressional staffer, declared as she recalled her experience of drafting antitrafficking legislation. Speaking of the original Chris Smith bill, she told me, "It had no labor component and that was a huge concern to us, not only because of the proportionality of labor concerns that were so immense, but also, honestly, it was a time when the kind of conservative and evangelical movements were becoming much more successful in human rights issues. . . . And there was a real concern that they were capturing this major issue, and not just as a kind of 'oh, it's ours,' but also that they were going to redefine it." Indeed, the placeholder *trafficking* presented an opportunity for conservatives and evangelicals to claim a stake in human rights and redefine the issue to reflect a particular set of sexual and moral values.

A Compromise in Vagueness and Utility

Ultimately, the parties involved in the drafting reached a compromise that reflected both of their positions. One of the main controversies during the compromise negotiations centered on the relationship between prostitution and trafficking and whether individuals participating in a criminalized act could be considered victims. Although the groups constituting the anti-prostitution sphere saw the negotiations as an opportunity to reframe all prostitution as trafficking and all prostitutes as victims, their position violated state laws criminalizing prostitution. As Paul, a federal policy advisor, noted,

> There are certain NGOs that wanted to focus only on prostitution, and they have a viewpoint that all prostitution is trafficking, and that was very difficult under U.S. law because the prostitutes in every state except for seven counties in Nevada are committing a crime, which by definition means that they are doing it knowingly and voluntarily. It doesn't mean they like the choice, but they are engaging in what states have decided is a crime. So there is a conflict between calling . . . all prostitutes victims of trafficking and what the U.S. law is saying. So we had some difficulty. We also did not want to give migration benefits and other benefits to people who were voluntarily violating state laws.

Paul continued describing the difficulty of reaching a definition that pleased all those involved: "We could not adopt a definition that, for example, would take people who clearly violated a state law, and a good example is these high priced call girls like in the [Elliott] Spitzer case.[62] There's not going to be a lot of sympathy for those women in the states who have criminalized that behavior to call them victims of anything. So because the states have chosen to criminalize prostitution, we couldn't just declare all of these people victims. We just can't do that, as the federal government you have to be sensitive to what states have decided to do." Legally defining all prostitution (coerced or not) as trafficking at the federal level, which is what abolitionists sought, was both unrealistic and a violation of states' rights.

The Clinton administration pushed to grant victim status only to those individuals *forced* or *coerced* into prostitution. As a result, the negotiations became very heated as antiprostitution feminists and evangelicals maintained that all prostitutes were victims. Paul told me, "It was very political, and it was very bitter on both sides. There were a lot of bad feelings. We were accused of all kinds of things, being pro-prostitution. It was ridiculous." By claiming that the Clinton administration supported legalizing prostitution, abolitionist interest groups manipulated the narrative of those seeking a broader definition of trafficking. Megan, a former congressional staffer, remembered, "It was this incredible, you know, 'Hillary has a whorehouse' [in reference to Hillary Clinton's role as head of the PICW]. Now you kind of forget, but in that period . . . the right wing rhetoric was really ramping up and it was extreme. . . . It was about sex, and it was about rape, and it was about . . . women's virtue, and if you had the labor definition then you were . . . complicit in the rape of thousands of young girls."

Partisan tensions and ad hominem attacks overshadowed any common interest that brought the two sides to the issue and ultimately were solidified in the law itself. Megan added, "One of the really sad things about this whole thing is that I was really involved, and I really cared, and I knew something about the issue, but the process was so unpleasant and so ugly and so nasty."

In the end, the compromise included three dichotomous elements that significantly influenced the way in which trafficking would be conceived from that point forward: (1) operative and nonoperative definitions of trafficking, which purposely conflated prostitution with trafficking; (2) a bifurcated operational definition of trafficking in which trafficking for forced commercial sex was marked as a special category; and (3) separate criminal statutes for sex trafficking and forced labor, which in turn created inconsistencies between who could be considered a victim of trafficking and what could be prosecuted as the crime of trafficking. It is worth unpacking each dichotomy in turn.

In the post–Monica Lewinsky years of the Clinton administration, Democrats had little ability to neutralize the sexual frenzy in which the TVPA drafting occurred, and sex trafficking was privileged in the law in several ways. The joint Smith-Gejdenson bill, introduced in November 1999, did conceive of trafficking broadly as involving all labor sectors, but it also addressed some of the concerns of antiprostitution feminist and religious advocates regarding the definition of sex trafficking. Ultimately, the new compromise bill,[63] signed into law in October 2000, incorporated multiple tiers of definitions of trafficking, embodying the social, moral, and political contestation surrounding the late 1990s conception of trafficking—one overarching definition triggers benefits and services for victims, one purely symbolic definition has no legal implications at all (but many social and political implications), and several new trafficking statutes define trafficking in the Criminal Code. These multiple levels and definitions of trafficking appeased the diverse groups with vested interests in the issue but also introduced significant confusion into the law and how trafficking is defined.

This tiered structure first shows up in the definitions section of the law, which establishes what I'm terming "operational" and "nonoperational" definitions of trafficking (one triggers victim benefits and the other does not). Although operationally the final bill took on the approach favored by practitioners and the Clinton administration (all forms of labor were included, and force, fraud, and coercion were required), it also contained symbolic definitional concessions to abolitionist advocates. In order to appease all sides, the drafters settled on an operational definition of "severe forms of trafficking" and a nonoperational definition of (nonsevere forms of) sex trafficking. Severe forms of trafficking (the core of the law) included

(A) sex trafficking in which a commercial sex act is induced by force, fraud, or coercion, or in which the person induced to perform such act has not attained 18 years of age; or

(B) the recruitment, harboring, transportation, provision, or obtaining of a person for labor or services, through the use of force, fraud, or coercion for the purpose of subjection to involuntary servitude, peonage, debt bondage, or slavery.[64]

Force, fraud, and coercion, therefore, became core requirements of the trafficking definition unless an individual involved in sex trafficking was under eighteen years of age. In fact, the definition requires the presence of three elements: (1) a process, such as recruitment, harboring, or transportation, (2) occurring by means of certain methods, including force, fraud, or coercion and (3) ending in exploitative conditions of labor or commercial sex. Those subject to "severe forms of trafficking" qualify for a range of assistance administered through NGOs. As I will discuss later, the TVPA also established related criminal statutes to prosecute perpetrators of the crime.

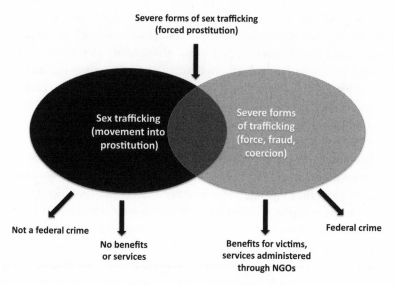

Severe forms of sex trafficking
(forced prostitution)

Sex trafficking
(movement into
prostitution)

Severe forms
of trafficking
(force, fraud,
coercion)

Not a federal crime   Federal crime
                    No benefits   Benefits for victims,
                    or services   services administered
                                       through NGOs

Figure 2. Severe forms of trafficking (adults only) versus sex trafficking.

Sex trafficking in its nonsevere form does not trigger benefits and services and is defined as "the recruitment, harboring, transportation, provision, or obtaining of a person for the purpose of a commercial sex act."[65] Thus, the TVPA defines recruitment or movement into prostitution (no force required) as trafficking in name only. This definition acts as a red herring, incorporated as part of the legislative compromise to assuage the concerns of feminist abolitionists hoping to diminish the boundary between forced and voluntary prostitution. The definition is distracting because it is not an operational definition—sex trafficking as defined here is not a prosecutable crime, and it carries no special benefits. In this way there are two definitions of trafficking but only one is operational (see Figure 2). Although highly confusing in practice, this was intentional on the part of the drafters. Representative Smith ultimately agreed with Democrats and the Clinton administration that the real focus of the law should be situations involving force or deception, but as Max, a congressional staffer who worked on the drafting, explained, "For presentation [to conservative constituents], Mr. Smith wanted to have a definition of sex trafficking that was without force, fraud, or coercion, and after a lot of debate we agreed to that even though in general the bill did not have criminal penalties or immigration benefits attached to sex trafficking." He continued, noting that the vagueness in the law was purposeful, "If you look at the bill, we did blur the distinction in certain places by not using the defined terms and by saying 'victims of trafficking' or 'assistance to prevent trafficking' . . . and therefore it was a little unclear what we were talking about. And that was purposeful under Mr. Smith's part. . . . So from the beginning we accepted a certain degree of ambiguity."

This ambiguity of language was a symbolic triumph for abolitionists. Although these concessions were disappointing for Democrats and other members of the human trafficking sphere, the legal ramifications were limited. Mark, a federal prosecutor, reacted to the compromise with frustration: "The two-tiered system in the TVPA was bullshit. To me it's complete bullshit, but it's what we have because that's kind of what you have to do to get things done up here [on Capitol Hill]." He nonetheless perceived the results as mostly innocuous. "Oh, it was basically a bone to Chris Smith. I mean that's exactly what it was. . . . The notion of having sex trafficking stay in the bill . . . it's like an appendix, or what's that thing we have that used to be our tail? The coccyx? So, it's like a coccyx or an appendix, although that's probably inflammatory to call it a coccyx. So it kind of stayed in there without much to do." While the legal consequences of the nonoperational sex-trafficking definition are minimal, as I will discuss in future chapters, the definition continues to influence conceptions of trafficking more generally by setting a legal precedent for describing prostitution as trafficking.

A second symbolic achievement for abolitionists was the bifurcation of the "severe forms of trafficking" definition with sex trafficking as a marked category. Although the definition is gender neutral and covers trafficking into all sectors, the two prongs implicitly limit and shift attention toward *women* trafficked for *sexual* labor by making a distinction in the law between severe forms of "sex trafficking" and other severe forms of unmarked trafficking— into agricultural, factory, or domestic work, for example. Trafficking for forced prostitution is separated as a special case, focusing on the *type* of work. Although I heard vague explanations for the split that alluded to commercial sex acts being illegal and thereby distinct from other forms of labor, there was no legal requirement that the two be separated. Max provided a more insightful take, noting that by conceding on the sex/labor split, Democrats were able to strengthen protections for all victims:

> It probably would have been possible to come up with some sort of definition that would have brought the two together, and we wouldn't have had to have the definition, but I think that in the political environment

in which we were operating in 1999 and 2000 . . . certain provisions of the law and certain benefits that never would have gotten into law were carried because people could talk about sexual slavery. . . . The idea that people [legislators] would not want to try to free and help people who had been enslaved for sexual services was such an anathema politically that you were able to bring additional things into it. So having a separate definition for trafficking into . . . services involving commercial sex acts created a framework that allowed the other things to be covered.

It was the emphasis on sex in the TVPA that created the bipartisan momentum to pass the law.

In addition to defining trafficking, the TVPA included several new criminal statutes to supplement the existing involuntary servitude and peonage statutes contained in Chapter 77 of the U.S. Criminal Code. These included Forced Labor (18 U.S.C. § 1589), Trafficking with Respect to Peonage, Slavery, Involuntary Servitude, or Forced Labor (18 U.S.C. § 1590), Sex Trafficking of Children or by Force, Fraud, or Coercion (18 U.S.C. § 1591), and Unlawful Conduct with Respect to Documents in Furtherance of Trafficking, Peonage, Slavery, Involuntary Servitude, or Forced Labor (18 U.S.C. § 1592).[66] Here again, as part of the compromise, sex trafficking by force, fraud, and coercion was separated from forced labor. Despite the split between labor and sex trafficking, there is nothing in the law to prevent sex trafficking from being considered a form of labor trafficking. Lynn, a federal prosecutor, told me that her office generally considers sex trafficking a subset of labor trafficking and charges sex traffickers with both sex trafficking and forced labor: "Legally you can charge sex trafficking always as forced labor . . . and we do. We usually charge them in tandem."[67]

On the criminal level, the sex-trafficking statute is broader in that it includes fraud as a means of trafficking, while the forced labor statute does not. The drafters narrowed the labor trafficking statute based on concerns that American corporations could be charged with trafficking if they misrepresented working conditions. Max recalled that the decision was made as part of the compromise:

> Mr. Smith made a very strong request, which was very difficult for us to accommodate, that would narrow the definition of trafficking into forced labor so that it couldn't be interpreted as criminalizing labor

law, that it was one thing to criminalize new forms of slavery, but . . . labor relations and inappropriate labor practices are governed by an entire statutory frame, which is essentially nonpunitive. It's regulated by the Labor Relations Board, and criminalization of these provisions were of concern to Mr. Smith . . . because of how that would be received by others in the Republican conference. So we had an elaborate discussion at like 2 a.m. . . . where we finally came up with the text which basically stayed unchanged in the process.

Although Democrats viewed defrauding someone into exploitative labor conditions as trafficking, the Republicans, who had concerns about alienating business sector supporters, fought to omit this element from the criminal statutes (but not from the victim definitions). Dean, a federal prosecutor, explained what these statutory discrepancies between sex and labor trafficking mean in practice. "For purposes of prosecution, the definition of sex trafficking is actually quite different than the forced labor definition. One big element is that [in cases of] sex trafficking, a method of coercion includes fraud, so if you are defrauded into commercial sex that is a prosecutable sex trafficking crime. If you are defrauded into a different form of labor, that's not a crime. So the sex trafficking statute is broader in that it reaches fraudulent means of exploitation and the forced labor statute does not." The crime of sex trafficking became an easier standard for prosecutors to meet.

The 2008 William Wilberforce Reauthorization Act (enacted after the completion of my fieldwork) attempted to partially fix this discrepancy, not by adding fraud to the forced labor statute but rather by creating a new federal crime forbidding misrepresentations designed to induce foreign nationals to come to the United States to work (18 U.S.C. § 1351). The new statute does not apply to misrepresentations to U.S. citizens. However, prior to this reauthorization, misleading an individual regarding the type or terms of employment was grounds for prosecution when it involved commercial sex, but the same was not true for other forms of labor. Additionally, the forced labor statute applies only to those who "provide or obtain" a person for forced labor, while the sex trafficking statutes cover anyone who "recruits, entices, harbors, transports, provides, or obtains"[68] or "benefits" from sex trafficking of children or by force, fraud, or coercion.[69] Dean continued reading from the U.S. Criminal Code, pointing out subtle but important differences between the forced labor and sex trafficking statutes:

And then also if you just look at the language . . . the forced labor talks about obtaining the labor of a person by coercion, so it's really focused on the labor. The sex trafficking statute, however, is focused on obtaining the person for commercial sex, so the sex trafficking statute is also broader because you don't have to have any commercial sex happen [intent is sufficient]. All you have to do is obtain the person for . . . the purpose of the commercial sex. So the statutes are actually written differently. They do have . . . some different effect. The two most significant being the fraud issue and the benefiting provisions that are both in the sex trafficking statute.

One significant consequence of these differing definitions for sex and non-sex trafficking is that an individual defrauded into forced labor could meet the definition of a victim of a severe form of trafficking and receive victim benefits and apply for the special trafficking visa, yet there is no prosecutable crime because the victim definitions differ from the statutory definitions (see Figure 3). The TVPA defined these people as victims but did not define what they experienced as a crime. Dean told me what this meant from a prosecutorial standpoint:

You could meet that definition, but there's no prosecutable crime. So for us, we don't have any involvement in those cases. There is nothing for us to do. There is no crime for us to prosecute. So where people are in labor by fraud . . . that's . . . not criminalized specifically, unless it rises to serious harm. So . . . if victims presented to us with those sets of facts, in our view we would not be giving CP [continued presence, a temporary form of immigration relief] to them, we would not be investigating or presenting for indictment because . . . the criminal statutes don't reach those conducts, so we'd have no jurisdiction or authority to pursue those matters.

In this way, a moral stance about the severity and "criminal" nature of defrauding individuals into commercial sex versus other forms of labor was incorporated into the law itself. On paper, these dichotomies appear largely symbolic because the law is inclusive of all forms of trafficking and establishes federal benefits and immigration relief for all types and genders of victims. However, these definitional bifurcations, and the implicitly gendered and explicitly sexual marking of trafficking, created the conditions for an imple-

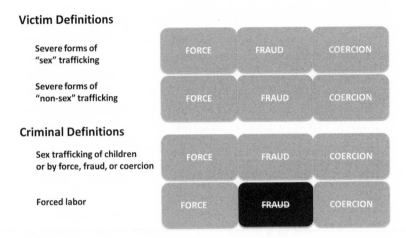

Victim Definitions

Severe forms of
"sex" trafficking

Severe forms of
"non-sex" trafficking

Criminal Definitions

Sex trafficking of children
or by force, fraud, or coercion

Forced labor

Figure 3. Victim definitions versus criminal statutory definitions.

mentation that is highly exclusive, as I will describe in the following chapters. As Patricia Ewick and Susan Silbey point out, "The multiple and contradictory character of law's meanings is a crucial component of its power."[70]

The Compromise Lives On

For Angela, the former federal policy advisor involved with the drafting, assigning meaning to the term *trafficking* meant transforming a complicated concept into a nameable and manageable crime.

> When people started talking about trafficking in persons . . . roughly ten years ago . . . we had to explain to people what that meant . . . so helping to attach some meaning to those words. . . . We needed people to understand, well trafficking in persons, what is that? Is it alien smuggling? No. Here's why it's different. . . . Here's what this is about. It's bringing in an understanding to the terminology of what this problem is so people understand it, know it, recognize it, can talk about it. You have to be able to name a problem to be able to address it.

Yet rather than resulting in a straightforward, agreed-upon definition, putting "trafficking" on the books meant codifying all of the contestation surrounding the issue. As Mark told me, "Unfortunately by adopting 'trafficking' as the operative term instead of 'slavery' or 'involuntary servitude,' continuing that as the basis, it basically brought that fight. And we've continued to have that fight ever since." Indeed, compromise over diverse notions of trafficking resulted in incorporating messiness and ambiguity into the law, as opposed to clarity. Although the TVPA provided a legal framework for addressing trafficking, and one by which those implementing the law are tied, it also left space to envision trafficking in varying, even contradictory, ways. Focusing on these definitions may seem overly technical, but it is this precise and subtle language of the law that reverberates today in discussions and implementation of U.S. antitrafficking law and policy.

As a cultural text, the TVPA illuminates the struggles and anxieties about prostitution, victimization, and women's sexuality that permeated its drafting. Ultimately the TVPA definition of trafficking is dichotomous because the effort to draft the law was dichotomous. The polarization around the issue of so-called sex trafficking resulted in a compromise that is functional yet value laden, prescriptive yet ambiguous, comprehensive yet bifurcated, and gender neutral yet gendered and sexually marked. The end product is a convoluted and layered definition that can be interpreted in numerous ways, allowing for varying conceptions of trafficking. Forms of sex trafficking that involve force, fraud, or coercion qualify as "severe forms of trafficking," while other forms of sex trafficking—absent any force, fraud, or coercion—are the law's vestigial organ: present, but not performing any function (such as prosecutions or benefits). The overlap of terms contributes to extensive confusion and mystification in the realm of policy, as well as in the implementation of the law in terms of who counts as a victim of trafficking. By incorporating a definition of "sex trafficking" minus any force, fraud, or coercion, the law (and its concept of "trafficking") remains ambiguous both legally and practically. These and other compromise elements in the law create the possibility to manipulate operational and nonoperational definitions, to frame trafficking selectively as related to either sex or to labor, and to distinguish between the trafficking that triggers victim benefits and the trafficking that constitutes a prosecutable crime. Each of the three bifurcated elements of the law complicates social and legal constructions of trafficking. As I argue in the following chapters, the multilayered law on the books leads to complexities in how the law is envisioned in the minds of those implementing it, resulting in uneven consequences for victims.

PART II

Thinking, Envisioning, and Interpreting Trafficking

Chapter 2

The Experts Make Sense of the Law

An interpretive approach to policy analysis . . . is one that focuses on the meanings of policies, on the values, feelings, and/or beliefs which they express, and on the processes by which those meanings are communicated to and "read" by various audiences . . . In analyzing public policies or the actions of organizational implementers, such an approach focuses on policy and/or organizational artifacts as the concrete symbols representing policy and organizational values, beliefs, and feelings.

—Dvora Yanow, *How Does a Policy Mean?*

I'm acutely aware . . . that there are lots of different definitions of trafficking, so as a criminal prosecutor I primarily look to the crimes of trafficking which are set forth in 18 U.S.C. Chapter 77, so I very much focus on the criminal elements of trafficking as a crime, but at the same time the victim definitions under the law are different, and in some ways broader, than the criminal definitions, so it depends on the purpose for which I'm analyzing it. . . . And I'm also acutely aware that that is all under U.S. law and there are a lot of different definitions under international law in other countries. . . . We are very focused under U.S. law on labor, services, or commercial sex, but other people will say "human trafficking" to mean any kind of exploitation of humans. . . . Finally, there is . . . a media conception of human trafficking that's just very general, and it's pretty much akin to any smuggling or movement of people, so people will throw that around to further complicate [things]. . . . I see a lot of

comparing apples and oranges in terms of . . . different definitions of
trafficking . . . so it's a big mess with the definitions.

—Katherine, federal prosecutor

As a result of the passage of the TVPA, professionals holding a variety of
worldviews and beliefs about trafficking are now investigating the crime,
providing services to victims, and implementing antitrafficking law and
policy. As the federal prosecutor indicates in the second epigraph above,
the law's many elements focus on interrelated but distinct aspects of the
forced-labor problem. So, depending on the role of the professional involved, parts of the law hold more or less relevance to their work. As various
individuals implement "their" pieces of the law, they translate the "law on
the books" into a working document that has meaning in their own minds.[1]
They may utilize all or part of the bifurcated operational definition and
draw on either criminal or victim classifications, depending on their professional functions. Although the law defines trafficking for these various
specialists, the compromise elements in the act itself create the space for
implementers to incorporate additional factors (e.g., professional biases,
past experiences with trafficking, and, as will be discussed in Chapter 4,
cultural and moral frameworks about sex) into their understandings as
they put the legal definition into action in ways that reflect their own values
and beliefs.

Two of the biggest obstacles to consistent and balanced implementation
are the law's newness and its complexity. Vast numbers of law enforcement
personnel, service providers, and government employees with varying levels
of experience may potentially encounter questionable situations and, as a result, be required to interpret whether what they are seeing is actually trafficking. Dean, a federal prosecutor, gets to the heart of the multiplicity:

You have literally hundreds of thousands of law enforcement in this
country that have to be trained and educated about this statute and
millions of citizens who are going to see and be able to also help identify this crime, so conducting the outreach and training in a consistent way and meaningful way is very difficult because . . . many people
have different definitions of trafficking, and every time people with
different definitions start talking it creates confusion, and what that
confusion does is it . . . either causes people to report lots of things as

trafficking or think things are trafficking that aren't, at least from our perspective, prosecutable. . . . Or it's so narrow that they think somebody has to be chained to a desk or something, that they overlook cases that could be prosecuted.

For some, all prostitution or all worker exploitation is mischaracterized as trafficking. For others, the category includes only the most obvious situations involving physical violence, to the exclusion of cases involving more subtle forms of coercion and control. Although there are obvious complications when those with limited expertise are charged with identifying the crime, the task is not much more straightforward among the most experienced, core group of antitrafficking professionals. It cannot be acknowledged enough: what constitutes trafficking is not always clear even among the experts—those dealing with trafficking victims and cases on a daily basis. Much of this confusion stems from the law itself, with its multiple goals (protection and prosecution) and layered notions of forced, defrauded, and coerced labor.

"It Comes Down to What Trafficking Is. That's Where It All Falls Apart."

As became abundantly clear to me as I delved into my research, those putting the law into effect are not always sure how to characterize the offense of trafficking, or they disagree on the precise factors that constitute it. I asked every person I interviewed, "How do you define trafficking?" The question revealed itself to be deceptive in its straightforwardness. I received complex and layered responses. Whether service providers, government bureaucrats, law enforcement agents, or prosecutors, my informants generally responded initially by emphasizing key elements of the severe forms of trafficking definition, but then they followed up with responses to the effect of "now that being said, you have to consider x, y, and z" or "that's how we define it as an agency, but I personally believe x" or "I define it by the TVPA definition but have a hard time getting recognition for my clients."

From talking with and observing professionals doing trafficking work under the TVPA, it was evident that, in practice, these individuals relied on the operational severe forms of trafficking definition (and related statutes) and ignored the extraneous and nonoperational portions of the definition. I found this to be the case regardless of whether my interlocutors were providing federally funded services, investigating cases, or prosecuting traffickers. NGO service providers need to show grant monitors that their clients meet the description of a victim of a severe form of trafficking (VSFT) in order to receive funds for case management, rent reimbursement, and other qualified expenses. Nancy, a case manager, told me that in her work, someone who is trafficked is "basically somebody who has been forced to do things against their will," and from that she extrapolates an understanding of the forced-labor problem itself. For Nancy, the TVPA concept of severe forms of trafficking dictated the type of client with whom she could work. Similarly, in law enforcement, the TVPA's criminal statutes prescribe what is prosecutable as a trafficking crime. When asked how she pins down the idea, Gwen, who works in federal law enforcement, responded, "It's really easy for us—the statutory definition. That's it." She went on, "We actually use the absolutes. We are a law enforcement agency. We have to use the definition in the law. That is what we have to hang our hats on. It's what provides our services under continued presence. . . . It's what our agents are required to swear to if they are going to do a certification under a T visa. So everything we do is statutory. We don't wiggle an inch." While the operational definitions generally directed how criminal justice authorities and service providers did their work, Gwen's comment does not concede that they also provided space for discretionary decision making and flexibility in case identification. A complicated feedback loop incorporating case evaluation procedures, media and advocacy messages, top-level policy, and personal moral frameworks, among other factors, also influenced implementers' conceptions and consequent implementation of the act's provisions. Further, the fact that criminal justice authorities and NGO service providers relied on two separate definitions of trafficking from the TVPA—the former using the criminal statutes and the latter the victim definitions—meant that their conceptions of trafficking itself were sometimes widely divergent.

Force, Fraud, Coercion

Ultimately, what distinguishes trafficking from other forms of worker exploitation is the presence of force, fraud, or coercion—the means used to hold someone in exploitative conditions of labor.[2] My informants used a variety of words to convey this concept, but their point was always the same. As Sara, a grant monitor for a federal funding program, told me, "I think there is a lot of gray area [around] labor exploitation . . . sometimes it can look like trafficking, and there is a lot of gray, but . . . the elements are the force, fraud, and coercion." Sara recognized those elements as the features distinguishing trafficking from other types of harm. Kyle, a federal prosecutor, put it this way: "We have a number of tools in the TVPA and the rest of the slavery statutes that we can use to prosecute crimes that fall under the human trafficking umbrella, but I think the common element to all of those crimes is that . . . somebody is compelled to provide work or services against their will." The use of categorical analogies was almost universal among my informants. Max, a congressional staffer, told me, "My own view is that trafficking is modern-day slavery, and . . . there has to be some sort of coercive element or some other element that deprives an individual of free will, so in that context I . . . say that anyone who is forced into any kind of conduct, whether it is legal or illegal, by force, fraud, or coercion or through some other means of deception that would take away the free will is a trafficking victim." Max described the factors that distinguish trafficking, sometimes termed *modern-day slavery*, from earlier definitions of slavery and involuntary servitude: today, the incorporation of the elements of psychological coercion and deception, rather than physical restraint, are most often central in keeping individuals in situations of servitude. Although there is a legal definition of trafficking upon which implementers rely, it is highly complex and layered, as was established in the previous chapter. I include these quotations from various individuals involved in carrying out the TVPA because they highlight the parts of the legal framework that resonate with each of them.

After thinking for a minute about how she conceives of trafficking, an immigration attorney named Jarrah responded, "It's easy but hard. We hardly ever think back to what we define as trafficking." Almost everyone I talked to had a good sense of what trafficking was—they knew it when they saw it—but it was difficult to put into words. Jarrah continued, "We say that anyone who is coerced to do something that they wouldn't normally do and is unable to leave the situation and that there is sort of a psychological climate of fear. So they may not be locked up, they may not be stuck in the house all day, they could possibly be able to walk down to the street corner, but for some reason they cannot separate themselves from a certain group of people or a certain person." This notion of a climate of fear is central to trafficking and one of the key features that distinguishes it from traditional notions of slavery and involuntary servitude. *Climate of fear* describes the kinds of manipulation and domination that violators use to keep individuals in involuntary situations, including holding the victim's documents, making threats to family and children in the home country, demonstratively beating other victims (and thus implying that the same could happen to the victim), threatening to report victims to immigration officials, and advising the victim not talk to anyone outside the situation or by phone because "the police are always listening." These factors conspire to build a web of containment around the targeted laborer. Fran, the director of a federal grant program, told me, "To me, the bottom line is if the person . . . either has a fear of what would happen to him or her or their family if they left the situation, or if there is something that someone else is doing to prevent them from leaving, then they are probably being trafficked."

When talking about what she viewed as the heart of the trafficking definition, Audra, an immigration attorney, agreed:

> The conditions under which they are working . . . for me, that's always been the emphasis of the analysis. Whether or not someone is working under conditions where they cannot leave, and they're not being paid, and as one colleague said . . . "operating in a climate of fear." I really like that definition because it, it encompasses . . . all of the evils that can be involved. It could be someone who is verbally abusing you, someone physically abusing you, sexual abuse, threats to your family abroad, so many different situations. The key component is that exploitation of labor and preventing the person from being able to leave from that situation.

She highlights what actually constitutes force, fraud, or coercion and what lies at the center of the offense.

The significance that these three words—*force, fraud,* and *coercion*—have come to hold since the passage of the TVPA is remarkable. Angela, a former federal policy advisor, told me, "It is interesting when you think about . . . how do you identify what the harm is and then reduce that to words in a statute, acknowledging that there are degrees of coercion along a continuum?" It is nearly impossible to avoid hearing the phrase "force, fraud, and coercion" when spending any amount of time in the antitrafficking field, yet as with the content of any statute, the words are open to interpretation. A great deal of fuzziness surrounds identifying the phenomena: in some cases, the force is immediately apparent to an outsider, while other times it takes a highly experienced professional to recognize the nuances of trafficking. Roxanne, a former immigration attorney, noted how challenging it could be to identify the manipulation that a victim experienced—precisely because that manipulation has distorted the laborer's experience so fundamentally:

> I think force, fraud, or coercion obviously can be manifested in different ways, and . . . definitely . . . there have been times when . . . I had to work very hard with my clients to . . . help them articulate what it was. . . . I just over time . . . honed in on how to make them articulate that, like what questions to ask them . . . because . . . I've had clients who could go in and out . . . it was a different type of coercion, so it might have been debt bondage or it might have been subtle threats to their family members or whatever, but basically there was something that prevented them from being able to leave, and so that's the way that I look at it.

Often the cases in which the victims have freedom of movement but are somehow being compelled are most difficult to recognize. Coercion takes many forms, at times very subtle and at others much more blatant, often requiring a great deal of patience and skill to uncover what could be misunderstood as a crime black and white in its heinousness.

Flexibility and Discretion

The complexity in definition means that what appears exploitative does not always quite add up to trafficking in the eyes of the law, as Molly, a federal prosecutor, expressed to me in response to the question of how she defined the crime: "I really don't like those questions [laughs]. . . . I suppose the right answer for me would have to be the way it's defined by the statute because things can sort of . . . look and sound and smell like trafficking, but if they don't have those elements I can't say that it's trafficking in the charging document." Meeting the criteria of the legal definition is critical for those whose business it is to prosecute captors and to secure legal provisions for trafficked workers. From a law enforcement perspective, the process for deciding whether a case meets the definition can be quite involved; it may include multiple conversations between agents, coordinators, and supervisors, weighing the circumstances of a case and comparing it to past cases to determine whether it meets the statutory benchmarks. Some criminal justice officials came by their expert status as a result of their experience and familiarity with the issue, receiving phone calls from agents from around the country who had never seen a trafficking case reaching out to determine whether what they were seeing constituted trafficking. I observed many similar discussions that followed the same pattern: service providers talking through potential cases and weighing the facts of a case to decide whether it rose to the level of trafficking.

From both the criminal justice and the service provision perspectives, three elements must be present to constitute trafficking. First there is a process, such as recruitment or movement into a particular situation, followed by the means by which the individual is maintained in that situation, whether by force, threats, or deception. That method of control is the second component. Some kind of end, which involves economic exploitation in which the victim performs labor or services without proper compensation, rounds out the trifecta. Although all three of these elements are required for any case to qualify as trafficking—that much is absolute—determining what circumstances and conditions constitute each of these elements is complicated. What exactly fits the statutory definition is discretionary and somewhat flexible.[3] Lynn, a federal prosecutor, articulated a kind of tension, with the statutory constraints operating among cases that are never textbook: "We define trafficking by the way the statute does. . . . Now that being said, definitions obviously could be more expansive or less expansive. . . . We do define it under the statute, but we obviously have . . . pushed the statute as far as possible, you know, expanding the coverage." Conversely, others used narrower interpretations of the definitions, homing in on those cases involving forced commercial sex, as I will discuss in the following chapter.

Each U.S. Attorney's Office has discretion over which cases it chooses to prosecute. Lynn continued, "A lot of what we do is discretionary. We obviously have systems in place to ensure that our office is being consistent within our office, but each office does decide things differently, and remarkably each prosecutor has a certain amount of discretion." She and a colleague worked on a case that pushed the limits of the statutory criteria in that the trafficker exerted control over the victim from across state lines: "The two of us looked at the statute and decided, you know what, this really does technically fit. This is an appropriate case to go forward. It's a totality thing; you weigh all the different equities. This was an egregious situation—we started out in our minds with how badly this woman had been victimized by him [the trafficker]. It fit within the definition . . . and we decided ultimately it was a case worth bringing." The "totality thing" is code for the subjective, nebulous, and slippery nature of assessing potential trafficking cases. Lynn went on, "It's very hard to . . . put that down into . . . a systematic, we don't weigh it, we don't come up with a score, but it's sort of everything—the evidence, the equities, the sort of justice aspect. . . . Would we be doing justice? The degree of harm and whether or not we think legally it's correct. And, we decided to do it based on all of those factors. . . . It was a really tough case, and quite frankly we could have easily lost, given all those factors." The precariousness of the case highlights the fine line between what does and does not count as trafficking, coupled with the elasticity of what constitutes force, fraud, and coercion.

An element critical to recognizing trafficking is the narrative of the victim—does he or she have a coherent story about what took place? Is it possible to get that person to articulate all of the elements of the story that make it trafficking? Even having a few elements suggesting the possibility of forced labor can lead to further investigation. Discretion and perspective influence not only whether to go forward with a prosecution but also how carefully a case is looked at to determine whether it "counts." Molly, a federal prosecutor, explained, "It's so discretionary. Interviewing a person is so dependent on the mood and the skill of the interviewer and the skill of the interpreter if there's . . . another language involved. There are so many variables in place; it's very hard to have . . . absolute guidelines for these things." Often agents and prosecutors do not know right away whether a case fits the legal rubric. The process of uncovering the whole story can be knotty. "Most trafficking victims cannot tell you what has happened to them when you first intercept them because they are too traumatized. They are too freaked out by being in touch with all these government agencies. If [the victims are] international, in their home countries they [law enforcement] are the enemy. They've been told repeatedly by the traffickers that these people are going to get them in trouble, that they're going to mistreat them, and all these other things. So there are a lot of things that just have to be addressed before the person can actually talk." Yet having this kind of time to devote to a single potential victim was uncommon, and criminal justice authorities often swiftly rejected potential cases on the basis of insufficient available evidence, subjective personal interpretive frameworks about trafficking, and simple intuition. When evidence pointed toward trafficking, agents or prosecutors at times solicited the help of service providers who had the time to devote to supporting victims and making them feel comfortable enough to share what happened to them. Often recognition as a trafficking victim, or even a potential victim eligible for NGO assistance, depended on the victim's circumstances and his or her story's ability to fit into the investigating agent or officer's own narrative of trafficking.

Brief and discretionary assessments by law enforcement lead to inconsistencies in victim identification, as many of my NGO informants reported. A service provider's client may be a victim in the eyes of one law enforcement agent but not another's. Many providers struggled with law enforcement's seeming fickleness in TVPA-related decision making. During a meeting of local service providers, Bridget, the director of one NGO program, expressed clear frustration with the mixed responses service providers received when bringing cases to criminal justice authorities: "The problem with federal law enforcement is that we never know what we're going to get in terms of cooperation. One ICE agent will have a totally different understanding of what trafficking is from an FBI agent. . . . We need to have a checklist!" Bridget and other providers favored the use of consistent criteria for establishing trafficking cases, but there were no apparent definitional standards beyond the law itself, which left considerable room for interpretation. These differences in law enforcement response manifested not at the agency level but often at the level of individual agents, whose knowledge of the issue and discretion involved in identifying trafficking and its components varied considerably. The dichotomous elements in the TVPA definition of trafficking set out in Chapter 1 create the space to incorporate flexibility, discretion, and subjectivity into assessments of what qualifies (see Figure 4). Because the TVPA includes both operative and nonoperative definitions of the central phenomenon, distinguishes "sex" from "non-sex" trafficking, and provides differing victim and criminal forms, professional contexts can influence which of these multiple and dichotomous definitions the implementers gravitate toward and depend upon most heavily. Thus, both service providers' and criminal justice officials' behaviors can be shaped by the number of trafficking cases they have worked on, the amount of time they have spent talking with victims, and— as will be discussed in the next chapter—their beliefs about what motivates individuals to migrate, as well as personal moral frameworks about sex and victimization.

While law enforcement officials rely on the criminal statutes to determine whether they can prove the crime, NGOs look to the VSFT definition to establish whether an individual qualifies for services and benefits. A victim for one type of agency did not always correspond to a victim for another. From service providers in New York and at national conferences, as well as from

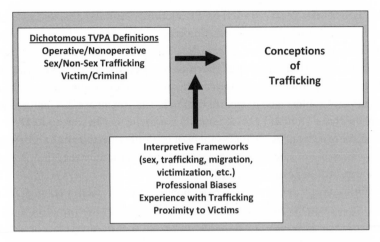

Figure 4. How subjectivity mediates legal definitions of trafficking

individuals in Washington overseeing social service grantees throughout the country, I heard consistently that NGOs see large numbers of survivors who are never adjudicated as victims by law enforcement. That is, NGOs are coming into contact with trafficked individuals who meet the TVPA definition, but who are not formally recognized and endorsed as victims, as I will discuss in Chapter 5. Fran, who oversees a federal grant program, told me about a confounding case from the Southwest United States: "[The victims] are from Mexico. The ICE agent, based on what he's heard, said, yes I think they are victims, but the trafficker has already left the country. There is nothing to investigate. There's nobody to prosecute. So ICE is not going to go out on a limb and say these women are trafficking victims. The women want to be repatriated, [so] they will never be counted officially as trafficking victims, but they are trafficking victims. And there's a lot of that."[4] While *victims* of trafficking and the *crime* of trafficking are two separate notions under the law, there is an uneven but symbiotic relationship between the two: a crime necessitates a victim, but a victim does not always necessitate a crime. Further complicating the situation, although an individual may meet the VSFT definition, if no corresponding violation exists (i.e., the individual was defrauded into forced labor) or the infraction is not recognized or considered prosecutable by law enforcement, then the violated person may not even be considered a victim.

From law enforcement's perspective, having a trafficker to prosecute is vital to their vision of trafficking. A victim without a perpetrator was viewed with disinterest. Who "counts" as a trafficking casualty is partly based on which cases are meaningful and time effective to officers of the law. Jim, a federal agent, told me, "A lot of girls the NGOs have were trafficked ten years ago, and we can't do anything. There are no records, we can't find the guy, and there's a statute of limitations with the law. Out of one hundred NGO victims that I interview, maybe four are viable." Yet a case not being viable in the justice system did not necessarily mean the victim was not truly trafficked. I heard from service providers of exploiters fleeing the country and of cases simply not being high priorities for law enforcement—but the victims were still in need of services.

Without a related active investigation, law enforcement personnel were reluctant to sign off on paperwork that would provide victims with immediate assistance. Although any individual who has the characteristics of a VSFT is immediately *eligible* for services, including case management and legal assistance, the timing of federal victim benefits (such as Medicaid, food stamps, and cash assistance) and immigration relief varies widely depending on whether law enforcement takes an interest in a case. Those victims whose traffickers fled the country, or from whose cases evidence was destroyed, or in whose cases law enforcement simply did not take an interest often experienced long delays in receiving benefits and protections.

Criminal justice authorities cited several factors that influenced case advancement, including the likelihood of the case standing up in court, the severity and size of the case, and the credibility of the victims. When asked how her office decides which cases to prosecute, Lynn responded, "Most often it's what case do we have enough evidence to go forward on. . . . How bad was the conduct? How good is the evidence? Sometimes how many victims, like is it a big enough case or is it just really a one-on-one situation where now the state could handle it [under the state antitrafficking law]? It's mostly driven by do we have the evidence to prove that this actually happened? Do we believe it actually happened, and can we prove it actually happened?" Belief that trafficking really occurred came up as an operative notion during several interviews with criminal justice authorities. Jim, a federal agent, told me he believed that NGOs helped their clients rehearse what to say to law enforcement so that they would be recognized as trafficking victims. "I think they coach the victims because the stories don't add up," he told me. Kyle, a federal prosecutor, agreed that potential victims sometimes lied, and he relied on intuition to assess the veracity of their claims. During a brothel raid, he encountered a woman who alerted him to some witnesses attempting to strategically misrepresent themselves. "She said, 'Look, I knew what I was doing; I wanted the money and those women did too, and they are back there talking that if they say *x*, *y*, and *z* they'll get benefits and that they don't have to be deported and they don't have to go back to Korea.'" While the immigration benefits for trafficking victims are highly desirable, the process of claiming them is so lengthy and complex (see Chapter 5) that, in reality, it is unlikely nontrafficked individuals would successfully obtain them without the truth emerging. Kyle noted that, in many cases, actual victims may not tell agents or prosecutors every pertinent detail of their experiences:[5] "They could be afraid of the trafficker, or they might not trust you, or all of those kinds of reasons that make them vulnerable. But, on the other hand, these women are subject to be dishonest to you because they know they can get money and they can get freedom. They could not be deported and they could have permanent [immigration] status." He continued, "The truth is like the golden mean in between those two extremes, and finding that can present a real challenge. . . . Basically the prosecutor has to believe based on his interview and any other evidence that exists, which [it] oftentimes doesn't, that this person is telling the truth. It's oftentimes a gut check." Relying on a "gut check" to determine authentic victimhood reflects the subjectivity inherent in identifying both trafficking victims and crimes—despite the apparent clarity of the law. Although criminal justice authorities are particularly sensitive to preventing individuals from "cheating the system," their unsystematic "gut checks" can also backfire, resulting in the deportation of victims who genuinely fit the definition.

Jim's and Kyle's comments reflect a tension between service providers and law enforcement and their varying goals in implementing the TVPA. While law enforcement agents are seeking out the so-called truth, service providers are often trying to assist victims in reconstructing traumatic experiences that may come across as fragmented and unreliable. I found that law enforcement agents in particular often accused victims of lying because their stories were incoherent or the agents had a *feeling* that the victims were lying. Yet, this kind of attitude on the part of officials failed to recognize as understandable the inability of formerly trafficked persons to provide a coherent narrative of their trafficking. Molly, a federal prosecutor who took seriously trauma's effects on recollection and communication, told me that she never gets the full truth in the first interview. The ordeal of an arrest combined with instructions from the trafficker ("never tell law enforcement the truth") result in initially incoherent stories. That recognition of subjectivity and persistence in identifying trafficking represents a consequential difference in perspective.

A Continuum of Exploitation

High stakes accompany the determination of whether trafficking has occurred, but many describe forced, defrauded, and coerced labor as part of a continuum. There is a fine line between trafficking and certain other forms of exploitation, and my informants often highlighted the difficulty of judging when that line was crossed. Trafficking occupies one end of a spectrum of exploitation, with those plotted at the "severe forms of trafficking" pole being a small subset of a much larger pool of mostly undocumented exploited laborers (the majority of whom were not trafficked). Fran, a federal grants administrator, noted, "The problem with the definition . . . is that it's like everything in life, it's a continuum, and where do you cross the line from economic exploitation to severe exploitation to trafficking?" She described a situation involving teachers from the Pacific Rim who were exploited but not trafficked; they were underpaid and promised things that weren't delivered once they arrived in the United States: "It's not trafficking. . . . The women could have left at any time." And although these women were not forced or coerced into these positions, their economic situation made them vulnerable to a type of injustice for which there is little legal recourse.

While much labor exploitation does not rise to the level of trafficking, many migrants share motivations for leaving home, whether trafficked or not, and service providers involved in this study recognized their clients as part of a much larger pool of migrants driven to risk their lives and freedom for the chance at better opportunities in the United States. Audra, an immigration attorney, told me, "From my perspective, there is a very large gray area between workers' rights and trafficking." As an attorney, she was well versed in the distinction between forced labor, on the one hand, and exploitation in which the workers were free to leave, on the other; however, she perceived a professional and political need to contextualize trafficking within the larger framework of undocumented migration and labor exploitation. While several scholars have critiqued the role of NGOs in what Laura Agustín has termed the "rescue industry" for their complicity in reproducing the trafficking framework, and with it the disciplinary responses of the state,[6] I found these assessments to be oversimplified for the majority of antitrafficking NGO programs in New York. In the sense that these NGOs accepted federal funds earmarked for those meeting the VSFT categorization, they did perpetuate that framework. However, they were not doing so blindly: the majority of providers I spoke with recognized the need for structural solutions focusing on prevention and greater protections for migrants and workers. They chose to help those in need within the existing system while gradually expanding the dialogue on servitude and exploitation as a continuum. With limited time and funds for advocacy, NGO service providers already found themselves on an uneven playing field with full-time antiprostitution advocates, who were steering the conversation further and further from the topic of labor and migration. Antitrafficking organizations found themselves poorly positioned to reframe the debate.

Nonetheless, many providers contested a framework that reinforced a restrictionist approach to immigration and one that deemed as worthy of assistance only a small subset of those exploited in the process of seeking a better life in the United States. As Chacon notes, "legislative revisions brought the crime of 'trafficking' into the prosecutorial mainstream, but did nothing to address the ways in which the preexisting legal regime upon which the TVPA is built actually facilitates trafficking."[7] There is an undeniable paradox between strict immigration restrictions and the demand for cheap labor in the United States: the law places so many limits on who can immigrate and work legally that many individuals are willing to take a chance, despite the risks, if it presents the potential for economic opportunity, love, or the hope of a better life in general. Undocumented migration itself creates situations in which predators can misrepresent opportunities and ultimately assert power and control over those who are seeking to improve their life chances.

A number of the professionals I interviewed envisioned a metric for determining what counted as trafficking that involved a comparison to what did not count (or what fell just short of counting) as trafficking. Lynn, a federal prosecutor, talked about evaluating the level of harm involved in a case: "The tricky thing . . . in the forced labor context is that very many situations are sort of on the line, in my opinion." She spoke of a case involving a couple who recruited a large number of migrant workers from South America, promised them jobs, and brought them to the United States. The couple helped the individuals find jobs and threatened to turn them over to immigration authorities if they did not pay back the money spent bringing them here. The exploiter housed the workers with thirty to forty people living in a single-family residence, sleeping on mats, and deprived them of sufficient food. The workers turned over the money they earned, and the couple applied the funds to the workers' debts and deducted amounts to pay for their food and housing, inadequate as it was. "So it ended up being sort of debt bondage, but it wasn't forced labor per se because [the couple] didn't actually make them work anywhere." Noting that the case ended in a plea deal,[8] Lynn continued, "In fact, if we went to trial in that case, it'd be difficult because it didn't seem as egregious, you know what I mean? We took the case, but it was definitely what I would call, if you will, 'trafficking lite,' and . . . sort of on the border, at the cusp of alien smuggling . . . and maybe extortion to some extent . . . and trafficking." She added that the sheer number of victims in this case was a key factor in pursuing it as trafficking, entitling the victims to receive services. Mediating factors such as the quantity of victims influence assessments of trafficking and can push a case over that all-important line in the eyes of criminal justice authorities.

Other factors, such as the nature of the relationship between trafficker and victim, sometimes influenced determinations adversely. Enforcement authorities questioned whether situations involving family members or romantic relationships were really trafficking, even when force or coercion was involved. Several service providers mentioned clients who were involved in servile marriage situations—they were brought to the United States through marriage and forced to perform household or other labor for their spouses. Nora spoke of a client who was deceived into marrying her trafficker and had great difficulty interesting law enforcement in her case. Although the situation fit the trafficking definition, certain characteristics were contradictory to law enforcement conceptions of the crime: "I think a lot of times people are trafficked and then it becomes very difficult for outsiders to see it as trafficking because the two may be related, or as has been the case in many of the cases I've worked on, there's . . . a relationship that's romantic, where I think investigators can be sort of skeptical about what was forced and what wasn't." Multiple cases have involved young women recruited through romance and then forced into prostitution, but because of the relationships, the level of force used was challenging to determine. Cases that involve fewer victims are much harder to corroborate and therefore more difficult for law enforcement to prove, sometimes resulting in what appears to the NGOs and victims as lack of interest in the case or a refusal to help. Conversely, some of these very cases were prosecuted because investigators found clear financial evidence and multiple victims corroborated the stories.

Another gray area affects trafficked individuals who themselves transition into roles in which they assist the exploiters or become enforcers over other victims. Especially in situations involving forced commercial sex, individuals may start out as victims but are then promoted to management-type positions in which they are called on to either recruit other women or manage newcomers. Responding to this type of situation, Nora told me, "It's very gray—not black and white at all—in terms of who is the good guy and who is the bad guy in the minds of the people we work with." She said her clients may conceive of certain individuals in a trafficking operation as criminal and others who are connected to it as undeserving of blame. "But even some people are only bad some of the time," she noted. Many survivors did not view their traffickers as corrupt all of the time because they relied on their captors for food, shelter, and basic necessities. In some cases, the trafficker had fathered the victim's children. However, law enforcement officers often viewed as complicity any acceptance of the trafficker on the part of the victim. "Not all victims are victims," Will, a federal agent, told me. He described an ongoing case involving a pimp and underage girls in prostitution— one girl in particular he adamantly believed was not a victim because she posted ads for the other girls on Craigslist. He told me, "The pimp will probably get fifteen years, and she should too." Legally, because this girl was under eighteen and in the service of a pimp, she fits the definition of a trafficking victim. Despite her age and the circumstances of her initial involvement, Will viewed her as a coconspirator because of her adopted role in the operation.

If articulating trafficking's meaning and its constituent elements of force, fraud, and coercion is complex for individuals working with trafficking cases on a regular basis, even greater challenges greet those who are less intimately familiar with the crime and the law. For inexperienced law enforcement personnel or those not directly responsible for implementation, confusion about what constitutes trafficking is magnified. As I will discuss in the next chapter, this becomes all the more complicated when commercial sex is involved.

Chapter 3

"Things That Involve Sex Are Just Different"

> Just as mystery writers use the pursuit of particular truths as a
> vehicle to propound general truths about the nature of evil, sex, or
> our "mean streets," so, too, do law's personnel, from police officers to
> high court judges, often make explicit and implicit assumptions
> about truth as such while going about their daily business.
> —Mariana Valverde, *Law's Dream of a Common Knowledge*

Sex as a Special Category

Reflecting on the sex/labor split in the TVPA, a federal prosecutor named Molly told me, "Things that involve sex are just different. I think because sex in every part of life is a unique and powerful thing. I think the kind of degradation that the victims of sex trafficking deal with is different. I'm not saying it's worse, but I think it's different than victims of labor trafficking." Like many prosecutors, Molly viewed trafficking for forced commercial sex and for forced labor as equal priorities, but her perception of their difference is commonly held by the American public and by many TVPA implementers.

What is it about sex that makes one form of trafficking so much more compelling and prominent than other types and allows it to take on such unique meaning? Over the course of my fieldwork, I repeatedly asked myself this, but I found that there is no one answer. For some, the concern is the exchange of sex for money. Others are troubled by the sexual harm, which is interpreted as worse than the injury caused by other forms of trafficking. Still others are swayed by the relative ease with which victims of forced prostitution can be identified because of their sometimes public presence. Certain representations are more "catching" and resonant than others[1] and the image of sexually victimized trafficking victims is one such representation—and it is easily sensationalized. Anthropologist Carole Vance notes that just as with the original nineteenth-century crusades against "white slavery," the preferred narrative frame for telling trafficking stories remains the melodrama: popular and media portrayals that favor stories of sexual danger compete with broader definitions of trafficking established under the law.[2]

Although my research does illuminate, and this chapter will reveal, various reasons that individuals assign special significance to trafficking for forced commercial sex, I am not interested in what makes this form of trafficking compelling so much as I am in unpacking the fact that inserting sex into trafficking results in a special category—and ultimately the exclusion of other types of trafficking and other categories of victims. The moral panic over "sex trafficking" distorts the notion of trafficking as an issue of forced or coerced labor or service by framing it purely as an issue of *sexual* violation.[3] That distortion has real effects for those in peril. As human rights lawyer and scholar Alice Miller has suggested, a hyperattention to sex has effectively excluded attention to other types of harm, including other forms of labor trafficking.[4]

In his introductory volume to *The History of Sexuality*, Michel Foucault raises the question of why sex and sexuality have come to be so widely discussed. Criminal justice, he argues, has intensified awareness of sex as a site of constant danger—and thereby created the impetus to talk about it as such.[5] Against that general landscape, the creation of the crime of "sex trafficking" has incorporated "trafficking" into the broader discourse about sex and sex into the broader discourse of trafficking, creating a discursive space for speaking about it in legal terms while expressing social and cultural norms and beliefs about prostitution, victimization, and appropriate forms of sexuality. Carole Vance describes gender and sexuality as "actively contested domains where diverse constituencies struggle over definitions, law, policy, and cultural meanings."[6] It is by infusing contested cultural meanings about sex into law that the TVPA has become a domain of special legal and social significance, with struggles over the meaning of trafficking and the value of different types of trafficking constantly being renegotiated through the implementation process. So we must investigate that process by which cultural valences compound the law's mechanics.

Many of the most common misunderstandings and oversimplifications about trafficking (inside and outside implementation) revolve around the special status assigned to sex and sex trafficking implied by the TVPA's two-tiered conceptualization, which also includes several bifurcated elements, meaning that individuals can focus on the part of trafficking's definition that best suits their personal or organizational values. This complexity affects both what counts as trafficking for various actors and also who is counted as its victim. The sometimes-counterproductive nuances surfaced in my interviews with professionals whose implementation of the law was also colored by the long shadow cast by sex. Some of my interviewees reinforced the notion of sex trafficking as unique, while others challenged such a belief. To highlight this diversity of perspectives, I begin with excerpts from interviews with four individuals that illustrate how they engaged with the subject of sex as it relates to trafficking. They were all experts in their respective fields, and all of their daily professional activities revolved around trafficking specifically. Two of the individuals—Molly and Jim—worked in the criminal justice sector, while the other two—Sheila and Charlotte—were based in the social service sector. Their views are not necessarily representative, but they do serve as vignettes of definitional dynamics in action.

The federal prosecutor quoted at the beginning of the chapter had been working as a government attorney on trafficking cases for four years when I met her. Despite Molly's belief in the uniqueness of sex trafficking, she was unable to articulate how exactly forced prostitution differed from trafficking into other labor sectors. In the face of a perceived difference, she believed labor trafficking cases could be equally brutal and cited one involving forced domestic work: "For example, the Sabhnani case that was out in Long Island . . . what those victims dealt with on a daily basis was really awful too. . . . There was nothing sexual about it, and those are incredibly vulnerable victims.[7] And so I think there are . . . different kinds of forced labor cases too." Molly's suggestion that trafficking occurs along a continuum also implies that some cases are worse than others; she added, "I think the domestic [worker] cases, to me, are sort of the saddest, maybe just because the victims feel like they're alone. A lot of times they're single victims who are serving a family, and I think part of the reason we don't see as many of them is that they're just completely invisible, you know?" Sympathetic intensity factors into identifying victims, as well:

Part of the reason, I think, that sex cases get a lot of attention is that there is a lot more contact, both with the public because of the customers and with law enforcement, not on the "we're making a trafficking case" kind of level, but your cops on the beat who know who the prostitutes are, they can tell where there's a brothel, there are raids that happen, and . . . virtually all of your sex trafficking victims have had prostitution arrests if they've been in the States for any kind of time. So there is contact there, and there's a visibility there that doesn't happen with a lot of the labor cases, I think.

If sex trafficking is more visible and more frequently encountered by law enforcement, we can see how the identification of vice crimes has come to be prioritized over identifying labor exploitation.

The kinds of trauma that victims experience are both subjective and dependent on the victim's particular circumstances, Molly suggests. During the same conversation in which she described the *distinctive* degradation experienced by victims of forced prostitution, she talked about being able to recognize trafficking victims by the expressions on their faces, noting that there is something unique about the experience of women who have been forced into prostitution in particular.

Sometimes if you interview enough of these people, you can see it in their face almost. . . . Maybe I'm looking for it, but I've seen how from . . . the first meeting to . . . when they actually . . . tell you the truth, what a victim's . . . eyes look like especially. They look dead when you meet them at first. I mean, especially sex work is so dehumanizing, and they are so distrustful and they've been so mistreated by the trafficker, both because they're being forced to be a prostitute, but also because they come home and they haven't made enough money. They're beaten, they get strip-searched, they've been forced to have abortions, they've lost their children that they have had.

In Molly's experience, she noticed something characteristic about the violation associated with sex trafficking: she believed it had a physical manifestation that could be observed in the victim's eyes. In her mind, being forced to participate in commercial sex compounded the other aspects of the trafficking experience.

Although the view of sex as somehow different was common among people working in the criminal justice field who interacted with victims sporadically, many of the service providers with whom I talked—who engaged with survivors daily—were reluctant to draw any distinction. Sheila was a longtime service provider and one of the first people I met while doing my research. We communicated regularly over the course of my fieldwork, and one afternoon I asked her if she saw any dissimilarities between trafficking for forced labor and trafficking for forced commercial sex. She responded, "Of course the nature of what people are doing, but I think all the other elements are the same." Perhaps betraying her inheritance of the very distinctions she resists, she went on, "To me it's not an either-or on the two groups. It's like both need a lot of attention." In contrast to Molly, Sheila did not view the sector into which an individual was trafficked to be a distinguishing factor in the experience of victims. In reference to recent increasing concerns over the issue of trafficking of U.S. citizen youth for commercial sex,[8] she added,

> We really need to look at this youth problem—these young girls—it's devastating. It's devastating to read about them and hear about them and so is the other worker exploitation. I think that somebody said that teen prostitution is America's dirty little secret. . . . I think all exploited labor is America's dirty little secret, but people don't have any idea that we're all complicit in it . . . in the clothing we buy, everything. So I think that that split, the argument, the dichotomy is really harmful to the whole field and it has really set everybody back.

Sheila notes the harm in drawing a distinction between forced prostitution and other forms of forced labor, one consequence of which is the invisibility of labor trafficking and the fact that the public is oblivious to its ramifications (e.g., clothing produced in sweatshops or produce cultivated by forced labor).

Sheila noted that the focus on sex trafficking was something that divided the antitrafficking movement, but she saw little evidence of victims of commercial sex differing from victims of labor trafficking. During negotiations for a New York State antitrafficking law, Sheila advocated for a single definition of trafficking rather than a bifurcated one: "The state thing really came down to the [abolitionist coalition] had been the loudest voice, and they convinced the lawmakers that sex trafficking was oh so much worse, and . . . we kept saying, sex trafficking is horrendous; it's horrible. Don't forget that in a lot of labor trafficking, domestic servitude, other kinds of labor, sexual assault is used as control or punishment. 'Oh I didn't know that,' would be some lawmaker's response. 'We've always been told that this is so much worse.' You know? So I don't think they should be separated." By contesting the dichotomy between sex and labor trafficking, Sheila learned that those supporting the distinction did not fully understand its consequences. Indeed, by bracketing out trafficking for forced commercial sex as unique, the sexual abuse often experienced by victims of labor trafficking was completely overlooked. Her experience underscored that concerns over trafficking were being driven by anxieties about sex and prostitution, not by concerns over the removal of free will, even when sexual abuse was the means used to establish control over another human being. Sheila was frustrated by advocates who had no experience working with victims portraying themselves as experts and pitching trafficking as solely an issue of sex trafficking: "I'm a firm believer that I cannot go out and give a speech if it's not backed up by something I really know, and what I found out was that the fourteen-year-old girl working in a sleazy bar in New Jersey and the thirty-five-year-old man from India had the same feelings about climate of fear, the same reasons for not leaving, the same feeling of helplessness and hopelessness." Sheila felt confident challenging normative assumptions about trafficking because her beliefs were grounded in her on-the-ground work with victims.

Charlotte was the director of a social services program and echoed many of Sheila's beliefs. She noted that service providers are well positioned to serve as advocates because of their extensive contact with victims. "I think it's a really important role because we are the . . . closest thing that comes to the survivor's voice. . . . So I see our role as really taking what we've seen in the implementation of what's going on—how it works and how it doesn't work—and being able to inform future programming. And I would like to think that we're doing it in a way that best serves the interest of clients." Based on her work with survivors of both forced prostitution and forced labor, Charlotte adamantly disagreed with the abolitionist focus on sex trafficking, which she viewed as running counter to reality. We discussed an advocate who had provided testimony at a congressional hearing and spoke about sex trafficking as though it were the only form of trafficking and also conflated it with prostitution. For Charlotte, and for other providers I spoke to, conflating prostitution with trafficking meant diverting attention away from those individuals who were most difficult to identify (because of their confinement) and most in need of services—those who had been forced or coerced into commercial sex or other labor sectors: "I have no idea why that voice is not being challenged. . . . We need to shift the debate . . . or nobody is going to ever understand our position." Indeed, the notion that sex trafficking equaled trafficking writ large was so dominant in the media and the public imagination that service providers were among a small minority who had the experience and knowledge to challenge this belief, based on their interactions with survivors.

Organizational limitations had to do with Charlotte's decision not to speak out publicly and challenge the abolitionist perspective herself. Because she is part of one program within a larger NGO, taking a political position on trafficking meant the entire agency would have to take on the issue: "It's really hard for our upper management to understand, not who cares about prostitution, but prostitution is not our issue. Why are we talking about this? What does that have to do with us? And it's really slow going to get them to understand that . . . unfortunately [the abolitionists] are making it our business . . . and even if our only response is trying to shift the debate or reframe the discussion a little bit, we do have to respond somehow." But responding meant engaging with a dichotomy that Charlotte viewed as false. "I don't like talking about sex trafficking versus labor trafficking because to me it's all trafficking. . . . I think it's detrimental to the trafficking movement to be so focused on sex trafficking. And they try to act like we are so focused on labor trafficking, but I don't think we're focused on labor trafficking. I think we're focused on trafficking. And it's not productive to be pitting sex trafficking with labor trafficking . . . saying whose experience is worse. I think it's about how to serve the best interests of clients." According to Charlotte, spending time debating the sex/labor split took valuable time and resources away from victims of all forms of trafficking.

Charlotte also struggled with persuading people to understand that focusing solely on sex trafficking was detrimental to labor trafficking victims. For outsiders to her line of work, forced prostitution always superseded any other form of forced labor because the notion of deliberate sexual harm was so foregrounded that it overshadowed even those forms of sexual harm that accompanied forced labor: "We get a lot of pushback and resistance even from within [our organization] of people not working on the issue, of how can you compare people who have to service five or ten men a day to somebody . . . working in a field or working at home? And I think that's really unfair to the labor trafficking person. No one can say whose experience is worse, and to pit victims' experiences against each other and to say one is more atrocious than the other, I think it's counterproductive to what we're trying to do." Charlotte addressed the issue in terms of victims' service needs.

> As far as needs when they come in, I don't think that it's necessarily the type of trafficking that they experience but their life skills and where they are. So somebody who was isolated in a home [doing domestic work] and doesn't have any experience in New York City could have much more intensive needs than a person who was sex trafficked and was out and about in society and living and having some limited freedom of movement and choice in their trafficking experience. So for me . . . it's the needs of the client; the trauma of the client isn't defined by their labor trafficking or their sex trafficking, but by their life skills that they bring to their experience.

The defining feature of a victim's trafficking experience, Charlotte said, is not the sector into which they are trafficked but the effect that trafficking had on his or her life and the types of assistance required to move on and achieve independence.

Following a meeting that Charlotte had attended on promoting trafficking awareness in New York City, she told me about a conversation she had with the head of an abolitionist-oriented organization: "She said, 'Well, you guys are the experts on labor trafficking.' And I said, 'No, our focus is on trafficking in general, and when we train we don't talk about sex trafficking or labor trafficking, we talk about both, and it's how to identify both . . . and people have the same signs even if they're coming from a very different setting.'" This abolitionist advocate assumed that Charlotte's organization must be "experts on labor trafficking" and that a clear demarcation was necessary in order to properly address what she viewed as two different types of exploitation. Charlotte continued, "I made a comment about a lot of our labor trafficking [survivors] having been sexually assaulted as well, and she was very taken aback by that and had no idea that in labor trafficking cases that there were sexual assaults. So I think that there is just a lot of misinformation out there. . . . I definitely think that they get a lot of misinformation about us and our philosophies." She went on, "I get so upset with the antiprostitution people sometimes because they act like labor trafficking is not a violation against women's rights, and it certainly is and even just as horrible as some of the sex trafficking cases that you hear about. But then again, that's leading into their saying one is more horrible than the other." Forced prostitution and forced labor, to Charlotte, are both women's rights issues, but the sex/labor division was deeply embedded within antitrafficking discourse and encompassed gendered constructions of harm, work, and victimhood. Consequently, any effort to contest this framework resulted in ideological clashes rather than positive outcomes for victims. Charlotte sighed, saying, "It's just so counterproductive, and I've never worked in a field where there is so much infighting about how to help people."

A federal law enforcement agent whose work centered primarily on investigating human trafficking crimes, Jim had worked on cases involving both forced prostitution and forced labor over the years. His quick response to my definitional question for him—he just said, "By the statute"—fell apart upon further prodding from me. "I don't see [trafficking] so much as forced labor. The cases I believe are more important are women coming and working as prostitutes." When I pressed him to talk about why he viewed them differently, he told me, "I think there's a huge difference between sex and labor trafficking. What happens in sex trafficking is horrendous. It takes everything away from a person." His assumptions about sex led him to make value judgments in his work about which types of trafficking were more repugnant and which victims more severely harmed.

Jim mentioned one labor trafficking case that had occurred in a neighboring district. Two women had been forced to perform domestic labor seventeen hours a day, seven days a week, for $100 a month. The traffickers verbally and physically abused the women, including beating and burning them. They restricted the women's movement and food intake and provided them only with thin mats for sleeping on the floor. Jim told me, "The women were locked up, but they still have some of their dignity"—as though forced prostitution is more degrading and a more serious offense than other kinds of trafficking. Jim based this judgment on what he viewed as the motivation of the victims, conceiving of survivors of forced prostitution as more authentic victims: "This whole thing, sex trafficking, sickens me. Most of the labor trafficking victims, they wanted to come here in the first place." In Jim's mind, sex trafficking was such a serious and heinous crime that the female victims could have no culpability in even wanting to enter the United States without documents.[9] Clearly uninformed about the circumstances surrounding *sexual* trafficking, he viewed forced commercial sex as totally repugnant, while the thought of men and women being forced into other types of labor and mistreated was much less so. The undercurrent in his comments was that victims of labor trafficking wanted to come to the United States and, therefore, knew what they were signing up for—although evidence suggests that many victims of sex and labor trafficking know the *type* of labor they will be performing in the United States, but when they arrive the conditions change and become highly exploitative.[10] Jim's views were driven by a sense of moral outrage that prioritized sexual victimization, especially when commercial exchange was involved, over other types of harm. Jim viewed women in forced prostitution as victims in need of rescue, while he saw men and women forced into other labor sectors, no matter how deplorable their conditions, as partly responsible for their suffering. Interestingly, Jim's views on how to eliminate sex trafficking were more in line with those of human rights activists than abolitionist advocates: "I think prostitution should almost be legalized if there's a way to monitor it, all the violence and drugs it generates."

Interpretive frameworks about sex intersect implementation of the TVPA, and the professionals involved integrate biases and ideologies into their antitrafficking work. Among implementers, there is no one vision of "trafficking"; there are many. Just as with the drafters of the TVPA, some professionals single out sex trafficking as imparting unique harm, while others contest this notion. We cannot assume that Jim is alone in thinking that trafficking for forced commercial sex is a despicable crime and its victims more deserving of protection and assistance than those trafficked as agricultural laborers or domestic servants, whom he viewed as partially responsible for their fate. On the other hand, Molly agreed that individuals trafficked for forced commercial sex are distinct from people trafficked into other labor sectors, but she nonetheless viewed all forms of trafficking as important and in need of attention. In contrast to Jim and Molly, both Sheila and Charlotte viewed the marker *sex trafficking* as generative of a false dichotomy causing additional harm to those trafficked into other sectors.

Sex acts as a key conceptual frame for trafficking in three important and interconnected ways. There is first and foremost a tendency to conflate prostitution with trafficking (i.e., all prostitutes are trafficked, or all migrant prostitutes are trafficked), and this conflation is codified in the TVPA via the nonoperational definition of sex trafficking. Second, there is a reductive trend implying that sex trafficking is coterminous with trafficking itself—other kinds of forced labor become afterthoughts or are completely ignored. Finally, there is an implicit undercurrent in the media, government policy, certain advocacy efforts, and even implementation of the TVPA that sex trafficking is the most important kind of trafficking. By keeping the attention on sex, each of these tropes transforms the meaning of trafficking and redirects the focus from trafficking in general to something that is both much more specific and much broader than the legally operative definition (sex trafficking is a subset of trafficking, while prostitution occurs in a number of iterations, usually without force).

The Conflation of Trafficking and Prostitution

While most of the professionals I met were experienced enough not to conflate noncoerced prostitution and trafficking, many of them spoke about the impact of conflation on antitrafficking efforts in terms of resources being diverted from severe forms of trafficking (both forced commercial sex and other forms of forced labor), the need for training on accurate victim identification procedures, and a misunderstanding of trafficking among the general public. I also witnessed frequent instances of conflation in the form of government policies, local law enforcement's trafficking-identification strategies, and educational forums held by antiprostitution advocates.

Conflation occurs on two levels—accidental and intentional. Much accidental fusion occurs in the media, either because journalists are making false assumptions (i.e., all migrant sex workers are trafficking victims) as a result of not thinking the issue through or they are relying on sources that intentionally equate prostitution and trafficking. As others have described, several feminist groups with roots in the antipornography movement deliberately conflate the two.[11] These "abolitionist feminists" argue that *all* commercial sex objectifies and oppresses *all* women, contending that no prostitution is voluntary, which makes it is impossible to distinguish between forced and voluntary prostitution. Over the course of the 1990s, abolitionist feminists became active voices in the trafficking dialogue and have remained so since. As described in Chapter 1, these feminists were part of the coalition that fought hard to maintain a definition of "sex trafficking" without any requirement of force, fraud, or coercion in the TVPA.

On a national level, what some of my informants referred to as the "abolitionist coalition" consists of a loosely affiliated group of feminist advocates and religious conservatives who have collaborated on key legislative issues such as the drafting and reauthorizations of the TVPA. Nationally and internationally, many types of organizations and individuals driven by various commitments identify as abolitionists in that they seek to end trafficking and slavery—and often prostitution, too.[12] While I did interview a small number of individuals whom I would characterize as members of the larger abolitionist movement, we should be careful not to characterize the movement as monolithic or to imply that its members have a single view of abolitionism. Talking to various people involved with the abolitionist movement made it very clear that their views were highly individualized and nuanced. In New York—the city and the state—the dominant voices in the coalition emanate from a small group of feminists who have been long-time antiprostitution advocates, and for the most part this is the specific group of abolitionists to which I refer. Because they were not actively *implementing* the TVPA, interviewing any of the feminist advocates who were the most vocal abolitionist spokeswomen in New York fell outside the purview of this study.[13] Although most antiprostitution advocates, in New York at least, do not prosecute traffickers or provide services to victims, it is important to include some of their voices here because so many of my informants saw themselves acting in direct opposition to these advocates.[14] I attended a number of events at which abolitionist feminists spoke, and I include some of their public remarks to illustrate the types of rhetoric to which many of my informants responded. My goal is not to further this debate; rather, I want to point to how the debate informs and enters into antitrafficking work on the ground.

When my informants professed objectivity—"We are a law enforcement agency; we have to use the definition in the law" or "I define trafficking by the statute"—they implied that they used the operational "severe forms of trafficking" definition in the TVPA precisely because that is the only definition that has legal power in terms of prosecuting traffickers. On the other hand, some feminists' effort to conflate prostitution and trafficking is primarily symbolic and ideological, but nonetheless their view is essentially codified in law and has material effects. Despite the fact that the nonoperational definition of sex trafficking has no legal consequences per se, it does have collective resonance. Because this subset of advocates uses this terminology to describe prostitution, this conflation permeates the media, the public consciousness, and even individual law enforcement agents' conceptions of trafficking.

So, who counts as a victim of trafficking? It depends on the mind in which the trafficking is being envisioned. When they refer to sex trafficking, abolitionist advocates are talking about something very different from service providers' and law enforcement's conceptions—the former refers to prostitution; the latter, to forced prostitution. In providing services funded under the TVPA, NGOs must rely on the operative definition—only a victim of a "severe form of trafficking" is entitled to services and benefits, so the terms *sex trafficking, labor trafficking,* and *human trafficking* always imply force.[15] In sharp contrast, abolitionist advocates continue to argue that all women moved into prostitution, even those somewhat intentionally working for a pimp or in a brothel, are victims of sex trafficking. As one abolitionist feminist stated in a 2004 speech, "The truth is that what we call sex trafficking is nothing more or less than globalized prostitution."[16] Many abolitionist advocates use the terms *sex traffickers* and *pimps* interchangeably, and they seem to describe some of the most dismal aspects of prostitution in order to equate it with trafficking.

At a conference I attended on trafficking from the perspective of violence against women, the head of a prominent feminist organization in New York City advocated conducting a block-to-block campaign to identify "sex traffickers." She proclaimed, "Trafficking is *the* issue. It's happening in our neighborhoods. It's like Starbucks. There is not a block in the city without a brothel." Her statement is emblematic of the definitional difficulties of the TVPA: advocates utilize the nonoperational "sex trafficking" definition to mystify what counts as trafficking. In this case, the advocate was suggesting that occurrences of trafficking were found at the same geographic density as Starbucks, presuming that brothels could be found at roughly the same rate as Starbucks in Manhattan, although I have come across no data to support this claim. The idea that trafficking is occurring in *every* brothel confuses prostitution and trafficking. If all prostitution is inherently exploitative, as this speaker certainly believed, all prostitution is trafficking. She declared that it was happening *everywhere* and, technically speaking, most prostitution taking place in brothels may fit the nonoperative definition of "sex trafficking" in the TVPA in that someone else is involved in helping, paying, or giving a room to a woman working in prostitution. But the TVPA neither criminalizes this "help" nor provides services to the women receiving this "help" unless force, fraud, or coercion is also present. The abolitionist's definition is nothing more than a legal mirage.

Many informants alluded either implicitly or explicitly to the rift between abolitionist advocates and themselves, whom they described as victim-centered service providers. Both groups identified as members of broad coalitions of feminists and providers, but they held differing ideological views regarding trafficking and prostitution. Over the course of my research, New York became a kind of microcosm of the larger trafficking debates taking place at the national level because of the concurrent efforts to pass a New York

State antitrafficking law and lobbying around the 2008 reauthorization of the TVPA.[17]

At a rally in support of New York State antitrafficking legislation, Sonia Ossorio, president of the NYC chapter of the National Organization for Women (NOW), talked about the vulnerability of victims of human trafficking. To emphasize her point, she read a quote posted on a blog by a john: "I asked her [the sex worker] if she minds doing this to men. After much pantomime and language barrier breakthrough, she said, 'Oh, for first six months I cry every night; now not so bad.'"[18] The use of this quote is problematic on several levels, the most important being that because it came from a website where johns rate sex workers—broadly speaking—there is no way to know whether the quoted woman was trafficked or not. Although the quote suggests that the woman was deeply unhappy in her work, there is no evidence that she was forced or coerced into prostitution. Yet this was the quotation the advocate chose to illustrate the need for antitrafficking legislation; from her perspective, all prostitutes are victims.

I witnessed this group of advocates making these kinds of conflations at numerous events that I attended over the course of my fieldwork. At one conference on trafficking as a form of violence against women, the director of an organization dealing with commercial sexual exploitation of children declared, "Everyone knows a man who has paid for sex. We have to take responsibility for allowing human beings to buy and sell other human beings." At the same conference, a feminist advocate and attorney defined trafficking as "the buying and selling of human beings as a commodity." Both of the speakers were referring to men buying sexual *services* from women but framed it in the language of "buying human beings," as though there were no distinction between paying a woman to provide sexual services for an hour or a night and buying or selling her as a piece of property to be controlled indefinitely. This kind of reductionist approach perpetuates confusion about what constitutes trafficking, and many of the service providers I came to know objected to using the language of trafficking to talk about prostitution. At the annual meeting of a national antitrafficking network, Jarrah, an immigration attorney, noted that the abolitionist coalition "is using antitrafficking as a platform for antiprostitution." From Jarrah's perspective, these advocates were taking advantage of the momentum surrounding the trafficking issue as a way to draw attention to their own efforts to eliminate sex work. Ella, another immigration attorney, viewed the conflation as driven by a need for funding: "It's like any concept of branding; it's, like, aim where the money is. If we can talk about an old problem in a new way and there's funding to go along with that, then let's do our best to put a spin on it." She continued, "I mean, do I think there should be services for people who no longer want to work in sex work or no longer want to work in prostitution? Definitely. . . . Should there be shelters or housing or job training opportunities? Definitely. But I think . . . when you're talking about a smaller pool of people [trafficked persons] and then all of a sudden it's a larger pool of people [women in prostitution], then who pays for what? I don't know, it just gets . . . confusing and overwhelming." Indeed, services for women wanting to leave commercial sex are sorely lacking. However, rather than lobbying for funding for services for this population, abolitionist advocates seek to conflate this "prostitution by circumstance" with trafficking and pimps with traffickers. As Jarrah told me,

> Well, okay, they want to get out of the sex work. It's one thing to morally chastise them like some organizations do, but how do we actually get them out of the sex work? They can't work at McDonald's; it doesn't provide a livable wage. So what opportunities do they have? They don't have resumes; they don't have past job experience or someone that can give them a recommendation. So we need services that provide for that, getting them typing skills, getting them . . . GEDs or vocational skills, things like that that are actually going to get them into jobs that pay a livable wage.

Many of the providers with whom I spoke were sympathetic to the lack of services available to women wanting to leave prostitution and agreed that sex workers should not be treated as criminals. They acknowledged the exploitation that many women experience in prostitution, but they drew the line at calling it trafficking precisely because referring to the two interchangeably diminishes the experiences of their clients and diverts attention from prostitution involving force, fraud, and coercion as well as labor trafficking. Roxanne, an immigration attorney, noted,

> There are literally people who are pushing for . . . the conflation of prostitution and trafficking, and that makes it much harder for those who have been struggling to access these protections and makes it even harder for them. It also helps . . . continue to frame the media message that prostitution is the same thing as trafficking. . . . We had

to train so many cops at different times, and I still don't think when we were done talking that they really understood that trafficking included labor trafficking. To them it's just prostitution and that's part of the messaging they are receiving, and so it's hard you, know?

There was a real disconnect between the image of trafficking presented by abolitionist advocates and the experience of trafficking victims who made up my service provider interviewees' client base. The idea that abolitionist advocates were propagating a contradictory notion of trafficking at trainings, conferences, and in the media was frustrating to providers, and they observed that law enforcement agents were developing preconceptions about trafficking as a direct consequence of the misinformation. Of course, this broad focus on all forms of trafficking by New York service providers is a phenomenon that may vary geographically or as a result of other contextual factors. While this proclivity was present among the providers I encountered in New York and among the national network of service providers to which most of them belonged, there are certainly variances in meaning in terms of how service providers in other regions define trafficking, with many organizations focusing their efforts solely on sex trafficking.

Trafficking as One End of the Spectrum of Sex Work

Legally, the TVPA differentiates trafficking for forced commercial sex from noncoercive forms of prostitution, and most of my informants viewed trafficking into forced prostitution as one extreme along a continuum of sex work. Jarrah, an immigration attorney told me,

> I usually . . . talk about a spectrum of sex work, so on one end we have persons who are trafficked who were forced into it and don't really want to do it, and then you've got the majority of sex workers in the middle who are doing it for circumstance, who would rather be doing other things, but because of lack of livable wages, etc., they cannot function economically without going into sex work. . . . And then we've got a minority of sex workers on the very other end that . . . have alternative means of financial stability, yet they choose sex work for whatever reason, you know, sexual autonomy, they find it convenient as a job opportunity, whatever. So then along that spectrum the needs of sex workers are extremely different.

For Jarrah and other providers I spoke with, separating forced prostitution from other types of sex work along this spectrum was an essential distinction. Immigrant women (and men) voluntarily working in commercial sex are not entitled to federal trafficking benefits, and NGOs cannot be reimbursed for providing services to individuals who do not meet the criteria for "victim of a severe form of trafficking" status.

Although abolitionist advocates continually tried to erode this distinction, a clear rationale exists for using force, fraud, and coercion as the defining features of trafficking. Mark, a federal prosecutor, told me, "I think that there is an understanding on the part of policy makers that there is a difference between a pimping case where someone gets hit and a case in which someone is enslaved, and figuring that difference out, obviously in some cases it's going to be difficult, but in other cases it's pretty clear. And in law enforcement we make those distinctions all the time." He elaborated, "There's a reason why there is first- and second-degree murder, manslaughter, and involuntary manslaughter, and part of our job in the law enforcement community is to figure out which one of those it is." A similar spectrum exists between sex work and forced prostitution: "[It's not just] the Mann Act, which assumes that the woman is a prostitute . . . and slavery, which assumes that the woman is being flat-out enslaved, with absolutely nothing in between the two. You know, [the law] attempts to actually fill in some of those in-between things, much like you have murder all the way down to simple assault." The abolitionist coalition of feminist advocates and evangelical Christians has been reluctant to recognize this spectrum, as Mark explained:

> The attempts to fill in those things have been misunderstood by that coalition because they think that it means that we are somehow saying that all cases should be done in one of those particular ways. It's almost like they don't understand the menu approach that we have to take, and . . . whether they do understand it and they're being disingenuous so they can fight a cleaner political battle, or whether they just don't understand it, and after eight or ten years you start to think maybe that's a willful non-understanding because anybody that's been to law school should understand this concept of how you set up an entire criminal law regime. And it's not a normative statement to say that something is manslaughter versus something being murder. You're not saying, "I value that person's life more than I value this other person's life." They're both dead and that's a tragedy. The dif-

ference is that there are other things that society has to take into account when setting up the criminal laws. And it's not that their life is worth less, it's that their death is more punishable based on the . . . evil intent of the murderer, as opposed to the "oops" of the manslaughter.

Mark's explanation raises two important issues. The conflation of trafficking and prostitution is both purposeful and political: antiprostitution advocates actively conflate sex work and trafficking as part of a larger strategy to eliminate commercial sex. And just as there is a range of crimes between manslaughter and first-degree murder, there is also a range of activities between voluntary sex work and severe forms of trafficking. A sex worker could be exploited by her pimp in various ways such that he could be prosecuted for pimping or pandering and various Mann Act charges, but she is still, in a practical sense, free to leave.

The process of determining whether cases meet the criteria for severe forms of sex trafficking—versus falling somewhere else along the spectrum of sex work—is instructive. Larry, a local law enforcement agent, told me, "We are getting a lot of phone calls [referrals], but a lot of them might be just straight up prostitution cases. . . . So we go out there and actually break it down—how were you forced? Where was your coercion in this? And you know . . . they pretty much say, 'No I want to do this, I like doing this, I do this strictly for the money, ya know, I work for a pimp'—but that doesn't meet the human trafficking [definition], so that's just a straight up prostitution arrest." He added that they close out those cases right away, and if anything, a detective from the vice team might pursue it. "But we wouldn't take it as a human trafficking case."

Being bound by the law, enforcement agents clearly made distinctions between forced and voluntary prostitution. Multiple informants also told me about encounters that were essentially variations on a theme: they confronted women involved in sex work who adamantly rejected the idea that they had been trafficked or victimized. Kyle, a federal prosecutor, is someone whom on many fronts I would describe as an abolitionist: he had volunteered for an international evangelical abolitionist organization at one point and characterizes that experience as deeply significant. Yet to me he spoke about trafficking as consisting solely of conditions involving force, fraud, and coercion. He told me about a case involving a raid on a Korean brothel. "I remember one woman; I can remember her face so well. She was not a victim; she was a voluntary prostitute. . . . And she said, 'Look, I knew what I was doing, I wanted the money and those women did too.'" Kyle went on to discuss the contrasts he observes between someone who has been forced into prostitution and someone who chooses it as the best of all of her available options:

> As someone who is deeply moved by the abuse of power and who . . . has seen firsthand the suffering that victims of trafficking can endure, I just have talked to lots of women . . . who have been through difficult circumstances but human beings who were in control of their faculties who told me, "I had other options, but I want to do this because I want the money. None of my other options allow me to make $10,000 a month, and I want to make $10,000 a month because I want these clothes, and I want to eat at these places, and I want to live in this place, and it's not that bad." And I think it's hard for some people to accept that reality because they may not have those same choices, but I've talked to plenty of people who do. And I've talked to people who have become victims and then rejected that and gone back [to working in sex work]. . . . There are people who would rather prostitute themselves for the amount of money they can receive for doing that than face the alternatives that they have and sort of live with a lot less.

Kyle's point that it is difficult for many people to understand how any woman could *choose* sex work over another kind of employment is one of the central points of contention among trafficking advocates and providers. As a result of the successful efforts of abolitionists to conflate prostitution and trafficking, the vital distinction between forced and voluntary prostitution has not taken hold in the public imagination. Rather, a vague and confused notion of trafficking in which all immigrant sex workers are in need of rescue prevails.

People who have been trafficked generally do not self-identify. They do not know the language of trafficking and sometimes even do not recognize that what has happened to them is a crime. Sheila, the director of a trafficking services program, had helped many survivors understand their experiences through the framework of trafficking and reacted vehemently to the assertion by some advocates that service providers also need to convince sex workers that they are victims:

People say very glibly, "Well, trafficked persons don't identify as victims." Well no, none of them do because they don't know that vocabulary, but I don't think it's a service provider's job to convince someone that they are a victim. I mean teaching someone the language [of trafficking] is one thing. "Is this what happened to you? Did you have a choice? Were you forced? Were you coerced?" Whatever, however you get the information out, and it either fits [the trafficking definition] or it doesn't. But . . . I've interviewed women who have said . . . "I know that it would help me if I told you that somebody forced me to do this, but I'll tell you, I paid money, I paid a lot of money to get to this country and this is what I did to pay it back. And then I saw how much money I could make. I should've stopped then, but I told myself okay I'll make $5,000 more and I'll stop, and I made $5,000 more and nobody made me do it, nobody told me to do it, and then I wanted five thousand more, and I have my own place and I'm treated well. Yes, people drive me from place to place and find the work for me, but I get money and I do this because I am addicted to the money." Now there are certain providers who say that those are victims of human trafficking. I can't say that because they are telling me that they are not, and I don't think it's my job to tell them that they are. And I'm a very good interviewer. I've interviewed thousands of people in my life, clinical interviews. If I've asked that a lot of different ways, and I don't think that they were coerced or that their freedom was restricted, then I am not going to say that they are a victim.

To Sheila's mind, these women had made a choice to come to the United States and enter sex work. During interviews with her, they asserted their agency and underscored their free will by emphasizing their deliberate decisions to come to the United States and undertake sex work as a way to make large amounts of money quickly. The women adamantly denied being victims, and although Sheila was well aware of the time required to draw out details of coercion from trafficked persons, these women's agentive acts and assertive demeanor convinced her of their autonomy.

The particular case Sheila referenced was one that both law enforcement agents and service providers described to me as illustrative of the distinction between "severe forms of sex trafficking" and what was referred to by some advocates as "sex trafficking." The case involved a large, resource-intensive, multistate investigation of Korean massage parlors and brothels but resulted in finding very few victims who met the "severe forms of trafficking" standard. Hundreds of sex workers were discovered, but the number of identified victims of severe forms of trafficking numbered in the single digits. Despite this low percentage and the fact that there were many other local cases that did meet the more stringent standard, antiprostitution advocates at events I attended continually referenced the case as trafficking, including at a congressional hearing. They were purposefully drawing attention to a case that was mistakenly designated as trafficking in an attempt to shrink the gap between sex trafficking and severe forms of trafficking. Although the majority of women working in the massage parlors under investigation fit the nonoperational sex trafficking definition in the TVPA in that they were moved or recruited into prostitution, they were never forced, defrauded, or coerced, so they were not victims in any practical sense. The case was described by advocates, the media, and even some criminal justice personnel as trafficking, but the designation served as more of a diversion from actual cases than anything else.

During the investigation, prosecutors wiretapped the phone of a man who transported the women from state to state to work in various brothels and massage parlors. From these taped conversations, it emerged that the women were paying approximately $15,000 to come to the United States. They knowingly arranged to pay off the money by agreeing to work in brothels. Based on the taped phone conversations and interviews with the women, it was evident that they would request to go to the location where they could make the most money and pay off their debts so that they could then make more money and return home. They were free to come and go and had possession of their passports. Lynn, a federal prosecutor, referred to it as a mass alien smuggling ring, and she did not view it as a trafficking case or a high priority for TVPA prosecution. She said that during interviews with women in cases such as this one, the women sometimes said that they felt they had to work in prostitution to support their families back home: "I consider this coercion in the bigger sense of the word, but it is not trafficking."

The matter of coercion marks another fundamental difference between abolitionists and other trafficking advocates and service providers. While many service providers I spoke to talked about coercion in terms of concrete examples such as holding the victim's passport, threats to the family, and so forth, antiprostitution advocates often invoked coercion in a much broader sense. At a conference on the intersection of trafficking and violence against women, one feminist scholar asked, "How can you presume that people under conditions of inequality are able to consent?" Essentializing, generalizing questions such as this one are key to the abolitionist platform and run counter to what many service providers consider a human rights approach that recognizes the ability of individuals to make their own choices, no matter how constrained their circumstances. An advocate at this same conference defined coercion as "the build up of control that is gradual, subtle, and controlled over time." Despite being an attorney, the definition she provided was vague compared to the types of coercion qualifying as trafficking under the TVPA. Her definition of coercion could be applied to almost any scenario along the spectrum of sex work, but she did not describe any specific types of compulsion or manipulation that would fit the "severe forms of trafficking" rubric. The TVPA defines coercion as (A) threats of serious harm to or physical restraint against any person; (B) any scheme, plan, or pattern intended to cause a person to believe that failure to perform an act would result in serious harm to or physical restraint against any person; or (C) the abuse or threatened abuse of the legal process.[19] Lack of economic opportunity, in and of itself, does not meet the TVPA definition.

Cases such as the one involving the Korean woman described above frequently became platforms for definitional debates among providers and advocates, with the former describing the women involved as sex workers and latter referring to them as "victims of sex trafficking." Ella, an immigration attorney, described to me her interactions with clients involved in a similar Korean brothel case:

> With a lot of the Korean women I spoke with it was like, "I have a lot of credit card debt" or "Someone told me that . . . I could work for two weeks and make five grand, and . . . I did it once and it wasn't so bad. I made a lot of money, so every couple of months I would just go work for a few weeks." And they were making like . . . three to five thousand for . . . a week or two of work. . . . There is this whole East Coast . . . I-95 corridor, and so a lot of times the women would go work in Virginia, but they live in Flushing. They said they would go down for . . . a couple weeks and come back. . . . It was like, "When I was done, I went home and I had my money."

The picture she paints is one of sex work, certainly—and sex work that presumably benefits not simply the women involved but the persons arranging the meetings. But choice, agency, and mutual benefit infuses Ella's recounting. She spoke about the reactions of some abolitionist-minded attorneys who were also involved in the case:

> Working with the lawyers that picked up these cases, I did intakes with [the women], but . . . I called back the agency that referred it and I was like, this person wasn't forced to do anything. To me that person is a sex worker, and a lot of people are uncomfortable with that term. . . . In these women's minds, or at least the way they articulated it, it was just to make really good money in this short stint. That's not someone who's raped and beaten and whatever. . . . Talking to the other attorneys, they would be like, "Okay well, [whispering] she was forced to work but she had her period. They forced her to work." It's like well, did she ask not to work? Was she only down there for a week? I mean, it sounded like there was a lot more autonomy in the situation. And then, "She had to work because she had so much debt, and people were chasing her." And, you know, started getting at the larger issues about . . . women and the economy and having access to better-paying jobs.

Given this gap in meaning of what constitutes trafficking, what constitutes coercion? Ella's account of this conversation with another attorney depicts the other provider as believing that lack of economic opportunity constituted coercion in that it motivated this woman to enter prostitution. Unequal economic opportunities do contribute to the phenomenon of trafficking, and many of the providers I came to know felt that addressing the issue was vital to reducing trafficking. They did not, however, view it as a coercive element by itself. As anthropologist Denise Brennan has noted, women rely on sex work (and migration) not only as a survival strategy but also as an advancement strategy, a means to get ahead in the world.[20] When women's options are constrained by both global and local forces, sex work and migration become creative responses for women with limited options. The exchange between Ella and the other attorney also suggests that at issue is not so much the woman's debt and economic standing but the fact that she was engaged in *commercial sex* to pay off her debts. The attorney probably would not have taken notice had the woman been working in a factory or a nail salon, even if she was earning far less than in commercial sex.

Feminist debates and narratives find their way into the broader public imagination—even law enforcement personnel were not immune to abolitionists' efforts to conflate prostitution and trafficking, which was in fact evident in the way the law was being implemented during my fieldwork.[21] Since the passage of the TVPA, there have been multiple instances of law enforcement investigating prostitution in search of trafficking. Although federal law enforcement has devoted a great deal of resources to raiding brothels across the country in search of trafficked individuals, this strategy has been largely ineffective—many brothel raids do not find any victims of severe forms of trafficking. When there are no victims, there are no TVPA prosecutions and certainly no benefits or protections for those undocumented sex workers identified during the raids. At a national conference, a federal prosecutor noted that the U.S. government was identifying more *potential* sex trafficking cases than labor trafficking cases. He said that sex trafficking investigations are "often extremely expensive and resource intensive but do not often yield the results we had hoped for. We know if people are immigrants and they are working in prostitution, but we don't know if they are trafficking victims . . . I struggle with whether we should be executing these large-scale raids." Often these types of searches identify voluntary prostitutes rather than trafficking victims.

Although conflation was common at the investigative level, all of the federal prosecutors who spoke to me clearly articulated the requirement of force, fraud, or coercion to meet the statutory definition of trafficking and were quick to assert that prosecution was not possible without these elements. This speaks partially to the fact that all of the prosecutors I interviewed were located in New York City or the HTPU at DOJ headquarters in Washington, D.C. As such, they all had dealt with a large volume of cases and were some of the most experienced trafficking prosecutors in the country. However, a few provided examples of conflation that they had observed in which prosecutors with less experience in other districts attempted to portray movement into prostitution (absent force, fraud, and coercion) as trafficking. Lynn told me that in the large Korean massage parlor case mentioned above, federal agents raided the brothels without having uncovered via wiretapping any evidence of trafficking. The attorneys prosecuting the case in another district—Lynn was not among them—charged the defendants with trafficking and several other infractions. Despite only having evidence of and securing a conviction for alien smuggling, the prosecutors publicized the case as trafficking. As Lynn put it, this "mis-advertises the issue and overstates the problem."

After already speaking with a number of people involved—including service providers and law enforcement agents—I observed one of the sentencing hearings related to this case. My informants made clear that the issue was clearly not trafficking. I was somewhat surprised during the sentencing when the prosecutor told the jurors, "*Sex trafficking* is a term that perfectly describes the evidence you've heard about in this trial, because it's all about movement—moving women from Korea, across state lines, taxi drivers delivering women. The wiretaps indicate, 'bring me a skinny girl.'" None of these conditions actually fit the operational definition of severe forms of trafficking. The prosecutor was referring to the *nonoperational* definition of so-called sex trafficking, and movement across borders has nothing to do with it. The misleading prosecutor said that whether the women consented to work as prostitutes was irrelevant to the charges.[22] Even when the women agreed to work in prostitution, she alleged, all of the conditions were stacked in favor of the underhanded entrepreneurs: they knowingly used undocumented labor, and the women didn't speak the language, were hidden away, were taken to unknown destinations, worked eighteen-hour days, and had to pay people all the way down the line. Although these factors do not paint a rosy picture, they also do not constitute severe forms of trafficking. An attorney for the government, the prosecutor used the term *sex trafficking* in a highly confusing way because it is not legally operative and replicates many of the abolitionist arguments that are not based on a legally tenable classification. Movement is not a key element of the trafficking definition. The women worked long hours and may have been exploited, but there was no evidence of force, fraud, or coercion. They came to the United States aware of the type of work they would be doing and the conditions under which they would do it. They were free to leave and bring any additional earnings home with them when they returned to Korea. The defendants did not "traffic" the women involved in any prosecutable way, yet the term *trafficking* added intensity to the prosecutor's argument.

Misrepresenting prostitution and trafficking as synonymous begins to look like a veritable strategy of law enforcement because all over the country government agencies devoted resources to investigating prostitution but produced few cases of severe forms of trafficking. More often than not, resources to identify trafficking victims contributed to identifying large numbers of voluntary sex workers because law enforcement assumed that targeting brothels would turn up situations of force and coercion. As Dean, a federal prosecutor, told me, "A lot of it is part of the difference in definition, all the confusion about the word *trafficking*. . . . Police are spending hours and months and millions of dollars focusing on every massage parlor that appears to have Korean women working in it, and the truth is they can't do them all. They pick one, you know, there's a hundred of them out there right? Four have trafficking in them. . . . If they're just going to pick one, they're probably not going to find one of the four. They're going to find one that's not. They're going to find one of the 96." While agent after agent told me that force, fraud, and coercion were the key elements of trafficking, these raids focused on a specific type of work rather than on detecting extremely exploitative conditions. Conflating prostitution with trafficking meant that many sex workers who were never trafficked were legally compromised, while others who had been trafficked were overlooked.

The Privileged Position of Sex Trafficking

Whether a conscious deception or just a misguided tactic, erasing the boundary between trafficking and prostitution happens widely. Another common but disadvantageous tendency—believing that forced prostitution is the only kind of trafficking or that it is inherently more important and serious than trafficking into other labor sectors—reflects deep unease over commercial sex as a site of trafficking but also assigns sex a sacred quality. The implication is that the act of sex for money breaches a moral and categorical boundary beyond the force and coercion that compel it. Although I encountered many professionals who disputed these claims based on their experiences of working with victims, I regularly found it promulgated by the media, abolitionist advocates, those at the highest levels of U.S. government policymaking, and law enforcement agents working on the ground. Policy makers manipulate cultural images of certain target populations, including trafficking victims, and enact policies reflecting these social constructions.[23] The social construction of trafficking as produced through U.S. policy during the George W. Bush administration had the overall effect of raising the visibility and import of forced prostitution and its victims while rendering all other forms of trafficking invisible. Although trafficking victims are commonly referred to as "hidden in plain sight" in order to make the claim that not enough is being done to identify trafficking (in some cases based on a faulty understanding of what constitutes trafficking), the fact is that a great deal of attention is devoted specifically to identifying sex trafficking, while labor trafficking receives far less consideration. As I will discuss in Chapter 5, the invisibility of labor trafficking results in those victims often facing a far more challenging path to protection than is open to their counterparts forced into prostitution.

I cannot count how many events devoted to "human trafficking" I attended during which the speaker would launch into orations about women and girls forced into prostitution without ever referencing any other types of trafficking, as though sex trafficking and human trafficking were synonymous. At one forum I attended, former Ambassador John Miller, director of the State Department's Office to Monitor and Combat Trafficking in Persons, remarked, "Coming here tonight inspired me to fire off a letter to the President of the United States requesting that in his upcoming speech on the state of the union he highlight sex trafficking."[24] Ambassador Miller, whose responsibilities included overseeing work on trafficking in *all* its forms, chose this occasion and many others to specifically speak out on the plight of women trafficked into forced prostitution. This privileging of sex trafficking was not surprising in the context of federal antitrafficking policy during that period, and President George W. Bush hardly needed a reminder to focus his efforts on sex trafficking in particular. Over the course of eight years, the Bush administration skewed enforcement of the TVPA toward eliminating severe forms of sex trafficking as well as prostitution.

Policy often reflects the interests of powerful constituent groups, and Bush-era antitrafficking policies replicated some of the most deeply held positions of abolitionists and evangelicals. A 2003 National Security Presidential Directive referred to "prostitution and related activities" as "inherently harmful and dehumanizing," adding that they "contribute to the phenomenon of trafficking in persons."[25] The administration promoted the prevention of prostitution as a strategy to prevent trafficking, so ending prostitution and ending trafficking became one and the same. This high-level policy directive set the stage for a single-minded and exclusive focus on prostitution (forced or not) to the exclusion of forced labor. Shortly following the issuance of this directive, the State Department posted prominently on its website a document titled "The Link Between Prostitution and Sex Trafficking."[26] The document cited research (conducted by well-known abolitionists) that has been widely critiqued on methodological grounds[27] yet remained on the website until the end of the Bush presidency.

"The current [Bush] administration doesn't want us to tell the truth," one of my informants, a federal grants administrator named Fran, told me after

I asked to tape our interview. The dominant discourse of sex trafficking found in Bush-era policies emphasized a particular way of conceptualizing trafficking and framing the issue—one in which female victims of forced prostitution were the most worthy of sympathy and assistance. Political scientists Anne Schneider and Helen Ingram note, "A great deal of the political maneuvering in the establishment of policy agendas and in the design of policy pertains to the specification of the target populations and the type of image that can be created for them."[28] As anthropologists of policy, Shore and Wright suggest normative claims are used "to present a particular way of defining a problem and its solution, as if they were the only ones possible, while enforcing closure or silence on other ways of thinking or talking."[29] Fran's anxiety about being quoted and potentially saying something not in line with the administration's focus on sex trafficking was palpable, but in truth, 60 percent of victims enrolled in federal service provision programs at that time were victims of labor trafficking.[30] Yet there was a sharp contrast between the reality of identified victims and the way the Bush administration represented the issue. While the focus of antitrafficking efforts has been broadened substantially with the shift in administration—in the 2009 fiscal year, 82 percent of identified victims were victims of "labor trafficking" and 48 percent were men[31]—eight years of "sex trafficking"–focused policies have lastingly influenced the way in which trafficking is conceptualized, which in turn shapes the way the problem is defined and how victims are classified from the highest level of government to the most practical level of implementation.

Sociologist Ronald Weitzer discusses the social construction of sex trafficking as a moral crusade spearheaded by antiprostitution feminists and institutionalized by the second Bush administration into government policy, legislation, and law enforcement practices, noting that shortly after the Bush administration took office, abolitionist views "were accepted, incorporated into official policy, and implemented in agency practices."[32] Throughout its tenure, the Bush administration actively consulted with Christian and feminist abolitionist activists on policy questions, posted links to abolitionist articles on federal agency websites (to the exclusion of other viewpoints), and limited antitrafficking funds to organizations with formal antiprostitution policies. The Bush administration was so committed to this particular political and moral agenda that it not only ignored other perspectives but members of the administration, along with abolitionist advocates, also accused service providing agencies that held alternative views of being "pro-prostitution" (even if they took no stand on prostitution at all), sometimes excluding well-respected organizations from events and trainings. Sheila, the director of one of the most esteemed trafficking services programs in the country, told me that State Department officials routinely questioned her approach because of its emphasis on fraudulent, coercive, and forced exploitation in all labor sectors: "They wanted to criticize us for our philosophy, but how can you criticize an agency that's got a constant flow of clients, that's well thought of by their law enforcement partners, by the community, by the clients . . . [and is] modeling best practices?" She felt that "they sort of punished us. . . . I got blackballed from some Department of State trips." NGO providers with whom I spoke were hesitant to directly counter abolitionist claims (even those with no empirical basis), often out of fear of losing funding. As a result, the abolitionist vision was continually touted as representative of trafficking. Charlotte, the director of one service-providing agency, noted, "I do think that [service providers] get scared of the name-calling and give in [to it]. . . . It's absurd to think that there are people out there that think that we're pro-prostitution." Yet the term *pro-prostitution* was used as a tool to silence providers and others advocating for a broader vision of trafficking grounded in the law and based on their experiences delivering services to victims.

Just as Bush-era policies led to uneven framing of the issue in many settings, their practical impact was varied, too. Providers, investigators, government bureaucrats, and prosecutors all made discretionary interpretations of law and policy, some challenging and others reinforcing normative assumptions about prostitution and sex trafficking. Steven Maynard-Moody and Michael Musheno remark, "With regard to what government actually does, as opposed to what it says it does, street-level workers are important decision makers. They deliver the services; they actualize policy, in this sense they are policy makers, at least metaphorically. Their decisions and actions are, however, localized and particularistic."[33] While abolitionist discourses were deeply embedded in U.S. government policy and practice, the voices of service providers illustrate the ways in which these assumptions were contested and fractured. Jarrah, an immigration attorney, noted that the Bush administration's focus on sex trafficking was influencing conceptions of trafficking among all levels of government. She reacted in an exasperated tone: "With the federal government screaming and shouting about sex trafficking, it's providing impetus for every level below them [to also focus solely on sex trafficking] until you get to the ground." She continued, "It's only the direct service providers who are saying whoa, stop, this is not accurate. Let's say there's ten layers in between [the top level of government and the ground]; you get all nine layers who are buying into that trafficking is only for sex work."

The image of trafficking presented by Bush administration officials and abolitionist advocates that emerged from my fieldwork did not concur with the experiences of trafficking victims as reported directly to me or relayed by the service providers whom I interviewed. Many professional implementers perceived policy makers, with their assumptions about sex trafficking, as overlooking the lived experience of actual victims. Bridget, the director of a trafficking services program, spoke about the ways that politics invaded implementation of the TVPA and conceptions of what constitutes trafficking: "I mean [local law enforcement agency] has . . . said that they are not even investigating domestic worker cases, or they only have task forces set up that are working with sex trafficking cases and stuff like that. Like, they haven't even tried to hide that. I think sex trafficking is assumed to be worse." She continued, noting the lack of evidence supporting the abolitionist claims guiding implementation, "Wasn't Melissa Farley [an abolitionist researcher] subcontracted by the government to provide guidance on the TVPA reauthorization? And it's clearly influenced by her. . . . it's clear that that their [abolitionist] views were woven into the law . . . that sex trafficking is worse, that the type of work is inherently somehow more dehumanizing, but actually I think it's not based on any evidence or data. So that's very dangerous when we are building an entire system of law based on assumptions or feelings."[34] Indeed, over the course of the Bush presidency, government policies, reports, and proposed legislation ignored the empirical observations made by service providers, instead incorporating abolitionist claims and ideology. Much like the antipornography crusaders of the 1980s, abolitionist feminists (some of whom previously identified more as antipornography feminists) preferred anecdotes to data.[35] Bridget mimicked the voices of abolitionist advocates, highlighting the nonempirical nature of their arguments:

"It sounds bad to me." "I would not want to be prostituted." "It must be terrible." That is not data! Or, "I'm scared of sex," or "I'm scared to, like, talk about it, so it must be really bad and scary." "Let's make the federal law based on my scary feelings." . . . If the data shows that, that's fine with me, but it's not enough to have the anecdotal stories that we don't even know where they come from. In my opinion, we really have to look at what are the factors that makes one trafficking worse than the other and base our laws on facts rather than this moral panic about sex.

A number of providers I came to know talked about their differences with the abolitionists in terms of experience (or lack thereof) working with victims, and the experiences of the service providers and survivors I interviewed (see Chapter 4) certainly did not conform to abolitionist arguments. Nonetheless, federal policy was absorbing that limited notion of trafficking.

While professionals implementing the law on the ground generally avoided empty rhetoric and held more nuanced conceptions of trafficking, government policy definitely influenced implementation, especially in the arena of law enforcement. In many ways, the service providers and law enforcement agents I observed and interviewed represented the two views of trafficking that have been in place since the drafting of the TVPA: service providers tended to emphasize the need to address all forms of trafficking, while law enforcement agents tended to view exploitation for forced prostitution as unique. Like many members of the broader public, individual law enforcement agents often assumed trafficking victims should fit the media-propagated image of a damsel in distress and took on a rescue mentality. Several agents acknowledged that their investigative focus was primarily on sex trafficking, and they viewed trafficking into prostitution as a more heinous crime than other forms of forced labor. Will, a federal agent, told me, "I would argue sex trafficking is more brutal than murder because of the damage to the psyche that occurs over time." Although Will had no training in mental health, much less the skills to assess varying degrees of psychological harm experienced by trafficking victims, he believed there to be something innately damaging about forced commercial sex. While discourses prioritizing so-called sex trafficking were deeply embedded in U.S. government policy and practice from the top down, in their roles as "street-level bureaucrats"[36] law enforcement agents also make discretionary decisions about what counts as trafficking from the bottom up.[37]

Law enforcement's focus on trafficking for forced prostitution meant the law was not living up to its potential of addressing all forms of trafficking. For Nora, a case manager who interacted daily with individuals trafficked into all sectors, the narrow vision of the crime meant that her forced labor clients effectively became second-class victims—a preposterous idea on its face. She articulated how the bifurcation in the law implicitly favored trafficking into forced prostitution: "I feel like even though it's not perhaps clearly stated in the law, that there is . . . a pecking order for these cases and there is . . . a top tier, which is trafficking for forced commercial sex acts, and then the second tier for forced labor. And I think that a lot of people who created the law felt like that type of trafficking was inherently more degrading to the person." In fact, Nora's assessment was spot on because the sex/labor split emerged as a compromise in response to abolitionists pushing for a sex-trafficking-only law. Nora continued, "I think in a perfect world the TVPA would have been written to not have these different types of trafficking separated out."

While the sex/labor divide was often referenced over the course of my fieldwork, it was also highly contested. The majority of service providers viewed the split as something imposed on them by abolitionists and others who framed trafficking as solely involving commercial sex. In response, service providers actively brought discussions of labor trafficking to the table, advocating for broader as opposed to more specific visions of trafficking. They were promoting a focus not on forced labor to the exclusion of compulsory sex work but on *all* trafficking, on male as well as female survivors, and on international and domestic victims.

Because the distinction between sex trafficking and forced labor permeates nearly all discussions on the issue, I asked all of my informants if they saw any differences between those types of exploitation. While many of them did not themselves see discrepancies, they perceived other professionals as drawing a sharp distinction between the two. Bridget, the director of a trafficking services program, responded, "I think the difference is who the police are interested in." She added, "I think that the way law enforcement approaches these cases because of the separation, actually not even because of the separation of the law, but because their own preconceived notions of a domestic worker, somebody who is a sex worker, I think has an effect on their interest in investigating a case or not and what type of resources they are willing to put in." Larry, a law enforcement agent, confirmed this and told me outright that his unit did not generally deal with cases involving labor trafficking, although it had investigated a small number of forced labor cases: "Labor's not one of our strong points. . . . Dealing with prostitution—that's easier for us to get into."

As a result of their divergent goals, service providers and law enforcement agents often expressed that their conceptions of trafficking were also wildly unaligned. Two related factors contribute to this incongruity: one based in the law and the other in the privileged position that many enforcement agents assigned to trafficking for forced commercial sex. The first contributing factor is the discrepancy between the "severe forms of trafficking" definition (which covers victim identification) and the criminal statutory definitions (which apply to prosecution) described in Chapter 1. Criminal justice authorities and service providers alike frequently recited to me the mantra of "force, fraud, and coercion" as the defining characteristics of trafficking. In actuality, the criminal statutes governing law enforcement did not include fraud as a means of trafficking into forced labor; statutorily, fraud was only a means of trafficking for forced commercial sex.[38] This small difference in definitions created a large gap in meaning and operations between service providers and law enforcement personnel. While an NGO service provider would consider someone defrauded into labor trafficking as clearly meeting the VSFT definition (which includes fraud) and therefore eligible for benefits and services, this same individual would not meet law enforcement's statutory criteria for forced labor. What legally constitutes trafficking for service providers does not constitute trafficking for law enforcement. To my surprise, I rarely heard service providers or law enforcement acknowledge this distinction in the law. For the most part, they viewed each other as having an incomplete understanding of trafficking. Law enforcement agents believed service providers were ill equipped to assess cases. For their part, providers viewed the disconnect as based in law enforcement's lack of training and privileging of sex trafficking cases, and in many ways the two were connected. The inconsistency in the definitions was just one symptom of the larger legal and policy slant toward sex trafficking.

Indeed, much of what drove the focus on sex trafficking was the social and political attention surrounding the issue, not an upsurge in actual cases. Despite the media sensationalism around forced prostitution, law enforcement interest in it, and its policy advantage, evidence suggests that the majority of trafficking occurring in the United States is for forced labor rather than commercial sex. A 2004 report noted that more than 50 percent of all trafficking cases documented between 1998 and 2003 involved labor trafficking in domestic service, agriculture, sweatshops and factories, food services and care, entertainment, and mail-order brides.[39] The typical view of a trafficked sex worker was not at all an accurate portrayal of the client base of the service providers I came to know. Ella, an immigration attorney, told me that approximately 60 percent of her cases were labor trafficking, with the remaining 40 percent involving involuntary prostitution. Many of her clients were domestic workers who had been trafficked by UN diplomats.[40] She had handled about twenty of these cases. Audra's experience was similar: "The vast majority of my cases are definitely labor. . . . I'd say maybe less than a third are sex trafficking cases and everything else is labor trafficking."

While many of the individuals I spoke with in law enforcement saw sex trafficking as somehow *special*, service providers, who worked much more closely with victims over the long term, asserted not only that they encountered more victims of forced labor but also that traffickers used the same methods, particularly sexual abuse, in all types of trafficking to assert control over victims. Nora, a case manager at an NGO, viewed the sexual assault that takes place in all forms of trafficking as separate from the type of work being conducted:

> Sexual assault is one thing. Now women who were . . . providing commercial sex acts . . . I really have not found this . . . inherent difference in the kinds of feelings that they have about that versus another type of forced labor. . . . Obviously clients are aware that there is a lot of social stigma around the work they are doing, but I think that what stands out for a lot of the cases involving sex trafficking is this initiation period where the trafficker . . . exercised their will over the person, and usually that's sexual assault, and that's what's really traumatizing to the clients. . . . Doing the work itself versus another form of forced labor . . . I can't say that there is a real major difference that I know, because I think a lot of things [are the same] like feeling they've been duped, feeling a sense of shame that they are not able to send money back home . . . that they didn't see it coming, or that they are not a good judge of character or that they just feel the rage of being cheated.

As many of my informants emphasized, sexual abuse is not limited to sex trafficking. Jarrah, an immigration attorney, put it clearly: "There is a little misconception that trafficking into sex work is a lot more emotionally troubling and a lot more serious versus trafficking into labor . . . but I think that the persons who are trafficked for labor are just as traumatized and just as nervous and just as scared as those that have been trafficked into sex work." In many cases sexual assault is used as a means of control and becomes an aspect of the climate of fear. As Kira, a federal victim witness coordinator, noted, "One thing that's become patently obvious over time . . . is to never make the assumption . . . that because you have a labor trafficking case or a labor trafficking victim that they won't have been sexually victimized. . . . The experience of trauma is so highly subjective that it's really impossible to generalize that a sex trafficking victim tends to have more issues related to trauma and long-term mental health issues and stabilization issues than a labor trafficking victim. It really just depends on what the totality of those conditions in the slavery situation are." My interviews with survivors of trafficking, which feature in the following chapter, reinforced Nora's point: the sex/labor split is false, especially when it comes to assigning severity to cases.

Based on their interactions with trafficked individuals, nearly all of the service providers with whom I spoke objected to the notion that forced sex work was somehow more horrific than other forms of involuntary labor. Bridget, the director of a trafficking services program, explained quite vividly,

> The brutality exists all across trafficking—like beatings, sexual abuse, all of those things are elements of trafficking in every sector, so we are talking about the commercial interaction of having sex for money . . . [people are] seeing that as inherently dehumanizing more than the other brutal situations that are happening across trafficking. But really that may or may not be true, but it depends on the perspective of the person—her own ideas about herself, her own resiliency, her own ideas about sex, where she's coming from sexually into that relationship. Also, is she getting support out of those interactions with the johns or not?

For Bridget, victim subjectivity was far overshadowed by cultural assumptions about the inherently horrific nature of commercial sex. In many cases she saw it was customers who had helped women leave the trafficking situation. Access to the outside world available through prostitution provided opportunities for escape. She continued, "It gives her [the victim] access to other sex workers and to the venues where they form relationships and help each other with resiliency, which domestic workers don't have. And together, a lot of those women devise ways to survive as a group. . . . What we see in our cases is that some of those women . . . emerge with more resiliency than the woman who was completely isolated in a home and a victim of that kind of brutality for years without access to the outside world." One simply cannot translate the underdefined legal categories directly into assessments of the severity or consequences of an individual trafficking case. The unique conditions of each situation, as opposed to the *type* of labor performed, affected the level of trauma that survivors experienced.

Even with situations lacking a sexual assault component, providers constantly stressed subjectivity. Ella, an immigration attorney, ruminated on the purpose of the law's split: "I agree [sex trafficking] is a terrible, terrible thing, but so is having a slave at home. So I don't really see what the difference is either way. I'm not trying to discount sexual assault or someone who's being forced into prostitution. I think that's really terrible, but I think it's terrible to force someone to sleep in a dog bed on the floor and not pay them and not feed them adequately and then expect that person to take care of your child." She continued, "I see the same themes with people that are victimized in either situation. To me, trafficking is all about a modern infliction of slavery and asserting power and control over someone else." Her definition is simple but sweeping and powerful. Cases involving severe coercion that nevertheless prompted no law enforcement action reinforced many service providers' beliefs that the sex/labor split did more harm than good. Bridget related one such harrowing tale:

> The client that I have that has the hardest time in life is a domestic worker. She was trafficked when she was under ten years old. She was in [the trafficking situation] until she was twenty-three or twenty-four, never went to school, was totally isolated, and when she finally got out of the trafficking situation, we helped her leave, she got agoraphobia. She was illiterate; she had panic attacks, major depression, eating disorders. I mean the amount of obstacles that this girl had was just amazing, but her case was never, like nobody [law enforcement] went after them. Nothing happened. It was just . . . brutal.

The general public may never associate those kinds of challenges with trafficking, but the individualistic and varied nature of cases is astonishing. Although I observed certain patterns that arose over my fieldwork, there was no typical case. As Gwen, a federal victim witness coordinator, told me, "We've rescued victims who have been held for twenty-five years in labor trafficking cases, so you've got this whole continuum of trauma and abuse versus maybe someone that's been involved in sex trafficking for two weeks. Both are legal cases." There are no standard scenarios, but when pressed, my informants would list certain patterns among clients while still generally reiterating the uniqueness of each situation. Ella, an immigration attorney, elaborated on the diversity of the clients themselves: "I have clients who can't read in their own language, and then I have clients who have college degrees or at least have attended some college. And I feel like I've had a really full spectrum of everything in between that, as well, and from all different countries."

Despite their varied experiences and regardless of whether they were forced to perform commercial sex or other kinds of labor, individuals who have been trafficked do share certain commonalities. As Nancy, a case manager, put it,

> They have all gone through difficult situations. They all have suffered . . . horrendous human rights violations. They all have the same issues in a way. What is going to happen to me next? How am I going to survive? How am I going to talk to people about this? How am I going to move on with my life and be a productive member of society? . . . I don't think there's a difference. I mean, the experience is different, but what comes after that, it's the same. What they worry about, what their hopes are, what their dreams are, you know, it's all the same. So I don't see any difference.

Chapter 4

Defining Trafficking Through Survivor Experience

There isn't one type of trafficking survivor.

—Nora, case manager

While the ways in which criminal justice authorities and service providers conceptualize and define trafficking are key to better understanding the TVPA's implementation, survivors' own conceptions—derived from real people's lived experience—offer a counterpoint that complicates and gives substance to the professional accounts. Trafficked persons are rarely given the opportunity to voice their own experiences. They are often viewed at one end of an uncomplicated binary—as either helpless victims with no control over their circumstances or criminals because of their social status, often as undocumented immigrants or prostitutes. Yet trafficking survivors and the situations they endure are not easily characterized, and there is no one typical trafficking survivor.

While the three dichotomous elements in the TVPA structure the ways in which implementers conceive of trafficking, the law's construction is irrelevant to survivors. The impression that trafficking can be bifurcated into "sex trafficking" and "labor trafficking" makes little sense when the messiness of lived experience is the lens. One victim of forced prostitution may have more in common with someone who was forced to pick tomatoes or into domestic servitude than with another victim of forced prostitution. Consonance depends on the circumstances of each particular case, not on the classifications found in or implied by the law. While the categories of sex and labor describe the types of work or services a person performs, that is the extent of their utility. In all trafficking, work and living conditions run the gamut. It is my contention that the experiences of trafficked persons challenge the received wisdom—legal and practical. The exploited individuals themselves attribute their suffering to a set of circumstances (e.g., isolation, deceit, threats to their loved ones) entirely different from those emphasized by many of the TVPA implementers.

The following five accounts are excerpted from life histories of trafficking survivors who had received or were receiving services at the NGO program I observed, Empower.[1] Individual profiles add context to these survivors' lives, which can be lost when extracting bits and pieces to weave neat accounts. I draw heavily on the words of the survivors I interviewed to give them a voice in their own narratives. These portraits are not meant to be typical or comprehensive (they are only a sampling of the survivors I met and the cases I observed) but to give a sense of the issues that survivors encounter. This focus on the particular underscores the uniqueness of each trafficking case instead of perpetuating the essentialized notion of "trafficked persons" as monolithic.[2] Although certain themes emerge in the stories these survivors tell, their experiences are far from formulaic. We follow the issues the survivors themselves chose to emphasize, including their prior lives, their memories of trafficking, the meanings they ascribe to their experiences, how they escaped, their interactions with law enforcement and service providers, and their efforts to rebuild their lives afterward. These are the experiences of those whom the TVPA was designed to protect and by whom the consequences of its implementation are most intimately felt.

All of the survivors I interviewed were women in their twenties and thirties because Empower had significantly more women enrolled in its program than men—at least partially attributable to law enforcement primarily referring female victims of sex trafficking. Although I was unable to interview any male survivors, I did meet and interact with several over the course of my fieldwork, and my observations reflect that. Interviews with male survivors would have broadened the scope of comparison, but the profiles I include strongly make the case that the conditions of trafficking transcend the type of work conducted.

Survivor Profiles

Camille

Thirty-two when I met her, Camille had only recently escaped her trafficking situation, and I got to know her over the course of her first several months at Empower. She allowed me to observe a number of her case-management meetings and consented to an interview. Originally from a southern African country, Camille spoke fluent English. She moved around while she was young, living with various family members over the course of her childhood. She eventually relocated to her country's capital city and secured what she described as a good job. She was planning her wedding when she was approached by the friend of an acquaintance who was looking for someone to come to the United States for two weeks to help with a catering event. Camille told me, "I never hoped to come here before," but the woman told her, "Go to America because they have very cheap wedding gowns . . . plus you'll have a lot of money." Despite not being much of a traveler, Camille was persuaded by the notion of coming to America for a short period of time to earn money for her wedding. She explained, "I'm the type of person who's not adventurous . . . I don't want to go away from home for a long time. I only came here because she was talking about two weeks. So I'm like, I can do two weeks; I won't be that homesick."

In reality, the agreed-upon two weeks turned into three years of domestic servitude. She worked seven days a week, was rarely allowed to leave the house, and saw none of the earnings she was promised. Camille was the only survivor I spoke to who equated her trafficking experience with slavery: "I had been with these people for three years and worked like a slave. . . . After being there . . . you think everybody thinks of you like that. . . . To be a slave, to work for someone and not be allowed to see my friends, not allowed to do nothing, just be in the house every day with this person, and you cannot do nothing." She worked long hours doing whatever her trafficker demanded and felt completely isolated—she felt owned by her captor.

Camille actually escaped one trafficking situation only to be retrafficked by the person who helped her leave. Her pseudo-rescuer forced Camille to take on domestic duties, including caring for her child. How did both traffickers maintain control over her? Camille explained, "My second trafficker, she knew what happened to me before, so she kind of did the same thing. She knew this lady took my passport and my [return airline] ticket and hid it. When my ticket expired . . . she said, 'Now you are in this country, and you can't do whatever you want because you are illegal. You cannot afford to go nowhere; if you go out, they are going to take you to jail and keep you there for two years.'" This threat of being sent to jail kept Camille from leaving the house, calling her family, or reaching out for help. "I was so afraid, I almost died out of fear. I was so afraid every day, like oh my God, like if I hear her come, maybe it's the police."

Four years after arriving in the United States and detained by her second trafficker, Camille finally reached a point when she could not endure these conditions anymore. The isolation and emotional abuse she experienced was so intense that she considered taking her own life. "I was tired of the whole thing; I didn't know what to do. I wanted to commit suicide," she told me. Taking a chance, she placed a phone call to a friend at the American embassy in her home country. Her friends and family had not heard from her since she left. When she explained the situation, her friend told her that what she had experienced was called human trafficking and that it was a crime in the United States. Camille told me, "That was the first time I knew what it was called." Camille's friend at the embassy reached out to a contact in the United States and eventually connected her to Empower. One of the case managers communicated with Camille and made arrangements to pick her up at the trafficker's home and transport her to a shelter.

When Camille told her trafficker she was leaving, the woman called the police. Camille explained, "She's like, 'I'm calling the police . . . because I'm going to tell them you are here in this country illegally.' . . . And she called them for real. They came to the house. I was so scared though, because all the time I believed they were going to take me for two years and whatever. The police came to the house and . . . I explained everything to them, how I came to this country, what happened." Camille described her escape as a turning point in her understanding of what happened to her. The police told her, "What happened to you is wrong; they should not have done this to you. You could have called us on them, not them calling us for you." She told me, "That was great for me just to hear that, because you know all this time . . . I believed I was really wrong for doing this, but my first trafficker she got me stuck in this country, she made me illegal so she could use it to torture me, to make me suffer."

Since leaving her abusers, she has finally felt cared for: "It's been wonderful working with these people and just to see how people care about you . . . the police and my lawyer, it's been great." She described her subsequent experiences as transformative and credited her therapist in particular:

It's helpful working with my therapist. I'm better now, because when I first came . . . my memory was messed up [from the trauma]; I was forgetting everything. . . . I was about to lose my mind for real, so working with her, it helped me a lot . . . just feeling good about yourself, not blaming myself about what happened, because I've been . . . [thinking] I should have known these people were lying to me. You know, I felt so stupid. . . . But my therapist . . . she's there for me . . . just to tell you why you're going through what you're going through, why your memory is so messed up, she helped me a lot.

Although she appreciated all the help she received, Camille did confide that she disliked feeling dependent on others.

Even though it was good help . . . I've been safe, everyone has helped me a lot, but . . . it's not me. I have never been in that situation where I'm so dependent on people. I need food, I have to come to Sadie [her case manager]. I don't have money; I need Metro Cards [for the subway], that's not me. I used to work and do things on my own and just live my life, and . . . as soon as I finished school, I started working, and I was on my own doing my own thing. . . . I appreciate what they do for me, but I still feel like that's not me.

She told me, "When I get home, I'm going to get a job and go back to that normal life I used to live. When I need something, I can buy it." Camille told me she planned to go back to her home country and study to be a secretary "and maybe continue my education from there." When I asked about her original marriage plans from before she was trafficked, she laughed, "Oh yeah. I was supposed to get married, so maybe in December we will."

Silvia

When I met Silvia, she was in her early thirties. She described her life growing up in Mexico, where she had graduated from high school and studied to be a secretary for three further years. Over two years of working, she really enjoyed her job. Much like Camille, Silvia was deceived into her trafficking situation but, as I will describe, the threats her trafficker used to keep her under his control took a different form. Silvia initially met her trafficker when he pursued her romantically. They began dating. After having a child together, the relationship changed. Silvia told me she never wanted to come to the United States, but her trafficker, whom she referred to as "the father of my children," sent her to Queens to work as a prostitute under the watch of some of his family members and associates. She said she was not allowed to keep any of her earnings but rather sent them back to her trafficker—she pronounced him only interested in "money money money." Although she had control over her own movement, Silvia felt that she had to continue working in prostitution because of her trafficker's threats to harm her children, who remained in Mexico with his family. When I asked Silvia if she knew at the time that she was the victim of a crime, she told me, "No, I thought life was as a robot. I did everything the father of my children told me without questioning it." Although she had felt powerless and unable to control her own actions, she told me, "The people I have worked with since leaving have helped me to see that I was the one who could stop this, and that I had a voice and a choice of when to stop it."

Silvia escaped after a friend directed her to a hospital psychologist. Silvia had never heard the term *trafficking* until the psychologist told her about Empower and referred her for services. Silvia said the program helped her "get out of the life and understand what I could accomplish." She credits her case manager and the program with a long list of beneficial services: "They helped me enroll in English classes, get my work permit and a social security number, helped me economically, helped me emotionally, and helped me see a doctor because I was having headaches." Being recognized as a victim allowed Silvia access to these basic social welfare services and benefits, but beyond meeting her basic needs, the assistance she received from social service providers helped her transform into a self-sustaining survivor.

When I asked about how her life had changed since she extricated herself, Silvia responded, "My life has changed a lot. . . . I see life in a different way now, and I am able to appreciate life and am in a place where I am able to deal with the suffering that I endured." She smiled, "Before I was just very afraid. I felt like I was in prison, and I couldn't do anything. With the help of [my therapist] and [my case manager] I saw that I could change things. I ask myself why I didn't do it before, and the answer is because I was scared. [My trafficker] would say to me that the only thing I was worth was doing prostitution and nothing else." For Silvia, though, the prostitution itself was not the heart of her suffering—she even noted that sex work was an attractive means of making money after escaping her trafficking situation. In fact, the devastating experiences that Silvia stressed to me were the manipulations that her trafficker used to control her: beatings, emotional abuse, and threats to harm her children.

Were someone else going through a similar situation, Silvia told me she would urge them to recognize "that people don't have the right to treat us the way this person has, and that if she wants to she can fight. It's hard. It's not easy. It can be difficult, but no one has the right to punish you. Even if you are illegal here, there is so much assistance. It can be hard to find, but if you want to, you can accomplish it [leaving, escaping]." Despite the suffering she endured, Silvia believed it was possible to move past the victimization.

Victoria

Victoria was twenty-six when I met her and had come to the United States from a South American country when she was in her late teens. The youngest of ten children, she told me, "My life . . . as a teenager and as a little girl, it was good. I came from a very humble family. My parents worked to give us the best they could. . . . I was happy back there." Her trafficking started when she found a job as a babysitter in her home country. After several months of working for the family, the husband, a diplomat, was relocated to the United States. "I was doing okay in school, and I was happy with my job and . . . they asked me to come. [They said], 'Oh, you're a good girl. We really like you; we trust you.' . . . They always gave me good compliments about my job. . . . I trusted them . . . so I said yes." She told me it was a hard decision to leave her family behind, but the woman she worked for made the opportunity sound very appealing. "She painted a beautiful picture . . . like you are going to go to school, you're going to have a better life, you're going to make good money, many things." For Victoria, it was a chance to move beyond her modest upbringing and move ahead in the world, gain an education, and help her family financially.

Victoria told me, "The first three months everything was good . . . and then she [her employer] changed thoroughly . . . She became very rough . . . and little by little she started treating me in a way that wasn't proper. . . . I lived with them for three years." The family paid Victoria so little, she told me she was embarrassed to say how much. They held her passport, allowing Victoria outside only rarely. "When I asked her to let me go out, she said, 'No, because there are bad people outside. They're going to kidnap you; they're going to kill you, think about that.' Psychologically she [controlled me]. . . . I wanted to leave, to go out, go to the mall, go to the movies, do something by myself like girls do, but I didn't have a chance to do. I hardly went to the supermarket to buy milk, and it was just three or four times." The intense psychological coercion led to her almost complete isolation from the outside world. The trafficker's home was like a prison for Victoria, with her formerly aboveboard employer's threats and lies keeping her there.

After an acquaintance of her trafficker observed how Victoria was being treated, she reported the situation to authorities, initially offering to help Victoria escape on her own. But Victoria told her, "I don't have my documents; I'm going to be illegal and I'm very, very afraid." If her trafficker meant to terrify Victoria into keeping silent, it was working. The acquaintance instead reported the situation to U.S. Immigration and Customs Enforcement. Victoria told me, "It was a very tough day. Immigration came to the house and they took me with them because I was underage and in the conditions I was working. . . . They asked me if I wanted to go with them or if I wanted to stay there. I said, 'I want to go. . . . This is my chance; I'm going to take it.' . . . I wanted to start a new life."

ICE's arrival angered Victoria's captor: "She was saying . . . 'I gave you a home; I protected you, and you repay me like this.'" Victoria responded, "No, I'm going away. My time finally came. . . . I'm very tired of you; you treated me really bad. You said you really liked me, and you would treat me like family. That's not true. You always treated me like a piece of shit." As disruptive as the whole escape was, for Victoria the hardest part of leaving was bidding goodbye to the boy she had looked after for three years. She recalled, "Instead of calling [his mother] mom, he called me mom because since he was born I took care of him. In the middle of the night, when he was crying for the bottle, he cried for me." Victoria said, "The only happiness I had in the house was the little boy because every time that I was sad I took him in my arms and I squeezed him, I cuddled him, and I called him my baby, and he made me forget about what was happening . . . and I always thought that we were going to be together like that." She told me on the day she left the house with ICE, the little boy "saw all these things, and he was crying and . . . he was grabbing me. . . . He was running behind me, and I said, [crying] 'It's time for me to go.' It's hard for me, that part." Her bond with the child was the only positive aspect of her otherwise abusive and exploitative situation.

Talking to law enforcement after she was rescued presented its own challenges: "They took me with them to downtown Brooklyn, to the immigration building. I was there almost the whole day. I was crying because I was very nervous because it was a new lifetime. . . . They asked me a lot of things."

With difficulty, she recounted her story to officials: "Now I'm ready, after five years, I think . . . telling you this story, to me, is more comfortable, but back then it was very difficult for me." Reliving her experience through the law enforcement interview compounded her trauma, but she agreed to cooperate with the investigation. "They asked me, 'Do you want to stay here, or do you want to go to your country?'" Victoria responded decisively: "I didn't think for a second . . . about going back to [my country]. Right away I said, 'I want to stay here. . . . I know that there are many tough times that are coming, but I can deal with it.'"

After spending three months in a shelter, Victoria made some friends and found an apartment. Then, she told me, "I remember the first thing I did was I went to school for English, and I studied nine months, full time." When I complimented her impeccable English skills, she explained her learning curve, saying, "I didn't even know when to say 'yes' and 'no' . . . just 'hello,' that was the only thing. . . . So I started going to school, and I learned English. I'm very proud of that." Her motivation was practical and aspirational: "I learned English because there are people who are here for years and years, and they don't know it. . . . I went to school, learned English, nine months later I was working . . . because I got my work permit and I started working, so I was much happier." Along with her improved immigration status, the services she received from Empower helped Victoria transition from a victim whose defining feature was her trafficking experience to a survivor flourishing in a new job with a new life. Her independence clearly buoyed her, and at the time of our interview she felt well respected on the job: "I've been working since thirteen . . . and I do not depend on anybody. I depend on myself. . . . At the end of the week, when I receive my check, I say to myself, I got this money because I worked hard and that's why. . . . I'm proud about it."

Like most of the other survivors I spoke with, Victoria acknowledged that she had never heard the term *trafficking* until she started working with Empower: "Before I didn't know about it or even know that it existed because in my country you don't hear those things. . . . We think that the United States is the country you go [to] and make a lot of money." The TVPA-authorized organizations, including Empower, that worked with Victoria changed her outlook as well as her circumstances—"I tell all these people that they are still helping me because they gave me so many things. They gave me money, they gave me support, they gave me clothes." Her case manager counseled her, liaised with the attorneys involved in her case, and assisted with the lengthy immigration applications. "She has an A in everything," Victoria declared.

Like many of the trafficking survivors certified since the passage of the TVPA in 2000, Victoria was waiting for the Department of Homeland Security to release regulations that would allow T visa holders to acquire permanent resident status.[3] She told me, "Every time that people ask me, 'When are you going to get your green card?' I say, 'Well I don't know when; I am waiting.' I already waited five years; I think I can wait two years more." A green card would afford her not just a more robust immigration status but also privileges that would markedly improve her life: "I have family back home, and I haven't seen them for like nine years, and that's one thing that I want to do. As soon as I get my green card, go back home and visit them. . . . I hope I have that chance."

Nadia

Nadia, an early-thirtysomething survivor, remembers fondly the capital city of the former Soviet republic where she was born and raised: "We had a central opera and ballet theatre which I lived right next to. We had a circus; we had all kinds of museums. It was very interesting culturally." The very bright daughter of two professionals, she excelled in school, had studied English since the age of six, and participated in numerous extracurricular activities. In college she worked toward a teaching career, but the conditions of her city deteriorated following the disintegration of the Soviet Union. "They started bombing buildings and . . . it became dangerous to even go out to attend college, to attend classes. . . . We went through the winter with no electricity, no gas, almost no water." Her parents moved the family to a small village in Russia, and Nadia reenrolled in college in a nearby city: "I was living in the University Center, and they were living about forty-five minutes away by local train, so I was not with my [mother and father] anymore, and I had to make it on my own."

After her college graduation, Nadia went to work as a teacher in a remote town. The tough economic times colored her everyday life: "That's when inflation started taking over, and the ruble dropped down; it had no value really, and the salaries were so low that . . . my teacher's salary was enough to just buy bread and milk for the whole month, that's it." As her parents aged, Nadia also had to take on the responsibility of assisting them financially, and she thought, "I'm now in this little town, I'm renting a room, but . . . now I have to feed myself . . . and I'm obligated to take care of my parents." Nadia supplemented her salary by tutoring but struggled economically.

One day Nadia saw an ad in the newspaper that offered jobs in variety shows in New York and New Jersey. Certainly, it crossed Nadia's mind that the ad might be recruiting women for sexual services, but she explained—in a way that rather astonished me—that most ads of that nature were upfront about the type of work involved. Unlike most of the other survivors I spoke to, Nadia had heard numerous trafficking stories prior to her own exploitation. Apparently, "At that time, everybody was talking about these deceiving ads . . . and [how] . . . once you get to the country, it's a completely different story." Nadia was nevertheless cautiously optimistic about the ad she read and decided to look into it. She went for an interview with the woman who placed the ad. "She looked just like a lovely woman, very open. . . . She presented it to me, she said it's fairly upscale, very beautiful, with an element of sexiness, pretty much like a variety cabaret show, and in my mind it was Vegas." Nadia did ask the woman whether the position entailed any sex, and she responded, "No, none whatsoever, absolutely no."

At the prospect of making $2,000 a week, Nadia was bowled over. Candidly she reported to me, "I was like, whoa. I thought I could never even dream of that kind of money." The job would be an opportunity to give her parents a better life: "I said, well maybe I should give it a shot because this woman, I really don't know why, but she doesn't look like a crook . . . she just seems reliable, trustworthy." Nadia said one peculiar element was that she was not required to pay any of her travel expenses; the recruiter told her, " 'You don't have to pre-pay anything.' . . . She said, 'Don't worry, when you start making money once you're there, you will pay us back for the ticket.' "

Within a few months Nadia was on a plane to the United States along with several other women who had been recruited for the so-called variety shows. Once aboard the plane, a woman accompanying them to the United States collected their documents. "They did take our passports from us, and they did take our tickets, explaining that they would be secure in their hands rather than us losing them or somebody stealing them." Once they arrived in the United States, everything was fine for a few days, but after Nadia and the other women had time to rest, they were taken to a club for what was to be their first day of work. "We walked in and there were nude girls dancing on stage, and I see that it is not what I was expecting. There is no glamour to it, there is no costume, there is no group performance. It's like . . . a regular strip club. Girls give lap dances, there are girls on the stage naked, and I'm like, 'What's going on?' This is like one of those nightmares that you didn't want to face, and immediately in our minds . . . [we recalled] all the stories that we had heard and had read about." Nadia was told she would be dancing at the club and would have to pay the people who trafficked her $200 a day, but when her traffickers realized she was not making as much money there as they had hoped, they transferred her to another location and forced her into prostitution. She told me, "They called me and they said, 'Well there are other alternatives since you're not making money dancing. You have to start paying us $200 a day." When they forcefully suggested she perform outright sexual acts for money, she said, " 'I don't think I can do it.' They said . . . 'Whether you make money or not today, you have to give us $200. Tomorrow you have to give us $200, and the day after that you have to give us $200, so make up your mind.' " The traffickers had collected phone numbers and addresses for Nadia's family back in Russia, and it was implied that if she did not pay the $200 a day, her family would be in danger. In addition to the $200 daily, Nadia had to pay for housing, food, and clothing. While engaging in sex work, Nadia was arrested twice over two-and-a-half months—both times she told the court-appointed attorney what had happened. And both times she was released with misdemeanor charges and returned to sex work the next day. Neither attorney recognized her as a trafficking victim.

The traffickers made clear that Nadia had to pay them off each day, but she was allowed to come and go on her own for the most part. She did not experience the same isolation that Camille and Victoria did, but there were clear elements of psychological coercion that made her afraid to leave. The prospect of sex work initially shocked her, and she never came to enjoy the work, but the destructive elements of trafficking that she stressed most emphatically to me were the deception she suffered and the fear she felt for herself and her family. After several months, Nadia decided to try to disappear, hoping that the traffickers would give up when they could not find her. She said everything was fine for about a week, until she received a phone call from her mother in Russia. "When I got on the phone my mom was frantic. She was crying, she was screaming, she was absolutely in shock. She said, 'Nadia, some people are calling us and threatening us. They are making particularly angry threats as to what they're going to do [to us].' " Shaken, Nadia received the unsubtle message. "Of course, I couldn't hide anymore." She called her traffickers, who threatened to kill her parents if she did not pay them the money she supposedly owed them.

While in the United States, Nadia had made a friend. When she told him what was happening, he immediately came over and brought a tape recorder. Nadia told me, "So they [the traffickers] called, I picked up the phone, recording the whole conversation. . . . He [one of the traffickers] starts making really severe threats to my family . . . like, you know, killing everybody, burning the house down, kidnapping my brother and doing all kinds of things to my mother and father in particular." At the end of the conversation, Nadia's friend took the phone and negotiated with the traffickers, threatening them with legal action. Although she did not know what was said or what happened after that, Nadia did stop receiving threats.

Two and a half years later, Nadia had moved on with her life, including marrying her onetime friend and negotiator. One day her husband brought home a newspaper featuring an article about the FBI's arrest of two of her traffickers. Her husband asked whether Nadia wanted to share with the authorities what she knew. "I said, 'I don't want to stir it up. It's been two and a half years and . . . I've tried to forget it. I will never be able to forget it, but I'm trying to put it in the back of my memory and not remember it.' And we didn't stir it up until the FBI came and found me." Ultimately, Nadia turned over the recordings and testified before a grand jury, which was emotionally difficult. "You know, it's one thing sitting here and talking to you about this kind of thing one-on-one and another thing sitting there in front of . . . twelve jurors." In addition to having to retell her story, Nadia was fearful of the legal process itself: "At the very beginning, I was very skeptical and I had no trust for the government and federal prosecutors. My attitude was they would only use you and when they are done with you, you're on your own." Although she understood that she was in some senses acknowledged to be a victim of criminal activity, she "was afraid that somehow or other they could've turned this prosecution against me. They could have said, and they tried to do that, they tried to say that we all were a part of the immigration fraud."

Ultimately, all of the traffickers pleaded guilty, and Nadia was referred to Empower for services. Although she was eligible to apply for a T visa, she applied for a green card through her husband. Seven years after arriving in the United States, she received it: "One day the approval letter came in the mail and . . . in big capital letters [it said,] 'Welcome to America.'" About a year after Nadia and I first met, she started her first semester of law school.

Simone

Simone was originally from a large city in Mexico. She described her family as "poor but happy." As a teenager she attended school and worked in her family's business on the weekends. One afternoon, a man approached her while she was working, complimented her work ethic, and asked her to come to the United States to care for his children. The man spoke to her father, promising opportunities for Simone to attend school and make money in the United States. "Now I understand, I am twenty-one, my life is very, very hard because I am alone here . . . but I've learned a lot of things now, and I don't want to say it's my dad's fault, but it's the guy [the trafficker]. . . . The guy had a bad heart." Immigrating to the United States was not a goal of hers: "I never thought in my life that I could be here. Now I think, oh my god, how it changed my life." After almost dying crossing the border into the United States, Simone was subjected to emotional and sexual abuse at the hands of her trafficker—all to exact control over her. She explicitly communicated her discomfort with reliving her experiences but hoped that my knowing would indirectly keep others from being exploited. This motivation for participating in my study—to help people in similar situations—was a thread connecting all of my interviews with survivors.

Although Simone's trafficker seemed pleasant and trustworthy when she first met him in Mexico, he changed when she arrived in the United States. Simone described working constantly, even sleeping with the children, and gardening and cooking during any down time: "I was working, working, and I never saw even one penny." She said the hardest part was not the endless work but, rather, not being able to talk to her family. "The problem is when I wanted to call my family, he always said the line is busy, tomorrow we call them. . . . He always gave me some excuse. . . . The job was nothing, I finished so, so tired, but . . . I [was] so depressed that I cannot talk to my family." Besides the emotional toll, not speaking with her family deprived her of the opportunity to alert others to her circumstances—she had no one to tell about her misfortune and exploitation. When Simone told her trafficker she wanted to go home, she said he responded saying, "You're stupid. You think you can go like this? Who is going to pay my money? You have to stay here and work and pay my money. . . . If you try to go, I will go to immigration; I'm going to tell them that you are here, and your dad can go to jail." Like the other women I interviewed, Simone alluded to her captor preying on her ignorance of U.S. provisions and using her lack of information and anxieties about deportation to put her at a disadvantage. His threats, combined with sexual abuse, contributed to the trafficker's control over Simone.

Simone eventually escaped with the help of a Good Samaritan, a friend of her trafficker's family who had observed his mistreatment of Simone. With this window of opportunity provided, Simone ran from the house and sought help from a local church. While she was initially relieved after escaping, her fears did not end there; she was terrified for her family's security in Mexico. "I was so scared because this guy had money, he had power, if he feels angry maybe he'll do something because he told me before, 'If you try to do something, I'm going to [kill your family].'" For safety reasons, Simone moved to New York. She told me, "I tried to start a new life, but I would always remember things, everything came in my mind, and it was so hard. But I had no choice, you have to live or you have to die." Making the move to New York was a turning point for Simone, and she began to see herself as stronger and more assertive.

With the support of a church friend, Simone decided to report her trafficker to law enforcement—"It was so so hard to do it." The interview process was particularly painful: "The hardest part was [talking with] . . . the people from the government . . . and these kind of people [law enforcement agents and prosecutors] they are nice, but . . . you have to answer, like exactly what happened, little by little, day for day, exactly what happened." For Simone, this brought back traumatic memories of her trafficking that she had tried to forget. "And oh my god, everything that comes in your mind, and if you try to forget everything comes again. . . . I think I closed this part of my life by coming to New York. I said everything is dead, and I will start a new life, but it's not." While she felt that the man who trafficked her was corrupt and had done something wrong, she did not realize it was a crime until the law enforcement agents explained the law to her. They also told her she was eligible for restitution of back wages. The money, she said, meant nothing to her; the real reason she agreed to cooperate with law enforcement was that she wanted to strip her trafficker of the ability to exploit anyone else. That message was her goal: "I don't want the money, but I want him to understand and not to do this anymore."

While in New York, Simone started working with a case manager at Empower who connected her with medical care and referred her to a psychologist, on top of helping her through the law enforcement investigation: "Definitely that helped me a lot. Three years ago until now is a big difference." When asked to characterize the aid she received, Simone explained, "They made me strong because before I was a very nervous person [on account of the trafficking]. Now I'm almost normal." The cultural adjustments took time, too: "Life here in America is so hard. . . . Definitely they helped, but the main thing is you have to help yourself here." Once subject to someone else's manipulation, now Simone is in control of her own destiny.

Indeed, her life had changed so much that she could not envision herself moving back to Mexico: "It's already passed five years, almost six, so I got older here. . . . I don't have a life over there. . . . Now I have other aspirations. I want to study; I want to do something for my family. Now everything has changed." Under the TVPA, Simone was able to petition to bring her parents to the United States as derivative T visa holders.[4] "I am very happy right now because I have my apartment, and I am just waiting for my family, and I am working very hard." In very clear English, Simone told me she wanted to continue studying the language. It was actually something her trafficker said that motivated her to continue her studies: "He told me many times, 'Many people they stay here in the United States the past twenty years and they cannot speak English. . . . The Spanish [speaking people], they have nothing; they just do the dishes.'" She added, "And now I think this is not right. The Spanish [speakers], they can go up. They can speak English, and they can do whatever they can do because the Americans, they don't have three hands or three legs or something different, so that's what I have in my mind." When I asked what she hoped to do in the future—she had just finished her high school equivalency—she told me, "To be a lawyer."

Simone's desire to help with the present research fit within her general campaign for betterment: "More than anything, I feel so angry when I see this kind of thing [trafficking taking place] because I say how come we don't have the information?" She placed herself in the context of change being made: "It's very hard for me to talk about this kind of thing . . . but I want this kind of information to come to other people . . . so I really want to help you."

Challenging Misconceptions

Opening a small window onto the lived experience of trafficked persons, the profiles of Camille, Silvia, Victoria, Nadia, and Simone begin to plot the diverse range of situations that survivors encounter. Camille, forced into domestic servitude, described her experience as slavery. She was threatened, deceived, and forced to work sixteen-hour days, seven days a week. She was terrified to leave the house, or even make a phone call, out of fear of being arrested and thrown in jail. Nadia, on the other hand, was forced into commercial sex but enjoyed relative freedom of movement and was able to make friends. Still, the threat that her family would be harmed if she stopped turning over earnings from prostitution loomed large. Similarly, Silvia was able to come and go, but her trafficker coerced her into prostitution through threats to her children. Contrary to the impression propagated by abolitionist feminists, for neither of these survivors was the act of prostitution itself the most exceptional element of their experience; rather, they were intimidated chiefly by the threats and deceit used by their traffickers to control them. Victoria's trafficker did not threaten physical harm to her or her family, but she was so psychologically controlling that Victoria left the house only three or four times in three years. Although trafficked into domestic work, Simone was sexually abused by her trafficker—prostitution was not the labor forced on her, but sexual violence was nonetheless an integral part of her oppression.

Each of these survivors endured unique types of control in diverse working environments, yet it was the force, fraud, and coercion that each of them emphasized as the defining element of their experiences. This certainly echoes the operational definition of trafficking we see in the text of the TVPA. And despite the emphasis given to "sex trafficking" by the drafters and certain implementers of the law, neither of the survivors I interviewed who had been trafficked into forced prostitution assigned the type of work they did any special significance. The notion of sex trafficking being *special* or uniquely *evil*, as imagined by some of my other informants, did not appear to hold true for these women. What emerged instead were the commonalities all of these women shared in terms of the qualitative conditions under which they were working and the ways in which they moved on with their lives after their exploitation.

In fact, several themes surfaced that are relevant to all of the survivors regardless of the type of work they performed. First, the term *trafficking* had little meaning for any of the survivors prior to escaping their situations and receiving assistance. While those working in the field use the term as though its meaning were self-evident, most of the survivors I interviewed had never heard the term prior their escape. Indeed, *trafficking* brings with it multiple undertones and connotations (e.g., white slavery, the movement of goods) that are completely irrelevant to these women's experiences. Audra, an immigration attorney, called the word an in-group, professional coinage: "*Trafficking* is problematic because it's a very ivory term, and people don't use it in everyday parlance. [It] has its own historical connotations too, like that it was originally about the sex trade of white women, and that's not necessarily applicable to the majority of trafficking survivors today. I . . . tend to use terms like *exploited labor, abused labor,* that kind of thing, and I only really use *trafficking* when I'm talking to other colleagues." Based on the experiences and subjectivity of their clients, many service providers contested the trafficking framework in this way and questioned its usefulness. Even for formerly trafficked persons, the word itself is not especially descriptive, and it tends to evoke images of movement and prostitution while ignoring key elements of deception and force.

Also striking is that in several cases, the survivors did not even know that crimes had been committed against them. Very few people self-identify as being trafficked, and as Ella, an immigration attorney, noted, "A lot of people think something bad happened to them or something wrong went on, but they're not going to say they were trafficked." She continued, "I think some people don't like to believe that they were duped. And again still even after you get them a T visa . . . people still . . . don't self-identify as trafficking [victims]." The label simply does not do justice to their experiences. Kyle, a federal prosecutor told me, "I think that *trafficking* can be a misleading term because . . . it sound[s] like movement is necessary, and of course that's not the case. . . . It's the compelled service that is at the heart of it." Audra, the immigration attorney who characterized the word essentially as jargon, avoids using it with survivors: "I start from the very beginning when I do an intake describing what trafficking is, and I don't necessarily throw out that term after that meeting. I'll say 'the person who treated you badly' or I'll say 'the person who didn't pay you,' as opposed to 'the trafficker' because it's such a loaded term. And I find that that's a little bit easier . . . to communicate."

Over the course of my fieldwork and subsequent analysis, I was struck by my interviewees' strength—and resilience. The women and men I encountered rarely conformed to the portraits of helpless victims produced by the media. Providers generally referred to their clients as survivors, rather than victims, emphasizing their very real agency and determination and challenging the image of trafficking as an insurmountable form of victimization—an image put forward by abolitionists. The "victims" I encountered were neither incapable nor helpless but rather had shown incredible strength during periods of intense hardship. Most had fallen victim to trafficking not because they were vulnerable and naïve but because they took a chance to pursue an opportunity they believed would improve their lives and those of their families. As Jo Goodey suggests, a distinction needs to be drawn between a woman's legal status as "victim" and her own identity as more than just that—namely, her existence as a human being with experiences and aspirations beyond the role of the proverbial victim.[5]

Some providers suggested that the term *victim* put their clients in the role of needing to be saved or rescued, while *survivor* implied empowerment. Sheila, the director of a trafficking services program, wanted to correct that impression: "The case management system can make it seem like something is wrong with clients because they have been trafficked. There is a list of problems funders require us to check off to prove that they are victims, but you can't assume that everyone who has been trafficked has PTSD and needs therapy. You also need to address strengths." Many reports of trafficking effects on survivors read like a laundry list of abuses—broken bones, contusions, headaches, poor nutrition, dental problems, dermatological issues, HIV, STIs, unintended pregnancies and forced abortions, sexual abuse, post-traumatic stress disorder, depression, sleep disturbances, substance abuse, and so forth.[6] In reality, no victim experiences all of these effects, and many emerge from their experiences resilient and driven to move forward. That evolution has become a programmatic goal; Charlotte, the director of a trafficking services organization, noted, "Our ultimate goal is to make sure that the victim who walks through our door becomes a survivor." Bridget, the director of another such program, told me how she viewed this transformation: "Success is . . . watching the clients succeed and watching them relatively rapidly grow and change in such a short period of time as three years. The resilience is amazing. Their inner strength is completely inspiring." What these individuals took away from this process was not so much a constructed identity of "trafficking survivor," but rather the ability to move forward and shape their own lives.

Most of the survivors I spoke to alluded to the difficulty of reliving their experiences when telling law enforcement what had happened to them. Nadia reports that the formality and scrutiny wore her down: "They were questioning me a lot, challenging me. . . . She [the Assistant U.S. Attorney] was . . . like, 'Why did you agree to do that? . . . Was it really forced labor or not? Why did you so easily agree to do this?' . . . It was especially hard for me to communicate with them and to try to explain the mentality [of the traffickers] to them." She told me, though, that this relationship softened: "Gradually . . . over time our relationship turned from almost adversarial to cooperative, and even like a partnership. . . . We started working with each other." Eventually Nadia considered herself a contributor to her trafficker's prosecution and even found the process satisfying.

Several of my informants found that sharing their stories in court was a turning point. Prosecutors told me that they made an effort to reach a plea deal in most cases so that victims would not have to testify, but the attorneys acknowledged that it was sometimes necessary and could be positive for victims in the rare cases that do go to trial. Katrina, a federal prosecutor, put it this way: "It's the victim's day in court, their opportunity to tell their story. It can often be an extremely rewarding experience for them after it's said and done, but also the jury needs to understand what happened, the real human costs behind what the defendant did, and it puts a face and a consequence to his conduct in a way that nothing else can." She gave me the example of one victim's reaction following her trafficker's conviction. "'I'll never forget . . . one witness who . . . we told her that the defendant was convicted, and she said, 'Do you mean that they believed me?' And that the jury validated her experience in that way was what she took out of it. [She] was like, 'I can't believe they listened to me. I was heard.' It was so valuable to her and she would never have gotten that if she hadn't come in and testified."

In many cases, not testifying during a trial but producing victim impact statements for sentencing hearings can be equally, if not more, rewarding. Several of my sources repeated a particularly empowering moment for one victim during the sentencing hearing of brothers Josue Flores Carreto and Gerardo Flores Carreto.[7] Molly, a federal prosecutor, called it "an awesome moment in the Carreto sentencing, which has become sort of DOJ lore, sort of how a victim can transform into a survivor." All of the victims had the opportunity to read victim impact statements. After the first of the two Carreto brothers was sentenced to fifty years in prison, the second brother's attorney asked to address the judge. Molly recalled, "So his lawyer starts tap dancing and starts saying, 'Your Honor . . . I've been a defense attorney for thirty years, and I've even worked on murder cases where someone actually died, and it wasn't that high of a sentence.' . . . And he's like, 'As bad as what these guys did . . . at least nobody died here.'" At that point, one of the victims who had already spoken asked if she could address the court again. Molly continued, "She stands on her own two feet, in a room packed full of people, and says, 'Your Honor . . . that lawyer . . . just said that nobody here died. Well, I don't think that's true.' She turns and she faces the defendant, and she points and says, 'That man forced me to have an abortion, so in my mind somebody did die, and I just wanted to tell you that' . . . So, it's really exciting when something like that happens." The second Carreto brother was consequently sentenced to fifty years as well.

Despite these banner moments, survivors and service providers have no illusions about the lengthy process of recovery and building a new life after trafficking, which Bridget, the director of a trafficking services program, said often takes years: "Most of the clients who stay with the program achieve their T visa and end up working and stabilizing within about two years. It's definitely a long, slow process." Independence does not come easily, said Nora, a case manager: "I . . . gauge success [by] the client not needing to be in touch with me as often because . . . they have their own job, they have their own . . . livelihood now and seem to be adjusting to . . . this kind of new life . . . where they're determining what they're going to do and the hours in which they're going to do it . . . noticing that the client seems to be a little more sure of themselves and feeling like they're making decisions and they've really come about it on their own." Numerous survivors allowed me to observe them struggling through the recovery process—navigating the bureaucracy of federal benefits, trying to find jobs, and working to bring their families to the United States. But I also witnessed many who had successfully moved on to the next stages in their lives. Several had enrolled in college, one in a fashion program, two in law school. One woman owned her own cleaning business, and a number of survivors reunited with their children from whom they had been separated for years. Malcolm, a young survivor who spoke at a conference, was enrolling in his first year of college. After describing the ordeal of being brought to the United States as part of a children's choir, forced to work long hours, denied food, and kept from attending school, he proclaimed, "It has taken me several years to become a survivor rather than a victim."

PART III

The Law in Action

Chapter 5

Intersections on the Ground

> Street-level decisions and actions are guided less by rules, training,
> or procedures and more by beliefs and norms. . . . Beliefs and norms
> are more elusive and resistant to change than rules and procedures;
> they are shadowy, never fully articulated, and often inconsistent.
> —Steven Maynard-Moody and Michael Musheno,
> "State Agent or Citizen Agent: Two Narratives of Discretion"

> The TVPA is a great idea . . . but . . . because it's somewhat a lofty
> idea, and people only . . . agree on the lofty ideas about it, rather than
> on the nitty-gritty details of what trafficking really entails, I think
> that's why we're having such a hard time at implementing and
> making sure that the law is as effective as it could or should be.
> —Audra, immigration attorney

In order to implement antitrafficking measures, NGOs and criminal justice authorities have to integrate sometimes-competing understandings of trafficking and of the TVPA—essentially, they have to find a way for the law *in their minds* to do the work of the law *on the books*. Professionals do subjectively assign meaning to trafficking. How do those conceptions intersect with the work they do, including providing services, identifying victims, prosecuting traffickers, and accessing resources? Survivors of trafficking can be affected by the variance, which produces tensions over which cases move forward, determines criteria for identifying victims, and prioritizes the timely distribution of benefits to some victims over others. As I have argued in previous chapters, the three dichotomous elements of the TVPA's definition of trafficking combine with interpretive frameworks to shape implementers' understandings of the issue and responses to it. While these factors partially explain enforcement's overarching focus on sex-based trafficking, specific characteristics of those involved—including their professional goals, level of experience with trafficking, and proximity to victims—color the TVPA's effects, too. No one group of professionals can be neatly characterized as thinking about or responding to trafficking monolithically; although some general patterns emerged during my research, the professionals implementing the law held highly nuanced views.

A New Law and a Multitude of Implementers

Over the course of my fieldwork, the newness of the law was apparent as professionals were still gaining experience and forming their working knowledge of trafficking. One criminal justice administrator told me that although the TVPA was passed in October 2000, it took prosecutors until 2004 to grasp precisely what the statutes covered. A steep learning curve attended the unique issues involved with trafficking: Dean, a federal prosecutor, "saw that the cases were more complex and a little bit different from our other cases, because they happened over time, the victim trauma issues were a little different . . . the nature of the offense and of the trials were different . . . The cases were different in that they were often multi-jurisdictional, or they had organized criminal networks." Complicated legal issues required extensive training and paradigm shifts in the years following the law's passage, particularly among prosecutors and law enforcement agents.

With so many federal agencies—the Departments of State, Justice, Homeland Security, and Health and Human Services, plus state and local law enforcement and victim service providers—working at and across different levels to implement the TVPA, collaboration was a challenge. The newness of the law sometimes resulted in a lack of consensus among the various agencies and professionals on interpreting the statutes, assigning responsibilities, designating the offices and agencies that would receive cases, and so forth. As Katherine, a federal prosecutor, emphasized, there is something particularly complex about antitrafficking work: "I'm not aware of anything else so complicated and needing so many players to all work together quickly, and everybody has concerns that are hard for the others to appreciate. . . . So there are things where it's just really hard to understand the institutional concerns and the substantive concerns of the other . . . partners that you need to work with."

Although NGO service providers and criminal justice authorities often praised each other's abilities, relationships between them could be tense and confusing because of the distinct organizational cultures. Working across sectors involved obstacles, and conflicting personalities impeded collaboration. In reference to an unpredictable relationship with federal law enforcement, Nora, a case manager, noted, "They reach out to us sometimes, but it's unclear when . . . and it's unclear who is calling the shots sometimes. It seems like a lot of it comes down to personalities." Service providers told me that while some law enforcement agents were highly compassionate and sensitive to victim needs, others were gruff and seemingly immune to the human challenges of trafficking cases. Even prosecutors, who shared a criminal justice framework with investigators, acknowledged that their relationships with agents were sometimes precarious. According to Molly, a federal prosecutor, "It comes down to the agents themselves because I have worked with brilliant ICE and FBI agents and detectives, and I've worked with knuckleheads. . . . Some of it's a personality thing . . . and some people are just naturally better at establishing a rapport with a victim." The mentality of many agents was changing as they gained experience working on actual cases. "I think with training and sensitivity, and the more agents . . . who have lived through a case with a victim, it's almost like a religious conversion. I've seen the roughest, grouchiest, gruffest guys become so sensitive to the needs of a young woman because they've seen what's really going on." Describing one federal agent with whom she worked closely, she divulged, "I think it would be fair to say people would describe him as abrasive, but he really knows how to talk to these girls. He is a good investigator and . . . he's talked to enough victims that he knows how to do it, so . . . it really depends on the individual investigator." Because of the complexity of human trafficking cases, individuals with divergent agendas representing disparate agencies were obliged to work collaboratively in the interest of protecting victims and prosecuting traffickers. Abrasiveness and other "personality" issues on the part of implementers could wreak havoc on an already complicated process.

The Law "in Action"

Given the multiple professionals involved—prosecutors and law enforcement agents on the criminal justice side, immigration attorneys and case managers on the service provision side—each responsible for implementing "their" pieces of the TVPA, gaps in meaning permeated antitrafficking work on the ground. Although some implementation conflicts could be attributed to the newness of the law and to "personalities," the larger obstacles erupted from the law itself. In many ways, the criminal justice and service provision aspects of the law were parallel but separate; in fact, different portions of the law governed them. The VSFT definition stipulates who is eligible to receive services and federal benefits—in other words, it says whom the NGOs can serve. In contrast, the criminal statutes govern the work of law enforcement agents and prosecutors and dictate what constitutes a prosecutable crime. As described in Chapters 1 and 2, the victim and criminal definitions do not fully correspond, particularly for so-called labor trafficking—that curious formulation that arises in response to the equally curious idea of a distinctly "sex" trafficking. On top of the definitional misalignment, criminal justice professionals and service providers possessed different professional frameworks for approaching cases, with the former focused on "making a case" and the latter committed to putting presumptive victims first.

While professionals in both sectors understood the importance of the other, they prioritized the dual objectives of the law according to their own functions—to protect victims and prosecute traffickers. NGO service providers strove to connect their clients with support and to assist them with accessing necessary benefits and immigration status. Participating in investigations was essential in that it helped achieve those goals for the client. In contrast, investigators and government attorneys prioritized identifying cases that could be successfully prosecuted and establishing adequate evidence to corroborate any trafficking charges—ensuring that a victim was supported was important to the extent that he or she was able to provide information and testify, if necessary. In essence, NGOs put the needs of the victim first while law enforcement agents put the needs of the case first, and both sides became frustrated when their purposes crossed. Many providers said they worked hard to understand the law enforcement perspective but questioned whether criminal justice professionals appreciated the nuances of the services they provided. Charlotte, the director of a trafficking services program, noted, "I don't think that they get what the social service needs of clients are, and . . . I think that NGOs do a really good job at understanding the law and trying to understand the perspective of law enforcement . . . but that they don't really get what we do." "Their intentions are very good," a local law enforcement agent named Larry told me, referring to the NGOs.

"I can see they want to help. They're at every one of our meetings, trainings, that sort of thing." He added, "But I wish they had a little more resources over there, more control over the victims." For law enforcement agents, like Larry, the victim was a means to an end—a source of evidence leading to conviction, which of course is ultimately a positive step against trafficking writ large. While law enforcement agents did not fully understand the role of service providers and the time required to stabilize victims, service providers also lacked an understanding of law enforcement processes, especially their bureaucratic delays.

Because many trafficking victims are undocumented migrants, connecting them with services is vital; without structural support, it is difficult to live independently in the United States, much less assist law enforcement with prosecuting their traffickers. Stable victims were valuable sources of information in law enforcement investigations into trafficking and key to a successful prosecution. The importance of NGOs was not lost on Molly, a federal prosecutor: "You can't do the case without a victim who is in shape to be a witness, and you can't have a victim that's in shape to be a witness without them having an inordinate amount of services because these people have been harmed for so long, they need counseling, they need housing, they need shelter, they need medical care, they need to be able to work, they need all of this stuff."

Service providers, and case managers in particular, worked intensively with clients over extended periods of time. Their more basic activities of referring clients to law enforcement and assisting them with shelter and food happen only in concert with more nuanced and holistic interventions. Case managers addressed complex medical needs by obtaining general screenings and addressing victims' gynecological, dental, oncology, and optometry needs. They dealt with mental health issues, including connecting survivors to counseling services—and moving clients toward even considering therapy. Acculturation issues fell under their purview as well, so they taught clients to use the New York City subway, introduced them to banking, and helped them enroll children in school. They accompanied clients to appointments and advocated on their behalf amid complex bureaucratic issues (accessing Medicaid, Social Security, and other relevant benefits); they assisted clients in enrolling in GED, ESL, and job training programs; they identified housing and negotiated with landlords when clients had no credit or job history. They liaised with law enforcement agents and prosecutors and translated (sometimes literally) complex information so that survivors could understand legal developments as they arose. Emerging from extremely unstable situations, individuals became stable and secure because service providers advocated for their needs.

Professionals working on all sides of the issue invoked the idea of a victim-centered approach. Providers used the phrase to describe their method of service delivery, the Department of Justice applied it to its prosecutorial model, and I heard it at nearly every training or conference I attended to describe efforts to put victim needs at the heart of any investigation. There was recognition on all sides that victims were more willing to cooperate if they had support and felt their rights were being protected; indeed, criminal justice authorities specifically prioritized victim recovery when it affected a prosecution. As Leila, a federal victim witness coordinator, pragmatically put it, "We are not going to have a successful prosecution unless we have a willing and stable victim." Although criminal justice authorities and service providers both supported victim assistance, their motivations differed. Dean, a federal prosecutor, emphasized, "Our job is to vindicate the interest of the United States, not just about any one victim that's in front of us, but all the victims present, past, future . . . but . . . the NGO's job is to . . . make sure that client gets what that client needs."

These goals often came into direct conflict. Max, a former congressional staffer, noted, "There has always been a little bit of schizophrenia in the bill. . . . Is it a human rights legislation . . . or is it a law enforcement legislation? . . . And those two appear to work against each other, to some degree." Many service providers viewed the law enforcement piece as dominating implementation, and in numerous ways it did: "There is this talk of [the law] being victim centered, but really it's criminal justice centered in a lot of ways," Radha, an immigration attorney, told me. With criminal justice authorities' and NGOs' different but overlapping goals (prosecution versus service delivery) and criteria for identifying trafficking (criminal versus victim definitions), their goals were often at odds. When these oppositions and overlaps in meaning and motivation led to complicated applications of the law in practice, it affected victims.

Worthy Cases Versus Worthy Victims

What Makes a Case?

While the core objective for NGOs is to provide services and obtain immigration relief for every victim of trafficking, the main goal of criminal justice personnel is to identify those cases with adequate evidence to prove the crime of trafficking. Certain circumstances—the availability of corroborating evidence, number of victims, visibility of the crime, and perceived level of harm experienced by the victims—that combine to make a law enforcement case for trafficking *also* combine to sharpen the focus on "sex trafficking." It's not possible to prosecute every trafficking case. Dean, a federal prosecutor, emphasized, "It's identifying the cases and smartly allocating our limited resources to the merit cases and not spending a lot of time and money investigating cases that aren't prosecutable." Inability to corroborate a victim's claim made any case dead in the water. Another prosecutor, Lynn, noted, "The most difficult thing . . . is [to] corroborate whatever the victim tells us because invariably they're going to tell us about some relationship they had that was coercive, but we have to prove that. If it just happens in the confines of a room like this [gesturing to the office we're sitting in], it's going to be very difficult for us to prove that they were . . . forced into it, unless you get something else to show that there was this coercive relationship." A victim statement alone was insufficient, especially in single-victim cases, such as those involving domestic workers or nannies; some form of corroborating evidence, such as hospital records documenting violence or proof that a door was locked from the outside rather than the inside, would be needed. "The prosecutor's core job," according to Kyle, a federal prosecutor, "is to . . . determine whether a crime was committed and if there was, to determine a way to prove that to a jury of twelve ordinary people beyond a reasonable doubt. . . . You also have to have evidence. That person's story alone it is not sufficient to convince the jury that a crime was committed beyond a reasonable doubt." Even if an individual is a genuine victim of trafficking, "You have to sort of pick and choose the cases that you think are really going to work," Lynn told me. With the criteria required to certify a victim of a severe form of trafficking in mind, she added, "There are people who I have even been willing to certify as victims for T visa purposes, but I couldn't ever make a case [prosecute] for that because the trafficker is long gone, or . . . the case is just too old, or the victim is very credible, but there is really no corroboration." In such cases, having a law enforcement professional, like Lynn, who was willing to certify a survivor's victim status despite the lack of a prosecutable case was essential but hardly the norm.

What a criminal prosecution requires contradicts the reality of victim identification. Radha, an immigration attorney, noted, "There is a really inherent difference between what our clients need and what the criminal justice system needs, and it's not the fault of prosecutors or agents; it's that they need really solid evidence. They need cases that are worth their time in terms of leads and investigations, and it can take our clients a long time [to be ready to cooperate]." Referring to some of the factors that make trafficking cases difficult to prosecute successfully, she added, "Our clients don't come packaged in these cases of ten women at a time, [who] recently left, and there's a good trail of fresh evidence there, the traffickers are all here [in the United States]." Often, victims would trickle into NGOs on their own, several years after escaping their trafficking situations, and long after their traffickers had returned to their home countries. Although these were authentic victims who met the federal VSFT definition, there was not enough solid or corroborative evidence to pursue in court. Dean, a federal prosecutor, told me, "If we believe that someone is a trafficking victim by the VSFT definition and the defendant engaged in trafficking conduct, but we may not be able to prove that, we may still prosecute the case using other statutes. . . . There could be a lot of reasons why you can't prove a case that had nothing to do with whether you believe the victim or not, you know? You've got to corroborate it."

In many cases, service providers perceived law enforcement as favoring sex trafficking and situations involving multiple victims to the exclusion of forced labor or single-victim cases. Nancy, a case manager, noted, "I always get a different response from law enforcement when it's sex trafficking versus labor or a domestic worker, or if it is sex trafficking with just one person involved in it without having a bunch of other people. . . . They don't even respond at all many times." When I mentioned this concern to Jim, a federal agent, he denied it: "Absolutely not. If there's one victim, it's too many." Katrina, a federal prosecutor, told a different story. When asked about how many victims were involved in the cases she had prosecuted, she responded that the cases were "mostly multivictim . . . the most I had was sixteen victims with a single defendant. The least I had, I think, was three or four." From a prosecutorial perspective, multivictim cases are easier to prove because the exploited individuals can corroborate one another's accounts.[1]

Federal prosecutors remained convinced that the government prosecutes all types of cases. Kyle emphasized, "We do the cases as we find them. . . . We've prosecuted sweatshop cases. We've prosecuted brothel cases. We've prosecuted . . . domestic cases . . . where there's a servant living in somebody's home. . . . There is no 'let's try to do more farm cases' or 'let's try to do more brothel cases'; it's just here's the lead, this is what the FBI needs to do, prosecute the case." In fact, all the prosecutors I spoke to, both in the DOJ Human

Trafficking Prosecution Unit and in the districts, reiterated that no preference should be given to any one form of trafficking over another. Criminal justice authorities have identified and prosecuted some major cases of forced labor since the passage of the law in 2000, and those numbers have increased, especially since Obama took office. However, over the course of my fieldwork, law enforcement identified only one labor trafficking case in New York City, in comparison to at least five times as many sex trafficking cases.[2] Clearly, the investigative lens was highly focused on this area, and the layers of meaning involved in interpreting and implementing the law (e.g., meeting definitional criteria, standards of evidence, and corroboration combined with investigative discretion) seemed to blind investigators to how their own work failed to align with larger patterns of trafficking.

Although federal prosecutors have, indeed, pursued a number of labor trafficking cases, many of my informants perceived law enforcement agents putting more resources into investigating forced prostitution. While prosecutors were theoretically open to pursuing all types of trafficking cases and held nuanced understandings of the similarities between trafficking into forced prostitution and forced labor, they also had heavy case loads and relied on law enforcement investigators to bring them meritorious cases. As the ones conducting investigations, agents served a filtering role and thus had some control over which cases ultimately moved forward—in many cases those involving forced prostitution, which were seemingly easier to identify and aligned with agents' interpretations of the law. The actions of individual law enforcement agents end up mirroring the TVPA's symbolic privileging of sex trafficking. Indeed, Lynn told me that although her office had dealt with more *victims* of labor trafficking (due to the large numbers of victims involved in a small number of cases), 90 percent of the *cases* they prosecuted were sex trafficking, as a result of referrals she received from law enforcement.[3]

Sex trafficking made up the preponderance of cases that law enforcement sent both to prosecutors and to NGOs. Ironically, many of the NGOs had more labor trafficking clients enrolled in their programs (identified through other service agencies or Good Samaritans), despite the number of sex trafficking cases they were referred through criminal justice channels.[4] This held true in the case of Ella, an immigration attorney: "Most of the labor trafficking referrals come from Good Samaritans or other agencies. Most of the sex trafficking referrals come from law enforcement." According to the U.S. Council for Catholic Bishops, 60 percent of their clients nationwide were trafficked into forced labor, but these numbers are not reflected in law enforcement referrals.[5] Service providers also reported that when *they* encountered victims first and *then* referred them to law enforcement, the response was always far greater for cases involving forced prostitution, as Roxanne, an immigration attorney, noted, "It was much harder for us to get law enforcement to investigate labor trafficking crimes. . . . I don't think once in my practice did I get a local cop to look at a labor trafficking case. And on the federal level . . . they would maybe interview our clients who we would refer to them, but I never had a case that was referred from law enforcement to us that wasn't sex trafficking." Labor trafficking cases could remain effectively invisible in the face of law enforcement's overwhelming focus on forced prostitution. Audra, an immigration attorney, said that she believed officials acted more aggressively on trafficking cases involving the sex trade:

> I've found that the response from law enforcement is always much more immediate for sex trafficking cases . . . than for labor trafficking, particularly if it's an isolated case of like one domestic worker in one household. I struggled very much to get someone to follow up and to get someone to officially open an investigation into the case. I know they have different priorities than we as antitrafficking advocates do, but from our perspective these are all victim witnesses that need to have their safety addressed. The perpetrators need to be kept away from the survivors, both here as well as abroad, and just some kind of sense of justice for the survivors so they can move on.

Providers told me over and over that law enforcement was consistently slower to respond (if they responded at all) to reports of labor trafficking, which suggests that a contextual and subjective—but by no means universally accepted—interpretation of the law (i.e., that trafficking equals sex trafficking) was influencing its implementation.

The fixation on sex trafficking emerges from a confluence of ideology, case identification methods, and the definitional splits in the law. Nora perceived law enforcement's focus on investigating sex trafficking as mirroring the focus of the Bush administration: "I think that there is clearly an agenda with the current administration and a lot of people who have . . . jumped on board with antitrafficking, and so it's really . . . very limiting because the cases that you mostly see are this one type of case—trafficking for forced commercial sex acts. And as long as that's the political agenda, then it seems like a lot of the agents of the TVPA, mainly law enforcement, will mainly look for one

kind of [victim]." New York City's DOJ-funded task force was meant to increase victim identification by bringing federal and local law enforcement and
nongovernmental service providers together, but many service providers told
me that despite NGOs' efforts to broaden the focus, their meetings focused
almost entirely on adult and domestic youth sex trafficking, with an almost
willful avoidance of labor trafficking on the part of law enforcement and task
force coordinators. Many municipal law enforcement agencies located their
trafficking units in their vice divisions, which by nature limited the type of
trafficking agents investigated to forced prostitution (also having the effect
of conflating trafficking and prostitution). Approaches were tied to the particular experience and focus of a department. Sheila, the director of a trafficking services program, noted, "Even the people that have worked a variety
of cases, when I've heard law enforcement participate in a training or a presentation they almost always only talk about sex trafficking. And I think
because they locate their law enforcement people within the vice squad . . .
that's a problem." By housing their human trafficking units within vice
squads, these agencies' views of trafficking became synonymous with forced
sex work. Pete, a federal criminal justice administrator, wondered, "They say
they will look at labor, too, but what kind of expertise do they have?"

On a practical level, case identification techniques also shifted attention
toward trafficking for forced prostitution, and criminal justice authorities acknowledged that it was more difficult to identify cases of forced labor. Trafficking victims tend not to self-identify, and it is more difficult for investigators
to gain access to the types of places where forced labor occurs. Some of the
contradictions inherent in law enforcement perceptions of trafficking that
led to higher rates of identification for forced prostitution are here raised by
Lynn: "We really haven't done as many forced labor cases. Part of it is . . . just
the volume we see, not the volume that exists, but the volume we see. There's
already mechanisms locally to find sex trafficking. You have vice squads out
there all the time. So that's where we get a lot of our stuff." She continued,
noting lack of visibility as a barrier to identifying labor trafficking victims,
"We certainly don't get them through the normal law enforcement mechanisms because they just don't come up as much. Part of it is the nature of the
crime because when you have sex trafficking, it's sort of a public crime. It requires other participants. Whereas when you have forced labor, like working in a sweatshop, you don't see it as much [there is no public interaction].
It really is a much more hidden crime, domestics . . . who are kept in people's
houses, you don't see it." Despite the volume of sex trafficking cases being

identified, Lynn's office had dealt with more labor trafficking victims—and in ratios consistent with federal statistics: "We've had like three forced labor cases. . . . If you're talking about ones involving sex, it's probably easily a four to one breakdown, so 20 percent of our cases are going to be forced labor. The other 80 percent will be sex trafficking. With the victims I would say almost exactly the opposite because the volume we get with a forced labor case is usually much larger. . . . If you count by victim, forced labor trumps because one case is thirty people. That's more than our entire docket of sex trafficking."

In terms of investigative efforts, some agents noted that they *responded* to labor cases but did not *look* for them. At a national conference, one federal agent noted, "I target brothels because it would be offensive if I knocked on doors looking for domestics. I'm willing to support agents working on worksite investigations. It is important, but I don't want to go into a worksite without a specific lead." For this agent, "knocking on doors" conveyed suspicion of the employers that he viewed as unwarranted in situations other than prostitution, in which criminality was already assumed. So although law enforcement conducted brothel raids under the assumption that trafficking lurks around prostitution, they did not use the same logic to identify labor cases (e.g., inspecting nail salons or factories for evidence of force or exploitation).[6] As Ella, an immigration attorney, put it, "Law enforcement isn't waiting . . . at Upper West Side homes looking for nannies that are trafficked." Larry, a law enforcement agent, confirmed this and, referring to the Sabhnani case (a high-profile labor trafficking case that occurred in Nassau County, Long Island), noted that law enforcement often has limited access to labor trafficking venues:

> Except for the one case on Long Island, I haven't seen any new cases of domestic work. Even that case, the lady was out walking around [the trafficked domestic worker had escaped confinement in the home] and somebody noticed her, so I don't think it's one of those cases where it's too much in the open like prostitution is because it's in the household. Who actually gets into that household except the people who live there, or actually somebody sees a lady like they saw in Nassau County walking around? . . . But in New York City, how many millions of people live here . . . for us to go into all these places and talk to nannies? It's just a very very hard case. I haven't seen any of them yet.

Investigators seemed to throw their hands in the air when talking about the difficulty of identifying these victims. However, Nora, a case manager, had several domestic workers as clients and believed law enforcement should be looking for exactly these types of cases: "It's troubling that there's this kind of disproportionate energy placed on one kind of trafficking, and yet the way we're going about finding those cases is very, very limited, versus all the other kinds of trafficking that could really be an issue in our country, and the investigative resources are not really being expended to find those cases. . . . A big reason we're seeing cases with prostitution is because those are the cases that people are looking for." Because it is a criminal activity, prostitution is a natural site for intervention. A common way for law enforcement to increase the number of identified trafficking victims without actually expanding investigative efforts to include labor is to focus on the problem of American-born girls being conscripted into prostitution here in their own country. Larry told me that cases of forced labor were not coming across his desk, so his office focused on domestic teen prostitution: "We haven't seen those numbers, so my turn was from international trafficking to more U.S. girls being recruited here in the United States." Larry believed the incidence of forced labor was minimal and that if there were actual cases, the victims would find a way to come forward. He protested, "We just can't find the crimes. . . . [If] people [are] being trafficked, then I would see a lot more cases like you heard about the Nassau County [Sabhnani] domestic case coming out. . . . In this day and age—with the media [and being] so accessible to cell phones or house phones, watching TV you see all these shows, everything else going on—I don't see why a lady can't pick up the phone and call." This view completely ignored what is known about the climate of fear that keeps many victims exploited—fear not just of their captors but of authorities, too. Interestingly, the domestic sex trafficking victims that Larry was identifying were not coming forward on their own, but Larry and his colleagues were seeking them out via targeted investigations. Will, a federal agent, agreed that if labor trafficking was a problem, he would see more cases: "It's not because we're not looking; it's because it's not there." He then told me most of the cases his unit identified were based on tips from existing informants rather than proactive investigation. Still, law enforcement's focus on sex trafficking did not necessarily produce viable cases, either. Often, the authorities were focused more on prostitution than on actual trafficking, which resulted in a zeal to raid brothels or massage parlors but very little force, fraud, or coercion found.

Providers noted that clients identified through other channels by NGOs were generally more cooperative than those identified through law enforcement raids; however, law enforcement continued to focus on raiding brothels rather than investigating NGO-identified cases. Service providers were baffled by law enforcement's disinterest in NGO-identified cases because the victims were generally more stable and willing to cooperate than those identified through raids. Radha, an immigration attorney, told me,

> Unfortunately, there seems to be an interest in . . . going out and . . . focusing on the sex, the prostitution . . . engaging in raids, so they can build a good case and then trying to prosecute those cases, as opposed to taking . . . clients that are . . . coming in on their own . . . but they also know and have acknowledged that it's clients who come in on their own, rather than through a raid, who are more cooperative and more interested in cooperating. It just doesn't seem to translate.

Bridget, the director of a trafficking services program, agreed that this focus on raiding brothels was detrimental to victims identified through other channels. "When they are putting resources into it, it's into raids rather than . . . processing paperwork for victims who have already come in or really doing investigations of victims that are coming in on their own, that kind of thing." The misalignment of resources and legitimate trafficking exasperated Jarrah, who told me, "We've got all of these sex workers that were forced into it [trafficked] . . . and we are bringing them into federal law enforcement, and they are not interested, and yet on the other side they are doing all of these raids into brothels and not finding any trafficked persons. And it's like, well there might be [trafficking victims], but that's not the way you find them."[7]

While the differences between criminal and victim definitions of trafficking partially accounted for law enforcement's focus on sex trafficking (after all, a victim could be defrauded into labor when there is no prosecutable crime), service providers noted that even with sex trafficking cases, law enforcement agents were often uninterested in or slow to respond to NGO-identified cases. Yet most victims (locally and nationally) were, indeed, initially identified by NGOs, not by law enforcement. Annette, who held a policy position in a federal trafficking office that oversees service provision for victims, told me, "The majority of our victims . . . didn't come originally from law enforcement; [the case] came from an NGO to law enforcement."

Gwen, who worked in federal law enforcement, noted, "We have a lot of referrals from NGOs. Some of our major cases came from NGOs." She mentioned one large labor trafficking case in New York in which the first victim was identified by an NGO: "[The NGO] ended up with the first victim that got out and brought the case to [federal law enforcement agency] and said, 'Hey, we think we've got something that's trafficking, can you look at it?' And without them bringing that referral and that victim to us, we wouldn't have rescued another ninety, ninety-five victims." NGOs provided law enforcement agencies with many leads, but investigators were selective in which cases they chose to pursue. Although this particular case was a success in that agents investigated the NGO tip, law enforcement's response was also incredibly delayed, and the victims remained in the situation for months after the NGO alerted authorities. Nancy, a case manager who had worked on that situation, told me how long it took to get law enforcement to respond: her supervisor "talked to [federal law enforcement agency] many times until they finally got interested in the case and they started making investigations and stuff. . . . And they kept telling us, 'Oh, we're going to do the raid,' and I think . . . they told us at the end of March, 'We are going to do it in April, we're going to do it in May,' and . . . finally they did at the end of June."

In general, providers perceived law enforcement response to cases as unpredictable. Bridget, the director of a trafficking services program, seemed exhausted by it all: "I really wish I could say these cases are the ones, and I used to say . . . they want the sex cases, and they don't want the labor cases, but I feel like I can't even say that anymore. . . . I don't even know if . . . we can tell you who they are going to be interested in because some cases they are just gobbling up and we don't expect to them to be interested, some cases that are just totally juicy cases and they just are not." Although service providers understood that a certain level of evidence was required for prosecution, they also questioned why law enforcement did not investigate certain cases that they, as service providers, clearly viewed as trafficking. Sometimes victims desperately wanted justice served or were fearful because their trafficker was still at large, but law enforcement would not pursue the case. Jarrah, an immigration attorney, told me, "We've got clients who they see their trafficker in the street and . . . federal law enforcement knows it, everybody knows it, but they are not going and grabbing these guys. And we can't really figure out why not, what the situation is." A similar account came to me from Nancy, a case manager: one of her sex trafficking clients had seen two of her exploiters in her neighborhood on multiple occasions, but federal law enforcement reportedly did not have the resources to investigate. The client was a victim of forced prostitution, so even the inconsistency in definitions could not explain this lack of response. Bridget noted, "There are a lot of cases where I think that the best thing for everyone is that there is not a prosecution . . . but there are cases that we really would like to see the people in jail that aren't pursued, so I think that's . . . difficult."

Not only did law enforcement hold different conceptions and rely on different definitions of trafficking from service providers; limited resources also meant that authorities had to make tough decisions in prioritizing the cases that moved forward. Jim, a federal agent, told me that his antitrafficking unit had been downsized in recent years, and they were often called to other types of cases: "We don't work only on trafficking. There is lots of smuggling and some gangs stuff." Lack of funding and competing criminal justice priorities hampered victim identification, according to Dean, a federal prosecutor:

> The big issue you're hearing from everybody is victim identification, and I don't know why we're not finding more victims. . . . Our biggest obstacle is it's a new statute . . . and then there is just a resource issue, you know? . . . There just aren't really the federal resources out there and . . . everything is so focused on terrorism and domestic security, and the war in Iraq has been expensive. . . . So the criminal justice process . . . has not had an increase in its capacity to match the enactment of the new statute.

With resources drained, a number of other factors went into making decisions about case advancement, ranging from the number of victims affected, the visibility of the case, the quality of evidence, and the value assigned to the particular form (or forms) of trafficking.

Two Obstacles to Certification: The Law and Law Enforcement

Despite the name "Trafficking Victims Protection Act," a combination of factors stemming from the law itself and from enforcement's interpretation has limited victims' access to immigration relief and federal benefits. While the TVPA established a battery of victim protections, law enforcement's role in evaluating cases significantly affected the timing and type of benefits. The drafters of the TVPA recognized that "victims of trafficking are frequently unfamiliar with the laws, cultures, and languages of the countries into which they have been trafficked, because they are often subjected to coercion and intimidation including physical detention and debt bondage, and because they often fear retribution and forcible removal to countries in which they will face retribution or other hardship, these victims often find it difficult or impossible to report the crimes committed against them or to assist in the investigation and prosecution of such crimes"[8] As a result, the TVPA provides assistance to victims, including federal benefits and immigration relief. The certification process makes a victim of a severe form of trafficking eligible for benefits and services to the same extent as a refugee, if he or she "is willing to assist in every reasonable way in the investigation and prosecution of severe forms of trafficking in persons" and "has made a bona fide application for a [T] visa" or "is a person whose continued presence in the United States the Attorney General is ensuring in order to effectuate prosecution of traffickers in persons."[9]

All victims of severe forms of trafficking are eligible to apply for the T visa, but it is that demonstrated willingness to cooperate in the investigation and prosecution of their trafficker that is so tricky. Willingness is usually demonstrated by submitting a law enforcement endorsement form (known as the I-914B) completed by a federal agent. Because the application process for a T visa can take several months to a year, and because prosecutors often want victims to refrain from applying for the visa until prosecution is complete,[10] law enforcement may apply for immediate temporary immigration relief called "continued presence" (CP) on behalf of those victims who assist in an ongoing investigation or prosecution (see Table 2 for a comparison of CP and the T visa).[11] Once certified by one of these means, a victim is eligible for federal benefits, such as Medicaid and food stamps, and receives a permit to work legally in the United States. In both processes (acquiring CP and application for the T visa) law enforcement plays a vital role in documenting that trafficking occurred so that the individual may become certified as a victim of a severe form of it, but the very requirement that victims cooperate in order to receive certification is problematic in two ways. Many victims are too traumatized or fearful to cooperate with law enforcement in the first place, and if a case is not prosecuted, law enforcement personnel are often hesitant to endorse even those victims who do cooperate.

Informants universally praised the law's inclusion of immigration relief but viewed as problematic the conditioning of relief on willingness to cooperate in an investigation. Of the many reasons to object to this condition,

Table 2. Comparison of Continued Presence to the T Visa

	Continued Presence (CP)	*T visa*
Eligibility	Victims who are necessary to an ongoing law enforcement investigation or prosecution	Any victim "willing to assist in every reasonable way in the investigation and prosecution of severe forms of trafficking in persons"
Wait Time	1–6 weeks	3 months–1 year+
Who Submits?	Law enforcement official	Victims may self-petition, but the application is very complicated; an 1-914B (completed by law enforcement) is not required but expedites the process
Expiration	1 year, with option to renew	4 years; after 3 years victims may apply for legal permanent resident status

retraumatizing victims is the most critical. Maribel, a service provider, noted, "That immigration assistance piece . . . it was very future-forward thinking. However, the whole willingness to cooperate with law enforcement and how that actually plays out on the ground is so detrimental. I think that the whole certification status is just a bunch of BS. . . . What other victim of crime at the federal level needs to be certified by a government agency that they are actually a victim of a crime? None. . . . This population needs to jump through so many hoops to actually be considered a certified victim of trafficking." The proviso of cooperation is one that other kinds of victims never need to fulfill. Many criminal justice professionals, on the other hand, viewed the requirement that certified victims be "willing to assist in every reasonable way" as essential to prosecuting traffickers. One of my law enforcement informants—Dale, an administrator—assumed that all involved parties have the same goals and therefore that successful tools for law enforcement should be very acceptable to service providers and victims: "We're just going to have more victims if we don't put the bad guys in jail. . . . And I think we've been fairly successful at helping victims and putting the bad guys in jail." Although pressuring victims to cooperate often resulted in access to additional victims, the requirement also had the effect of pushing certain victims away.

Service providers reported that the cooperation requirement was indeed a barrier, and as a result, certain victims elected not to pursue the T visa. Roxanne, an immigration attorney, told me about several clients who chose not to report their cases to law enforcement (and therefore to go without certification) because they were fearful that the traffickers would retaliate against their grown children living in their home country once it was known the victims had cooperated with law enforcement: "They just didn't want to take the risk because the adult children were back in the home country and then the traffickers might know where they lived." One survivor, Nadia, told me that after she escaped, her traffickers' associates called her parents in her home country, threatening their lives unless she paid back the money allegedly owed them. Nadia did not come into contact with law enforcement until several years after she escaped the trafficking situation, but she questioned whether she would have trusted any protections that they could offer:

> I don't know how things would have played out had I met all these
> people [law enforcement and service providers] . . . when my parents
> were still threatened. . . . I don't know. . . . I truly believe that there was
> absolutely nothing they could have done for my parents in Russia. . . .
> Once they said, 'We have people on the ground.' I said, 'Where my
> parents live? Even if you have guys in Moscow, St. Petersburg, this is
> nowhere near there.' Don't be ridiculous, telling me you have some
> FBI agents in Russia was going to save my family."

It can be hard for outsiders to understand the downsides to victims' aiding the authorities, but Roxanne reinforced Nadia's point: "I think there is this perception that once people cooperate with law enforcement, it's kind of like what you see on TV . . . the Witness Protection Program, and there's no protection, and so they are really, really vulnerable."

There is an inherent contradiction in compelling undocumented migrants—who are afraid of being deported and may come from countries where law enforcement is corrupt—to cooperate with officials in order to access benefits and services. Sheila, the director of a trafficking services program, disclosed, "I think this victim cooperation piece is a nightmare. To have that requirement at the same time that immigrants are afraid to reveal themselves in any way, how can you expect this to work?" Misunderstandings about the role of law enforcement—sometimes as a result of genuinely prob-lematic past run-ins with authorities—and ignorance of the laws at play can incite concern on the part of victims like Rocio, a survivor who had been traf-ficked into forced prostitution: "I was afraid at any moment they would ar-rest me . . . and I thought they were going to deport me. . . . I knew they could deport me for the kind of work I was doing." Rocio was identified during a law enforcement raid, so her options were to cooperate or be deported. Al-though she ultimately agreed to cooperate, victims identified through chan-nels other than in-person criminal busts have a greater incentive to remain under the radar and avoid any contact with law enforcement.

Fear and trauma are the most formidable barriers to victim cooperation, and service providers encounter these factors often. Sometimes criminal justice authorities wanted to pursue a case, but the victim was not ready or willing to cooperate. Indeed, victims were often retraumatized by retelling their story to law enforcement. The providers I spoke with told me that up to 50 percent of their clients would disappear because they did not want to in-teract with law enforcement; they essentially chose to remain undocumented and without access to services or benefits. Jarrah, an immigration attorney, noted that numerous victims were coming forward but disappeared once they learned of the cooperation requirement: "Our worst-case scenarios are the ones where they come in, we tell them about our services, but the U.S. gov-ernment provides so many restrictions on how they can get these services—like cooperation, not being able to work in prostitution, and not being able to leave the country, that clients disappear . . . because it's too overwhelming and there's too many restrictions on how to get the status."[12] Another immi-gration attorney, Ella, told me that she believed the cooperation require-ment was detrimental to her clients' well-being:

> I dread working on cases when there is an investigation. I dread it. I hate it. I don't like dealing with law enforcement. My clients don't like dealing with law enforcement, but in order to get the T visa you have to cooperate with law enforcement. Of course, on the other hand, when it's a successful prosecution or an investigation that's really done right, it's a win-win for everyone, except for the trafficker [laughs]. But when it's this . . . weird tug-of-war dynamic over law enforce-ment trying to get their claws into your clients, and the client is too scared to cooperate, like trying to find a balance in those situations has been really negative and really stressful.

The idealized image of a victim desperate to abet law enforcement in retribution for her suffering may seem commonsensical, but my informants asserted that this inclination was not the norm. Jarrah noted, "All the clients, even if they end up cooperating, are terrified of cooperating. None of them want to, but the ones that really want that immigration status do it because they know that that's the only way . . . they're going to be able to get immigration status." Indeed, the promise of immigration status served as a hook to persuade victims to cooperate in law enforcement investigations in which they otherwise would have had no interest.

Although some victims were certainly reluctant to interact and cooperate with law enforcement, others were highly motivated to access immigration benefits or to assist in punishing their traffickers. Yet criminal justice authorities, and law enforcement agents in particular, were often inconsistent gatekeepers in terms of granting CP and endorsing victims for the T visa. This is not surprising: their role as arbiters for federal benefits and immigration status could only ever be subordinate to their primary goal of investigating and evidencing crime. Whether and when to endorse victims was a highly discretionary and subjective decision. While the providers I spoke to viewed these immigration remedies as essential to the law, every single one emphasized the enormous obstacles, and the often-lengthy process, that stood between victims and certification, and with it immigration status, benefits, and the ability to work legally in the United States.

Continued presence, the key to the most immediate immigration relief and benefits, hugely contributed to stabilizing undocumented survivors who recently escaped a trafficking situation. At a congressional hearing I attended, Marcy Forman, the director of the Office of Investigations at ICE, touted continued presence as part of the agency's "victim-centered approach" to trafficking.[13] Hugely important for those victims who received it, CP was never obtained by the majority, despite provider efforts to advocate for it. Consequently, providers viewed the process as anything but victim centered. Over and over, they told me of their difficulties getting law enforcement to respond to requests for CP for their clients, or even to interview victims to assess the viability of their cases to see if they *might* qualify for CP. Fran, a federal grants administrator, confirmed this lack of response from law enforcement, calling it a national problem: "Some of our victim service providers say they spend weeks or months trying to get someone from law enforcement to come in and interview a victim, that the victim is willing but they can't get law enforcement there." Without even an interview with authorities, clients experienced long delays in certification and consequent benefits, and they would never receive CP. Audra, an immigration attorney, acknowledged the competing goals of law enforcement and service providers, but she questioned the lack of concern for victim needs: "I certainly agree that there are different priorities and limited resources that they have available to them . . . and I acknowledge that they have a different goal and agenda than my own, but I feel like that's not an excuse for refusing to do even the minimum in terms of responding to the minimum needs of our clients." For Audra's clients, an interview with law enforcement was the difference between potentially immediate upgrades in immigration status, with the ability to work legally in the United States, and having to wait months or years to access these same benefits. Unless law enforcement would assess their situations' fit with the rubric of trafficking, these clients saw their road to documented status lengthen into the distance.

A number of providers told me that even when victims were actively collaborating in an investigation, law enforcement agents were still often reluctant to grant CP and would sometimes withhold it or refuse to sign a T visa endorsement. This issue went beyond New York City, as provider after provider at a national conference cited examples of stalling. Although nearly every provider I spoke with complained about the obstacles to getting CP for clients, when I asked Jim, a federal agent, how long it takes to get a victim CP, he told me, "As soon as a victim is identified, the CP paperwork goes in so they can get services, and the NGO can handle it." Speaking at a national conference, Gwen, a federal victim witness coordinator, agreed: "We don't have to have a trafficking prosecution to grant a victim CP; we do have to have an investigation." Providers told a different story. Bridget, the director of a trafficking services program, told me of law enforcement, "I would say the obstacles are refusal to give continued presence, even when a client is actively working and helping them with a case. That's for me the number one hurdle, terrible thing." Clients might actively participate in law enforcement investigations but not receive CP in return. Bridget continued, "We have a client who was driving around in a car pointing out places her traffickers lived, identifying people left and right, like you'd think she should be on the payroll over there as much as she was helping them." But the client never received CP. Compare this account from Jarrah, an immigration attorney:

The most frustrating part of working on these cases . . . [is] we've done extensive intakes, the person is clearly trafficked, we will take them to ICE, even to meetings of two hours each, all this information. . . . We are giving phone numbers, we're giving addresses, we're giving money orders, we are getting photographs, all this information, and the ICE agent will look at us and say, "I personally believe that this person is trafficked, but I have to corroborate all of this person's evidence or information and we need other witnesses, or we need to go to these houses," and then the case just gets lost, and they drop the case and they don't do anything about it, and we have to make a gazillion phone calls to try to get ICE interested.

In practice, if a case was not prosecuted (for whatever reason), the victims did not receive CP.

Most victims, even after agreeing to cooperate in an investigation, had to wait out the long administrative process of applying for a T visa. Without CP, victims remained "pre-certified" until their T visas were approved (see Table 3 for a summary of protections available to pre-certified and certified victims). This could mean months of waiting without any legal immigration status in the country and consequently no ability to work legally or access benefits—a bureaucratic wrinkle, perhaps, for authorities, but a significant and lengthy burden for victims. For their clients, case managers see certification as a practical matter and a symbolic, psychological boon as Nora, a case manager, told me: "To help them get these documents that identify them . . . that's so empowering when you're able to do it, and it's so disempowering when you're not because you have these clients who continue to live kind of underground and . . . having to . . . wait out the long process of applying for a T visa." During my year of fieldwork with Empower, some clients who entered the program shortly after my arrival still had not received their T visas upon my departure. These survivors continued to work without documentation because they had no other options for supporting themselves—and, in some cases, their dependents.

The drafters' goal of victim protection was not being met in a consistent or timely manner—all the more unfortunate when one realizes how willing the victims are to perform legitimate labor. Sheila, the director of a trafficking services program, told me, "The worst thing we can do to survivors is make them wait to work. I've never known such a motivated group of people who want to work and are determined to work." Pre-certified clients still had needs for food, shelter, and medical care; although NGOs, with their grant funding, were able to assist with some of these needs, undocumented victims

Table 3. Protections Available to Pre-certified and Certified Victims

Protections	Pre-certified Victims	Certified Victims
Social Services	✓	✓
Federal Benefits (Medicaid, food stamps, cash assistance)		✓
Immigration Status		✓

lingered in a precarious situation. When victims remain pre-certified, they are unable to work and do not have access to public benefits or health care. Although some victims sought out jobs in the informal sector, others were too afraid of being deported to work without a permit. The unfortunate disparities between certified and noncertified clients were remarkable, Nora said:

> You can . . . see . . . the second-class citizen thing with clients who aren't certified and those who are because you have all these legal documents that . . . put them on the map for everybody in the community who employs them, who provides medical care, who . . . they might . . . open a bank account with, versus the clients who don't have any of those documents, still may have suffered a severe form of trafficking, and may not be able either to convince [the government] of that or are in the process of getting all of that ready. And there's all these things that they really need that they can't get in the same way or with the same ease that other clients have.

Certification became one more bifurcation in the process of TVPA implementation; those who were not certified remained invisible.

Applying for the T visa came with hurdles of its own, many of them similar to CP. In some cases, willingness to cooperate was itself sufficient for victims to receive an I-914B, the endorsement from law enforcement that hastens the process. Even if law enforcement chose not to pursue the case, the agents could still agree to complete the endorsement in support of a victim's visa application. However, during my fieldwork, providers traced a shift away from this stance, which was initially the status quo following the passage of the law, and toward a more stringent standard for endorsing victims based on whether corroborative evidence was available and prosecution possible. The law does limit CP to those victims needed for a criminal investigation, but the T visa only requires willingness to cooperate. Law enforcement, however, often used the same criteria for completing an I-914B as for granting CP. Corroboration is required to prove most crimes, but victim benefits are not generally contingent upon it. As much as law enforcement personnel emphasized the importance of victim cooperation to identifying additional cases, they often shrugged it off if it did not serve their purpose. Rather than endorsing any victim "willing to assist in every reasonable way," authorities tended to endorse I-914Bs only for those victims with prosecutable cases, causing additional delays in visa approval and consequent benefits eligibility. Jarrah told me,

> We do not understand why because, under the law, a trafficked person just must abide by reasonable requests for cooperation, and "reasonable" is kind of subjective, but if our clients are saying that "I'm willing to cooperate as far as ICE or FBI or the AUSAs want to take this case, I'm giving you all this information, I'm here, I'm ready to do whatever it is they're asking me to do," to me that is cooperating with reasonable requests for cooperation. And these clients . . . they're going to these meetings, they're offering up all this information, and then ICE or FBI or the AUSA is actually requesting a stricter standard than what the law requires.

The unrequired stringency made no sense to her.

> We've actually had one of the . . . division heads . . . say to us . . . "We've got too many cases coming in. Look, the requirement for us is that a trafficked person must have an idea of where the trafficker is, preferably in the United States, and the trafficking cannot have happened over five years ago." Well, that doesn't fit into most of our clients. Most of our clients, it takes them, especially when they're trafficked into sex work . . . we are averaging five to ten years before they come out and tell anybody that this is what happened, so that's a huge problem.

Even if these victims were willing to cooperate, law enforcement agents generally would not accept the cases and, thus, would not endorse them for the T visa. Criminal standards of evidence were getting in the way of survivors accessing victim benefits, which should be a completely separate issue.

NGO service providers acted as mediators between their clients and state actors but had little power to change law enforcement practices. Jarrah, an immigration attorney, wondered, "What are these people supposed to do if . . . a law enforcement agent doesn't want to help our clients? What do we do?" I sat in on a meeting between a victim, Camille (who had been trafficked into domestic work twice), and her case manager, Sadie. They had called the DOJ hotline to report what had happened, and the victim confirmed she was willing to cooperate.[14] After several months of waiting, unable to work because she was undocumented and at a virtual standstill in her life, Camille inquired of Sadie, "Why don't they believe me?" Her impression was that because the government had not expressed interest in her case, they must not find her story credible. Camille had taken a risk in reporting her abuse to authorities, yet the lack of response suggested that her story had fallen upon deaf ears, and more tangibly that her ability to meet material needs (such as food and shelter) while in the United States was quickly dissipating. Audra, an immigration attorney, cast this trend in the context of a broader shift in the development of the TVPA in action: "When it first passed, everyone was really concerned . . . about survivors' willingness and comfort in talking to law enforcement. And obviously that's still a problem, but now the problem seems to be getting law enforcement to cooperate with the clients, and that's an additional hurdle that they shouldn't have to go through." She continued, "Even making that step is so huge and then to be practically slapped in the face by law enforcement who is like, 'That's not a trafficking case, and we're not going to help you' or just dragging their feet and then not being as responsive for whatever reason." The frustration that service providers and survivors felt when they went out on a limb and made the decision to cooperate with law enforcement but received no response or validation is itself a significant force in TVPA dynamics. What Audra said she needed from law enforcement to move forward with a case was fairly mechanical: "I perceive law enforcement's role as . . . taking the report down, taking the facts down and then . . . reporting it to the local AUSA or the DOJ. . . . If they don't want to take the case on, fine, but then it's their responsibility to say 'Yes, client X met with me on September 1, 2007. She reported these facts,' signed John Doe. That's what I need, you know?" Having this signed endorsement greatly sped up the T visa application process, granting victims access to protections sooner. But federal agents often told providers that a particular case was not trafficking, my informants told me—despite their strong assertion that the victims fit the criteria for VSFTs.

Among groups of professionals working to fulfill their own particular aspects of the law, discord was often driven by conceptions of "what counted" as trafficking. Perspective matters: the criminal criteria conjure a vision of trafficking that is markedly different from the victim-centered definition. While service providers believed meeting the VSFT definition and being willing to cooperate should meet the standard for granting CP or completing an endorsement for the T visa, law enforcement personnel used adequate evidence to prosecute a criminal case as their criterion. For example, Gwen, who worked in federal law enforcement, framed lack of law enforcement response in terms of lack of evidence: "Nongovernmental agencies only have the story of the victim. That's it. When an investigative agency gets involved, they are able to look at cell phone records, work records, entry and exit records from the United States, who they are talking to on the phone . . . when they were at certain places, and so we have access to huge amounts of information during our investigation that the NGO has no idea about, and so there is a reason that the agents probably have not done the continued presence because they are not sure it's a trafficking case."

Whether law enforcement had evidence to prosecute a case or not, victims were forced to submit T visa applications without I-914B endorsements and just hope for the best. Rhada, an immigration attorney, complained, "There's problems with how the cooperation element gets interpreted in that all you can do is be willing to cooperate, but law enforcement sees it as being committed to an ongoing prosecution or ongoing investigation." She was aware that the frustration arose from purposes not in alignment: "I think they are looking at everything as a standard of evidence to get a conviction, whereas we are just trying to show cooperation. We're showing that . . . there is a reasonable belief that this person is trafficked and they are willing to cooperate. We are trying to get documentation from them that someone has cooperated, and they are trying to say, 'There is not enough evidence,' which is not relevant at all to someone's immigration application."

The law does limit CP to those victims who are necessary to an ongoing investigation or prosecution, but willingness to cooperate is sufficient for the T visa, meaning at times service providers were expecting too much regarding CP and that law enforcement were often overly discriminating in granting T visa endorsements. Curiously, although law enforcement's main objective was to investigate cases, they held a remarkable amount of authority over whether and when victims became documented; *criminal* definitions and prosecutorial standards of evidence became the primary gauge for endorsing *victim* benefits.

"The Agents Are Doing What the Traffickers Did"

Law enforcement agents often used a carrot and stick approach with CP or the endorsement for the T visa, sometimes withholding the paperwork indefinitely, which essentially recreates the control used by traffickers, who coerce their victims to cooperate through false assurances. When it served their interest, investigators used promises of protection to elicit information from victims. Ella, an immigration attorney, told me, "Sometimes . . . law enforcement will want tons of information from someone, and they'll be like 'Yeah, yeah, we'll get you CP,' and then they'll drag their feet on it, and it's very frustrating." Delays are one thing, but complete withdrawal of support is quite another, as Radha, an immigration attorney, divulged: "It is problematic when we have a client who has been cooperating for months on end with this carrot and stick, [with law enforcement] saying that they are going to get continued presence, and then they don't get it." A case manager named Nora had been through that process as well: "I've had one . . . case that was brought to me by ICE. They said that they were going to help [the victim] out, that she had told the truth . . . and they said that they had written an application for her certification. But then . . . they just dropped the ball, and I called and called and called and called, and it wasn't a priority for them to fix it."

All this prioritizing, strategizing, and sometimes manipulation led to a bizarre reversal of roles: law enforcement agents making decisions that affected victim benefits and immigration status while service providers and victims were collecting and providing evidence of trafficking. Sadie, a case manager, lamented that law enforcement would even ask victims to provide corroboration for their own trafficking: "The burden of proof shouldn't fall on the clients. The victims shouldn't be doing investigating, and the lawyers shouldn't either. Law enforcement are asking clients to plead their case." One survivor, Camille, spent months cooperating with law enforcement but never received CP. Two months after she agreed to cooperate with federal authorities, I sat in on a call with Camille, her case manager Sadie, and the agent assigned to her case. When Sadie inquired of the agent whether any progress had been made on getting CP for Camille, the agent responded, "No," explaining that because no "official" investigation was underway, nothing could progress in that department. Even though Camille had already participated in two day-long interviews with the agent and was regularly providing names and addresses of people relevant to the case, the agent maintained that she considered this "information gathering" as opposed to an "investigation." Camille was torn about staying in the United States to pursue her case, but her family encouraged her to wait out the process and seek justice against her traffickers. As the "information gathering" stage of her case dragged on, Camille began to run out of options for remaining in the United States without CP. Her stay at the NGO-affiliated shelter was about to expire, and Camille was hesitant to work without a social security number. All the while, the federal agent declared that CP required "too much paperwork." As the process proceeded and the agent continued to ask Camille to remain in the United States to provide information and testify before a grand jury, Camille told me, "The agents are doing what the traffickers did. The just say, 'Stay a little longer, stay a little longer.'" Clearly, by the time Camille testified before the grand jury, an investigation was underway, and yet she received none of the benefits to which she was entitled under the law. In this case, the agent's inexperience with trafficking cases was a key factor. She was not well versed in completing the "lengthy" paperwork required for CP or the needs of victims. While Camille was entitled to protections under the law, the agent's lack of training and experience resulted in an implementation failure.

Agents also used threats when a victim did not "cooperate" to their satisfaction. During a staff meeting I attended at an NGO, Nancy, a case manager, reported on a client who had been promised CP and a work authorization card from the federal agent investigating her case. When Nancy spoke to the agent about getting the documents (I was also present for the phone call), he told her he might not give the client CP after all. He said the victim had not disclosed to him some (seemingly irrelevant) details about her health. According to Nancy, the agent said that this omission made him distrust the rest of the victim's story—he told her, "Maybe she's not going to get an EAD; maybe the next thing she'll get is a one-way ticket back to [her home country]." Withholding this documentation was a way to assert control, replicating the power dynamic between trafficker and victim. In a sense, the agent could be seen as the "good guy" or "rescuer" for even considering providing these documents in exchange for the victim's cooperation, but the tactics were far too familiar to the survivor.

Law enforcement agents would also withhold CP because of a survivor's current actions. Bridget, the director of a trafficking services program, described a situation in which law enforcement agents refused to grant CP because the victim had reentered sex work of her own volition: "One of the reasons they can't get CP is when they start working on the investigation, the cops say you basically don't deserve it because you are still a sex worker, so we don't really believe that you are a victim. They can't conceive of the fact that a person could have been trafficked, had left, and then continued to work for themselves in sex work. And that has been, I think, a huge obstacle for them." For many victims without paperwork, sex work was their only option for earning a living wage. Any labor they did would be outside the bounds of legality—at least sex work paid relatively well. Were they to receive a work permit, they could stop, but law enforcement viewed this as a deal breaker. Bridget noted,

> There are so many problems with continued presence. It's like a child begging a parent for candy . . . and they [law enforcement] have all the power . . . and it's so much faster and easier for them to get the ball rolling for continued presence. . . . Continued presence can take as little as two weeks, maybe a month. A T visa, from the minute you send it could take as long as four months before you get a response [and much longer to prepare and get final approval], and four months is a long time to not see a doctor, to not . . . get counseling or whatever other benefits you need.

Some clients put considerable effort into cooperating, often at great personal risk, without receiving the immigration status they so desired: "They might've gone through all of those hoops and still not get anything for it. And that's really really hard for our clients because I have clients who will say, 'But what did I do wrong? I did what they asked me, why won't they help me?' And it's really heartbreaking to have to tell them that they have to wait a little longer because I'm still trying to get a response from any given agent."

Lack of Standards Leads to Lack of Protections

A general lack of clarity surrounded victims not receiving CP—even those in the criminal justice field were not certain of the specific requirements. Lynn, a federal prosecutor, noted that victims have no control over whether an investigation proceeds, but she was unsure how this should affect certification:

I think technically what is required is if the person is a victim of a severe form of trafficking, and they're willing to cooperate in, I think in a federal investigation or prosecution. What does it mean though if there isn't going to be an investigation? Does that mean they don't qualify? Obviously, on its face, that seems unfair because it's not their fault there won't be an investigation. The reason there may not be an investigation is not necessarily because you don't believe them; it's because there's no good corroboration, we can't bring a case, we can't find the guy, she can't identify the person, or whatever it is. . . . In fact, ICE or FBI will probably take the view of, hey listen there is no investigation—they can't cooperate, therefore they can't qualify for CP. That doesn't bar them, though, from qualifying for a T visa.

Not only does vagueness surround the requirements for CP, making determinations is itself highly subjective, and victim certification is tied to the quality of evidence or viability of a criminal prosecution. The professionals I spoke with repeatedly emphasized that there was no stable standard for granting CP or signing off on the T visa. As Lynn told me, "All this stuff about the victim benefits and what qualifies is so ill-defined ultimately. . . . There are no strict rules or qualifying criteria that can be applied . . . across the board. . . . I think every office . . . every agency is different on how they apply this." Her personal views on endorsing victims highlight how discretionary the decision is:

Some agencies will take the view that even if you believe them, if there's no way to bring a case and there's no way to corroborate . . . that they're a victim of trafficking, you may not even endorse their T visa. . . . They can still get the T visa without the endorsement of the agency, but it's a whole lot harder. . . . My view is if we believe they're a victim of trafficking, even if you can't bring a case, fine, they haven't gotten CP, then you maybe should at least endorse them for purposes of that. . . . Congress hasn't given us enough guidance. . . . I can't argue that ICE is wrong, but I do believe that sort of a more humanitarian point of view would be to give them the T visas. . . . The truth is that people are interpreting these statutes to mean that if you can't prosecute, you really can't certify. I think that's probably wrong for the purpose of the T visa and probably right for purposes of CP.

Many providers disagreed with what they perceived as law enforcement's overly strict standard for granting CP or T visa endorsements. Radha, an immigration attorney, attributed the high bar for granting CP to a desire to shrug responsibility: "Everybody wants to cover themselves; they don't want to be handing out documents that grant illegal immigrants status just like candy, so they create obstacles." Agreeing, Nora told me, "There is . . . an element of self-preservation and not wanting to sign off on anything that could possibly come back to haunt them somehow, such as a case being somehow connected to terrorism and then that impacts the agent's career." One federal agent's hesitation to grant CP stemmed from a fear of being liable if the victim committed a crime: "We're not a social welfare agency; we're an investigative agency," Will said as justification for not endorsing victims for CP. Audra noted, "It's just really challenging because I'm still getting the same kind of responses from law enforcement saying, 'Oh, well we don't want to take on the responsibility of . . . opening an investigation or writing even a letter,' because of I don't know why. They don't ever get to the point where they explain why. To me it sounds like it's too much paperwork maybe, or I don't know." A federal criminal justice administrator, Pete, assured that law enforcement should not be granting CP selectively: "We don't want law enforcement to have a group of victims but only want three of them to testify and receive CP. The goal is to get all the victims CP and T visas." Unfortunately, this point of view was not reaching agents on the ground, and victims suffered because of it.

Some criminal justice personnel were more willing to assist victims but clearly perceived signing off on endorsements for victim certification as secondary to their investigative and prosecutorial work. Speaking highly of NGO service providers, Dean, a federal prosecutor, nevertheless emphasized that their priorities were often different from his:

> We really couldn't do the cases without them. . . . I think where we have breakdowns are timing—they want things to move quickly. We don't always want things to move as quickly. . . . We are doing a lot of different things that aren't related . . . specifically to their client's T visa application. We're subpoenaing the records, we're investigating the defendants, we're trying to identify the victims, we're trying to corroborate. . . . I mean, I'll give you the I-914B if you cooperate, but that's really not my main goal to fill out an I-914B. My main goal is to prosecute the defendant.

Certainly, Dean was willing to provide T visa endorsements for victims, but he was also dismissive of the urgency of accessing immigration relief for victims.

Service providers at a 2007 national antitrafficking conference questioned a high-level prosecutor about the seeming arbitrariness of granting CP. The prosecutor responded, "The examples you are giving seem so outrageous. It only serves law enforcement to grant continued presence because it helps the case." Of course, helping a case only matters if law enforcement believes a case exists and is prosecutable. He added that CP should be granted immediately to anyone assisting in an investigation—if it was taking more than a month, he wanted to hear about it. While this official seemed well intentioned, interviews with professionals in service delivery and at various levels of government indicated that there was a disconnect between policy intentions and actual implementation: as one case manager stated at a meeting of local service providers, "This is more an issue of implementation than a legislative issue." Because the law was unclear on requirements for granting CP and no regulations existed to offer guidance to law enforcement, decisions were left to the discretion of individual law enforcement personnel.

"We've Given Up on Law Enforcement"

When law enforcement was uninterested in a case, failed to grant CP, or did not sign off on the I-914B, NGOs proceeded on their own in trying to gain T visas or other forms of immigration status for their clients. Nora, a case manager, noted that law enforcement took on less than half of her clients' cases: "The others just are sort of still waiting for a T visa, but law enforcement never had any interaction with them or never took interest in the case. They interviewed them and said, 'No, we're not going to work with this.'" Without official documentation of a victim's willingness to cooperate, the T visa process was much more difficult, leaving the onus on victims and their providers to demonstrate their intent to help in any way they could. Even obtaining law enforcement documentation of victim status was exceedingly difficult, according to Audra, an immigration attorney: "If they are not willing to open an investigation, that's fine, but . . . they can give the courtesy of submitting some kind of letter saying that cooperation was made. That's all we really need at that point. And I think that's a more than fair exchange." As director of a trafficking services program, Bridget took a more matter-of-fact approach: "They [law enforcement] haven't proceeded with most of our cases . . . so we don't work with them a ton, except for the initial, like trying to get [an endorsement], they refuse, they don't want to talk to us, and then we do the T visa without them." Radha, an immigration attorney, said that she and her colleagues took matters into their own hands when necessary: "There are a lot of cases that don't go smoothly because we bring them to federal law enforcement, and law enforcement just drops the ball, either by saying that they don't see it as a trafficking case or saying that they don't have the resources to investigate, and then at that point you've got somebody who has shown a willingness to cooperate, but we have no documentation for it, so we create our own documentation." Absent support from law enforcement, service providers looking to ease the path to a T visa were forced to be creative. Jarrah, an immigration attorney, told me that she documents victim cooperation on her own to submit in place of the I-914B with the T visa application: "We've actually given up on them [law enforcement] . . . what we've actually done is say, okay, well we are going to call law enforcement. . . . We're going to tell them the story, and if they're not interested . . . we do our own legal affirmation of all the times we tried to contact them, and we're applying without law enforcement, because we just don't know what to do." One client's experience stood out as exceptionally dire:

> Our worst-case scenario . . . she . . . was trafficked by someone she believed would be her boyfriend and take care of her and love her, brought here, forced into prostitution and then had a son by the trafficker; she was forced to leave her son with the traffickers. We took her to law enforcement. The traffickers are still here in the U.S.; she still runs into some of the brothers and sisters of the initial recruiter in the streets to this day. She gave over all this information, and they're [law enforcement] just not interested, and the biggest worry is that her child is held hostage in [home country]. She wants the child here, and without law enforcement involved in the case, it is going to be extremely difficult to get that child out of [home country]. And that's been our worst-case scenario. And we recently applied for a T visa without law enforcement certification, and so we're waiting to see how that's adjudicated.

Such cases strained relationships between service providers and law enforcement—relationships that were essential for meeting the needs of survivors—creating additional implementation hurdles.

Although many of my informants agreed that the implementation of the TVPA had been positive in certain ways, their comments also pointed to the intense frictions inherent in working across sectors, with a multitude of professionals with different priorities who rely on different definitions and conceptions of trafficking. As a result of discrepancies in both definition and interpretation, large numbers of victims experienced long delays in receiving protections and benefits, were denied the opportunity to seek justice against their traffickers, or were never counted as victims at all. The TVPA in action reflected the complicated intersections of the law on the books and the law in their minds, creating a vortex of tension, confusion, and ambiguity.

If It Doesn't Count as Trafficking, Do the Victims Get Counted?

Quantifying trafficking is exceedingly difficult due to its underground nature, yet statistics on trafficking are thrown around quite casually by the media, NGO advocates, and government spokespeople. The most recent government statistics estimate that between 14,500 and 17,500 people are trafficked into the United States each year, but there are no reliable estimates of the number of domestic trafficking cases.[15] While many have questioned the estimates circulated by the State Department (especially when those figures are compared to the number of victims actually identified), several of my law enforcement contacts referred to the numbers as "inflated." Jim told me, "I don't believe any of the numbers," and Will concurred: "I can't stress enough how inflated the numbers are." Although there are serious methodological concerns in terms of how the estimates are calculated,[16] many service providers with whom I spoke suggested that low numbers of identified victims were partly a consequence of law enforcement not looking in the right places and not recognizing or certifying the victims whom NGOs brought them.

Because the U.S. government only collects data on the number of trafficking cases that are prosecuted and the number of victims who are actually certified, informants noted that large numbers of people who met the definition of a VSFT were never officially counted. Any victim who was not certified was not counted. Although the government tracks how many individuals receive CP and how many are awarded T visas, there is no way to know how many people were too scared to come forward, were unable to articulate exactly what had happened to them, never made it to a service provider, or gave up when law enforcement expressed no interest in their cases. Providers noted that many clients sought services because they needed immigration help, not because they were victims of trafficking (though they were). Jarrah told me, "We're helping a lot of clients . . . but there is a larger number that we're missing out on . . . that they're not getting the services that they need, and that's a huge concern." For many, the cooperation requirement was a significant barrier—with it in place, victims were unable to receive benefits simply on account of being trafficked. Agents' reluctance to provide CP and T visa endorsements kept the certifications numbers low, so the simple solution would be to certify more victims. Lynn, a federal prosecutor, certainly thought so: "We should certify these people because there's a difference between how many cases we can bring and who actually qualifies as a victim." Yet the process for obtaining a visa was often filled with obstacles, and not every victim who applied received one. Nora, a case manager, noted,

> There is this limit in capacity of . . . the types of cases that can be certified and prosecuted versus those that can't, and really what can minimally be done for those that aren't, and you hope it's the immigration route with the T visa, but we're starting to see that there's major rigidity, that it has to have a law enforcement endorsement, or it has to reach this threshold of collaboration with law enforcement . . . but I think that limits the number of people that you can really find and help, and it also doesn't really make the trafficking survivor in the front seat of their own process.

Because law enforcement's priority was to get a conviction, having those officials in control of victim benefits confused the process.

Providers reported that adjudication of T visas (done by the Vermont Service Center of the U.S. Citizenship and Immigration Services, or USCIS) often involved hurdles similar to those that crippled the CP process. Even after law enforcement had signed off on CP or provided an endorsement for a T visa, the Vermont Service Center would sometimes decline the paperwork. Even though she experienced this push back, Ella, an immigration attorney, divulged, "I find that on the sex trafficking cases I tend not to get requests for additional evidence because I think it's just more obvious." Obviousness is, of course, subjective, pointing to a problem about which providers frequently complained: Vermont Service Center employees were not well trained on trafficking and would only immediately approve the most sensational cases involving sexual assault or physical violence. Sadly, this affects attorneys like Jarrah's recommendations to clients:

> We joke about this. In our applications . . . it is helpful if the client has a worst-case scenario. The application will get more easily processed, and it will go faster if there is physical or sexual violence. And so we really ask our clients, "Did he beat you, did he hurt you, did he or she do this or that?" It does make everything go faster, and I think that is the lack of training and also the salaciousness in the news that it's not trafficking unless she or he was beaten to a pulp. . . . So there's just a lack of education and a lack of knowledge about how scared a person can really be without being physically violated.

Obstacles like the lack of training of the adjudicators in Vermont were not rooted in the wording of the law but rather emerged as implementation issues. While the TVPA acknowledges that no physical or sexual violence is necessary for trafficking to occur, government bureaucrats drew on their own impressions to determine victim status. In many cases, these interpretations were insensitive to the subtleties that constitute the climate of fear experienced by many trafficking victims.

Because the T visa process was so burdensome, providers would often seek for their clients other immigration remedies that they viewed to be faster and easier. The most common alternatives were the U visa (for general crime victims) and Violence Against Women Act (VAWA) self-petition (for women who are married to U.S. citizens or lawful permanent residents and are victims of domestic violence), but other survivors sought asylum, applied for green cards through their spouses, or filed for Special Immigrant Juvenile Status (SIJS). In other cases, victims sought no immigration remedy and instead chose to be repatriated to their home countries or remain in the United States without documentation.

Trafficking statistics also fail to account for victims who were deported rather than receiving the benefits to which they were entitled. In several cases, Sheila, the director of a trafficking services program, suspected that law enforcement had deported potential victims before investigating for trafficking. When we spoke, she was at a loss for any valid reason for preemptive deportation: "It's not just because they didn't know. It used to be you could say, 'Oh well, they didn't know what to ask,' but, 'Hey, this is too much work, it's a headache'? These cases are a headache for everybody. They're hard. What do you do with these people? How do you take care of them?" Deportation seemed to occur as a result of law enforcement's inability to elicit a full account of the circumstances surrounding victimization, but as discussed in Chapter 2, persistence was always key to identifying victims. Molly, a federal prosecutor, told me, "The first time you interview a victim, you never get the truth." Jim, a federal agent, noted, "We've never had a girl come in and say this is what happened. You've got to pull her teeth out to get the information. They are reluctant." He told me that during the Carreto case, he and his fellow agents interviewed the women five to six times, with the women always saying they were working voluntarily, as they had been coached to do by their traffickers, before opening up about what had really transpired. Often, those suspected of being exploited would not divulge the details of the situation, which limited Jim's professional options: "We'll get the NGO to talk to them, and if they still don't come forward, they will be deported." NGO service providers, as mediators between survivors and the state, worked hard to uncover victims' experiences and advocate on their behalf to law enforcement, although they may not be consistently given the opportunity. With hasty deportations, law enforcement sometimes preempts the intervention of willing service providers. Charlotte and Nancy told me about a case in which two of Nancy's clients who had previously escaped had tipped ICE as to the whereabouts of their traffickers. In a raid, ICE arrested one of the traffickers and detained several women. Charlotte offered her assistance but heard nothing back and was later told that the potential victims were all deported before service providers had any chance to speak to them. These particular traffickers, Nancy told me, had repeatedly instructed her previous clients to throw law enforcement off by saying they were working voluntarily. Charlotte and Nancy were familiar enough with the players involved to know not to accept that story at face value, but the police, Nancy told me, "don't understand how much time it takes for a story to come out." In addition to not taking the time to get the victim's story, law enforcement likely overlooked numerous cases meeting the VSFT criteria (with victims who would be entitled to T visas) but not the criminal definitions.

Undocumented victims fearing deportation had good reason to avoid identifying themselves to law enforcement. One federal agent told a conference audience, "There is a lot of training in ICE, but there is no will to pursue trafficking. The focus is on forced removal. At the end of the day, this is what agents get recognized for." Audra, an immigration attorney, agreed:

Figure 5. ICE "Hidden in Plain Sight" campaign billboard. Image courtesy of ICE.

ICE thinks that they have addressed that tension by having specific task forces [and] . . . units specifically focusing on trafficking. And I've had agents explicitly say when they interview clients, "Oh, you can tell me everything; I'm not here to deport you." . . . And as much as I appreciate them saying that, I don't wholly believe them because even if that agent might not do so, they still work for an organization that is about deporting people, and . . . to have that kind of power and discretion is dangerous . . . because that's what makes people reluctant to come forward in general.

ICE's reputation fits exactly with the horror stories traffickers tell their undocumented victims. As Sheila, the director of a trafficking services program, opined, "How can you convince people who look at the news and see ICE doing a raid and sending innocent people back to a country that they haven't been in for umpteen years, splitting families apart, and then the next day tell them that ICE will help them?"

Toward the end of my fieldwork, ICE launched a public awareness campaign, placing on subway marquees and bus shelters posters with a photograph of imploring eyes and the words "Human Trafficking: Sexual Exploitation. Forced to Work Against My Will. Hidden in Plain Sight." The ICE logo and a phone number to report possible trafficking followed (see Figure 5). A related public service announcement for the ICE hotline posted on the agency's website ends with the text, "If you see me . . . you can help me by calling." Making no reference to the inherent contradiction posed by asking the public to report undocumented immigrants who may or may not have been trafficked, special agent in charge of ICE's San Diego investigations Miguel Unzueta asserted in a press statement, "ICE is asking for the public's assistance to help us recognize and identify the victims of modern-day slavery who are in our midst." My research complicates his next statement, as powerful and well-intentioned as it may be: "ICE is committed to giving trafficking victims the help they need to come forward, so we can put an end to this reprehensible form of modern-day slavery."

Chapter 6

Moving the Antitrafficking Response Forward

> In a perfect world, the TVPA would have been written to not have
> these different types of trafficking separated out.
>
> —Nora, case manager

"The Best It Could Be"

Trafficking's highly contested and politicized place in the United States
rules out easy solutions to the quandaries posed in these pages, but my
hope is that this ethnography will serve as an instrument of institutional
change. The experiences of actual implementers and survivors highlight
without pretense the inconsistencies in the law and the imperfections in
its implementation. I began this ethnography by invoking the successful
pre-TVPA response to the Paoletti case involving fifty-seven Mexican nationals forced to peddle trinkets on the streets and subways of New York
City; I would like to end it with the post-TVPA success of the Carreto case,
the response to which many informants cited as a best-case scenario, and
use it as a jumping-off point for imagining how the current study might inform future trafficking policy. Although many cases did lead to tension and
divisiveness among antitrafficking professionals, at times NGOs and criminal justice authorities worked astoundingly well together. The Carreto case
became a textbook example of multisector collaboration, but because few
cases meet such paradigmatic, quintessential conditions, it has proved a difficult model to replicate.

The case involved two main codefendants, Jose Flores Carreto and
Gerardo Flores Carreto, who forced young Mexican women into prostitution

in brothels throughout the New York City metropolitan area. Law enforcement stumbled onto the case when a woman in Mexico called to report that her daughter had been kidnapped. Using a photograph and a phone number, ICE tracked the woman to an address and spotted her going into a laundromat. The rest of the case unfolded from there. After identifying the first victim, the agents arrested ten individuals, including the two Carreto brothers. Their victims had been forced into prostitution through a combination of threats, coercion, and isolation tactics. Some of their children were being held by the Carreto family as collateral in Mexico, but the women had been coached to always say they were working voluntarily or face retribution. Because the agents had resources available and took their time, the women—who were hesitant at first—gradually began to divulge what had happened. The agents and prosecutors were able to corroborate the women's stories, collecting financial receipts and other evidence; they even traveled to Mexico and ultimately extradited the Carreto brothers' mother, who had been overseeing the Mexican side of the operation.

Tess, a service provider involved with the case, explained that it went well because of the dedication of the criminal justice authorities involved. Applauding all of the professionals, including local assistant U.S. attorneys, Justice Department prosecutors, federal agents, and others, she told me, "They were working on it without turf battles. . . . They really worked well as a team." Her praise continued, "They involved us as service providers from the get go; they gave access to the immigration attorneys representing the women. They utilized a team, and that's the way it's supposed to be. The ICE agents were fabulous. . . . The case managers were fabulous, and the women trusted [the case managers] so much they actually helped them find other victims of the case and gave permission to pass that on to the prosecutors." Summing up why the case was such a success, she said, "I think that that law enforcement used enough resources in their investigation, that they really valued information that [our] staff could give them, ICE did, everybody did. . . . It wasn't without its major bumps in the road, but I think you always have that because [of] people working on it who don't look at things the same way, but the end result was fabulous. So that was the best it could be."

Ultimately, the two main codefendants accepted a plea deal the day before the trial was scheduled to begin. Although the survivors were not required to testify, several of them made victim impact statements at the sentencing, and the brothers each received fifty years in prison, one of the longest sentences ever imposed in a trafficking case. Nora, a case manager, told me about the atmosphere: "It was such a great day. Everything came together. All of the case agents were dressed to the nines, and service providers were all in the room. Despite the politics that sometimes come between us, we were all one united front celebrating the outcome—fifty years." Tess noted, "When it works, it works well. When a case works, like the Carreto case, it's great. But I don't think that's happening enough."

Service providers and criminal justice authorities alike characterized the Carreto case as a shining example of cross-sector collaboration, but the factors that made this case so (in a sense) perfect shed light on some of the struggles inherent in the TVPA's implementation. The case involved forced prostitution, so there was no discrepancy between criminal and victim definitions, and it appealed to those agents who prioritized sex trafficking. In other words, the conditions of the trafficking were such that it "counted" as a case for service providers and law enforcement agents both. As a result, authorities were sympathetic to the victims and sensitive to the NGO's role in assisting them. The evidence was also strong, and law enforcement had the resources to collect it and to wait for the victims to stabilize and tell their stories. Consequently, there were no struggles over CP or T visa endorsements, and all of the victims received benefits and immigration status quickly and easily.

Responding to the Less-than-Ideal Response

While the Carreto case became a model of sorts, very few forced labor situations fulfill these ideal conditions; imperfect implementation is far more common, raising questions about how best to respond to cases that challenge dominant cultural narratives about trafficking. During my fieldwork, I found that tensions over what constituted trafficking, over prioritizing cases, and over determining the victims who are worthy of benefits were much more typical than the resounding success of the Carreto case. The competing pressures and outright conflicts that I have described here plagued implementation of the law as I observed it. Despite the good intentions of the TVPA's drafters, blurriness about definitions and procedures has prevented the law from reaching its full potential, particularly in terms of meeting survivor needs. Although titled the Trafficking Victims Protection Act by Congress, implementation has been skewed toward the criminal justice aspects of the law, with victim protection taking a back seat. Indeed, victims have the most at stake in the law's implementation and suffer the negative consequences of uneven implementation. Because sexually infused social anxieties and cultural assumptions are incorporated into the policy's application, victims for whom these factors have no bearing are the ones suffering defeat. Debates among advocates have become conflicts among implementers, who unwittingly but decisively create separate categories for deserving and undeserving victims. When law-enforcement-identified cases are privileged, large numbers of victims are not being recognized, most notably those trafficked into forced labor in sectors other than sex work and very often men—even though those victims are no less addressed by the letter of the law. Rather than assisting and protecting all victims, the TVPA is effectively harming those rendered invisible through the continued focus on sex trafficking, both symbolically on the books and in actual practice.

Arising from the multiple actors, agencies, and agendas involved in antitrafficking work, a cacophony of voices and narratives emerges. Each professes a particular meaning of trafficking, a favorite—if, perhaps, implicit—hierarchy of value accounting for different "types" of victims, and pet goals for the law itself. Although all are at work on the large problem of trafficking and guided by the legal text (the law "on the books," as I have described), a plethora of additional factors contribute to implementers' visions of the law "in their minds." As a result, the law "in action" is a translation of the law as written, reflecting the text (itself embedded with cultural anxieties, norms, and assumptions) but also accumulating cultural interpretive fragments along the way that emerge during implementation. The bureaucratic process of identifying trafficking involves a tremendous amount of subjectivity and thereby moral, emotional, and cultural frameworks that contribute to the law in their minds.

Although all work toward a common goal of addressing trafficking, diverse implementers were propelled by idiosyncratic sets of objectives and motivations, as well as attention to different aspects of the law. Yes, the goal of the law was to help victims and punish traffickers, but profound gaps in understanding plague application as service providers and criminal justice authorities strive to collaborate and perform their duties. In some ways implementation resembles the law on the books in that the text governs those practices; however, in other ways some readings seem far removed from the material text of the law and rather reflect its cultural production. Ostensibly, the TVPA's inclusion of trafficking into all labor sectors was a victory for those who advocated for a broad and fair-minded approach to the issue. In practice, though, the law's interpretation is very much skewed toward the sex-trafficking-only approach favored by abolitionist advocates. The social and political contestation that pervaded the drafting of the TVPA still haunts its execution.

A Slippery Split

Compromise was necessary to move antitrafficking legislation forward, certainly, but some of the most serious repercussions, with potential for additional harm to survivors, are only becoming apparent several years after the law's passage. Buoyed by their symbolic successes with the TVPA, abolitionists have continued to advocate for an even greater focus on so-called sex trafficking. For example, during the 2007–2008 legislative session, a coalition of antiprostitution feminists and conservatives[1] lobbied to change the law to more directly connect sex work and trafficking; their efforts were so successful that the House passed a reauthorization bill that effectively eliminated the distinction between severe and nonsevere forms of sex trafficking. The bill removed the elements of force, fraud, and coercion from the sex trafficking definition (labor trafficking did remain the same). In the proposed bill, the inoperative definition became operative, and anyone moved into prostitution, with or without force, was considered a victim of trafficking. Opponents (including a national network of service providers and the Justice Department) objected to the federalized criminalization of prostitution, which was previously only a criminal offense at the state and local levels, and argued that the changes to the law would detract from the most serious cases of trafficking—those involving minors and force, fraud, and coercion. Ultimately, the Senate's reauthorization bill maintained the original definition of trafficking from the 2000 TVPA, and the House changes were dropped from the final reauthorization compromise.[2] However, the proposed changes to the definition in the House bill illustrate how the cleverly negotiated compromise definition of trafficking created room to further push the categorical limits and the meaning of trafficking, including widening the void between "sex" and "non-sex" trafficking.

Abolitionists also continue to push for a stronger link between trafficking and prostitution in domestic youth sex trafficking—the movement of young U.S. citizens into prostitution. While the TVPA formulation of "severe forms of trafficking" includes any movement into prostitution in which

the individual is under eighteen regardless of force, fraud, or coercion, in recent years abolitionists have attempted to redirect efforts away from *international* trafficking of adults and children into forced commercial sex or labor
and specifically toward *domestic* youth sex work.[3] Some providers I worked
with believe that this move—to include in the "severe forms of trafficking"
definition individuals recruited into prostitution absent any force, fraud, or
coercion—confused the issue. But they nonetheless recognized these youth
as victims under the law; Ella noted, "With underage prostitution I have a
bit of an issue with the conflation of trafficking and prostitution. . . . I see
where the overlap is, but then I think things get mottled and confusing when
you talk about them being the same thing." Even Dale, who directed a federal office devoted to child exploitation, told me,

> The core issue . . . is different for [domestic youth trafficking victims]
> than it is for the little girl from Moldova who was brought over here
> thinking she was coming . . . for one thing and ended up being in
> prostitution. . . . They're victimized in a core sense in the same way,
> and they were both prostitutes; they were both subjected to sexual ac-
> tivity that they shouldn't have been, but one of them may have
> thought they wanted it and the other one may have thought what the
> hell's going on, you know what I mean? It's just very very different.

Although a number of my informants were perplexed by the law's inclusion of domestic minor sex trafficking, they nonetheless saw it as an important issue needing to be addressed. However, service providers were alarmed
at abolitionist advocacy efforts to shift attention *away* from other forms of
trafficking and *solely toward* domestic minor sex trafficking, a move that
would sharpen law enforcement's existing focus on cases involving commercial sex. Over the course of my fieldwork, numerous informants mentioned
their fears about government funding shifting to domestic minor sex trafficking to make up for the low number of victim certifications. Sheila, the
director of a trafficking services program, baldly confided, "To me, it's not
an either-or on the two groups. It's like both need a lot of attention."
    Others questioned the motives of organizations promoting an exclusive
focus on domestic minor sex trafficking. Maribel, a service provider, told me,
"I find some of the work of [organization devoted primarily to domestic minor sex trafficking] anti-immigrant and racist." She brought to my attention
a cartoon included in a report published by that organization: it depicted sev-

eral women of color entering a door marked "foreign girls" while a pouting Caucasian girl walked away from a door marked "American girls" blocked by a "closed" sign.[4] The cartoon reflected the feeling that American youth trafficked into prostitution were not receiving the level of service afforded to international victims. In fact, American citizens were *already* entitled to the same federal benefits, but the TVPA specifically made this assistance (along with case management services) available to international victims who otherwise would *not* be eligible for them because of their undocumented status. Over the course of implementation, it became clear to providers that navigating the federal benefits system could be just as difficult for an American citizen with no support system as for an international victim of trafficking. The difference was that international victims had access to case management services specifically for survivors of trafficking, while domestic minor sex trafficking victims did not.[5] While this disparity was problematic, efforts to pit one group of victims against another raise questions about what types of victims are worthy of saving. These efforts to direct attention even more sharply toward commercial sex (forced or not) illustrate how easily the issue of trafficking can be reenvisioned to take on the characteristics of particular interest groups and the need for further research on the consequences of the TVPA and the transformative capability of trafficking as a social and legal issue.

Ethnography as an Instrument of Institutional Change

In response to abolitionist attempts to further conflate trafficking and sex work, some argue that the antitrafficking paradigm is ineffective and that the issue needs to be reframed.[6] Indeed, there are many problems with our working notions about forced labor, whether sexual or not. The antitrafficking response is deeply gendered and trades on cultural myths and stereotypes about female victims as weak, unagentic, and in need of law enforcement's rescue. The current framework is prosecution driven, favoring criminal justice and ignoring the continuum of exploitation that could be much better appreciated were efforts focused on addressing trafficking's root causes and reducing vulnerability. While assistance is available for identified victims, it could be argued, for example, that the number of T visas being granted is so inconsequential in comparison to the larger number of exploited migrants that we as academics should no longer engage with the concept of trafficking because it detracts from these larger, yet less alluring, issues.

I wholeheartedly agree that there is a need to appreciate the antitrafficking movement's place within the broader context of migration rights, sex worker rights, labor rights, ending poverty, and reducing gender disparities. Those excluded by the trafficking framework experience a range of harms. However, throwing our collective arms in the air and acting as though trafficking does not exist just because the legal response is unsuccessful does not solve much. While the current approach undoubtedly isolates the most egregious cases of compelled labor and ignores larger structural factors driving the problem, the fact remains that the TVPA filled a number of gaping holes in the previous criminal code and has been used to put abusive traffickers behind bars, preventing them from inflicting further harm. It also provides protections that were previously unavailable for individuals suffering serious abuse; to date, thousands of survivors and their families have benefited. Not only was the law a step in the right direction, there is more it can accomplish in the future.

I hope that my research draws attention to the very real problems plaguing implementation, including the consequences for survivors, and that changes can be made to improve the law's effectiveness. Political rather than practical feasibility is often the biggest obstacle to solving complex social problems like trafficking. Everyone agrees trafficking is horrific and wrong, but arriving at a solution that is popular *and* meets the needs of those it impacts is the formidable task before us. A number of policy changes are needed, both in terms of everyday implementation[7] and structural prevention,[8] but I will focus on two that I see as crucial to survivor outcomes, based on the evidence I collected: (1) establishing a nonbifurcated definition that eliminates the symbolic focus on sex trafficking in the TVPA and (2) putting survivor experience at the forefront of policy development and implementer training.

Since trafficking first entered the legislative agenda in the United States, the phenomenon's contours have been highly contested. Two broad coalitions advocated for two highly divergent conceptions: one focused on the *type* of work and the other on the *conditions* of work. As a compromise, the TVPA covered individuals moved into *all* sectors by force, fraud, or coercion but drew attention to trafficking for forced commercial sex in particular. The dichotomous effort to draft the TVPA, and the resulting bifurcation of the trafficking definition, shapes the ways in which various professionals think about trafficking and affects implementation. Although the players have changed somewhat over time, the core issues and disputes remain the same. The marking of sex trafficking as a special category (along with the gaps between the victim definitions and the criminal statutes) means that NGO service providers struggle to serve and advocate on behalf of those trafficked into other labor sectors. Law enforcement agents define trafficking "by the statute," but their conceptions are sometimes limited by the balkanized legal construct. As a result, the cases that are recognized and prosecuted and the victims who swiftly access protections and benefits reflect Molly's axiom that "things that involve sex are just different." The symbolic sex/labor split has resulted in hierarchies of application: officials are responsible for enforcing "the law," but the legal text created the ability for investigators to compartmentalize different forms of trafficking and respond only to those cases fitting whichever conception is convenient.

·   In the short term, the most obvious solution to many of the implementation problems described throughout this book is an amendment to the TVPA's definition of "severe forms of trafficking" to eliminate the sex/non-sex split, the most significant source of inequity in the law. If the law is truly going to protect the victims for whom it is named, then any opportunities for bias must be removed from the framework. Compromise was critical to moving antitrafficking legislation forward during the TVPA's drafting, but hindsight has shown that the agreed-upon definition of trafficking has resulted in harm for those victims overlooked or made invisible by the bifurcation. While all laws are viewed through the cultural lenses of those implementing them, establishing a unified legal definition of trafficking would be a concrete way to eliminate the current implicit hierarchy and set the stage for a broader envisioning of trafficking that effects more positive change.

In addition to legally integrating sex and non-sex trafficking, the United States must put survivor experience at the forefront of policy development and training, and those with the most experience—rather than the strongest opinions (and largest pocket books)—must be recognized as experts. The sex/non-sex split reflects a cultural ideology rather than the reality of trafficking, and it is not too late to adopt a more balanced approach and to incorporate the experiences of actual victims into the government's antitrafficking response. The textual intersections between the demarcation of so-called sex trafficking, its elevated status for law enforcement, and its domination of investigative efforts on the ground are all functions of social and cultural assumptions about sex as a special category, overriding the lived experience of trafficking survivors and the observations of service providers. Survivors have the most at stake in the TVPA's implementation and the most to reveal about the reality of trafficking. It is crucial to look at the full spectrum of victim experience and draw on survivor narratives to inform policy development, to educate law enforcement, and to help forge a deeper understanding of trafficking more generally. If the TVPA is to truly meet victim needs, policy makers and law enforcement alike must acknowledge and respond to the experiences of survivors of all stripes—not just those who fulfill popular perceptions of what human trafficking victims look like.

Even when survivors are unable to organize and advocate for themselves, their voices—whether trumpeted through research such as the present study or via service providers who are well situated to understand the needs and experiences of survivors—should feature more prominently in policy discussions about how best to respond to trafficking and how to improve TVPA implementation. The accounts of actual survivors transgress notions of the "typical" and reveal how the loss of free will cuts across all trafficking. Recall how the narratives of Camille, Silvia, Victoria, Nadia, and Simone call into question the assumptions about the privileged position of sex trafficking. The detrimental aspects of trafficking that these survivors themselves assigned the greatest meaning were isolation, control, deceit, fear, and threats to their families.

Survivors of trafficking have not yet organized en masse, but small groups and individual survivors are beginning to speak out. Former clients of the Coalition to Abolish Slavery and Trafficking (CAST) in Los Angeles have organized to form the Survivor Advocacy Caucus, lobbying for policy change and speaking publicly about their experiences. The CAST website describes a campaign in which the caucus successfully entreated DHS to improve procedures for T visa holders to access green cards:

> Caucus members used a CAST-designed strategy to record their testimonies regarding the inefficiency of the system to procure Green Cards to T Visa holders within a promised two-year period of time and the impact that the delay had on their health, economic, and social stability. Members sent this document to the Department of Homeland Security (DHS) in collaboration with CAST partners. As a result of this advocacy effort, the DHS issued regulations allowing victims to adjust their status and apply for Green Cards in a shorter amount of time. These regulations fulfilled the congressional intention of the original Trafficking Victims Protection Act in 2000, as it allowed survivors freedoms such as visiting family and getting better jobs.[9]

Survivor voices, whether projected directly or via intermediaries, must also inform how law enforcement personnel and other TVPA implementers are trained. The service providers with whom I spoke often attributed their critiques of law enforcement—for deporting victims, focusing investigative efforts on forced prostitution, and not endorsing victims for the T visa, for example—to a lack of training and relevant education. Jarrah noted that if service providers had more opportunities to train law enforcement, identification could be improved: "I think they really need to get trained by service providers and really hear what's actually happening to victims and what kinds of clients we're getting." She added, "We need to change the paradigm . . . in their minds as to what exactly is a trafficked person, and then also train them all in not just looking always toward trafficking into sex work or trafficking and prostitution." Such critiques were not reserved only for law enforcement, and NGO service providers often expressed belief in the need for training government bureaucrats, such as Vermont Service Center employees, refugee benefits administrators, court employees, and staff at Children and Family Services, among others.

Because of their close connections with survivors, NGO service providers are specially positioned to educate other professionals in the trafficking field. As mediators between victims, criminal justice authorities, and the state, service providers possess specialized knowledge about victims and their needs—and they know it. Charlotte, the director of a trafficking services program, told me how she viewed her position: "I think it's a really important role because we are the closest thing . . . that comes to the survivor's voice . . . so I see our role as really taking what we've seen in the implementation of what's going on, how it works and how it doesn't work, and being able to inform future programming. And I would like to think that we're doing it in a way that best serves the interest of clients." Service providers interact with victims on a daily basis; listening to their experiences and the types of meaning and value ascribed to them so personally leaves NGO professionals with an uncommon fluency, so to speak, in the language of trafficking victims.

As conduits to survivor experience, service providers are well positioned to speak to the needs of survivors, yet the demands of providing direct services, along with limited budgets, often prevent them from disseminating their expertise. One is reminded of the success of abolitionist advocates in convincing the House to expand the definition of sex trafficking during the 2007–2008 legislative session. No united and effective service provider front spoke up. Abolitionist-feminist policy organizations and conservative and religious coalitions dominated lobbying efforts around the reauthorization, while the expertise and experience of service providers and victims were largely absent until the final stages of the reauthorization. Ella, an immigration attorney, told me that she vehemently opposed the abolitionist effort, but she and her service-provider colleagues had neither the time nor the money to lobby Congress: "It's important for . . . lawmakers to hear the voices of the people who provide direct services . . . What's challenging is [we] don't have any time to run around and do a lot of policy work. At the same time, some of the groups that only do policy I don't feel . . . effectively carry the voice of the victims." Victor, a congressional staffer, told me that many congressmen and congresswomen did not have the time to untangle the competing arguments about trafficking and prostitution. The fact that the abolitionist coalition had the ability to bring together feminists and evangelicals was enough to convince many legislators that the arguments presented by the abolitionist coalition must be widely shared: "They've got Gloria Steinem and the head of the Southern Baptists. And so the combination of moral suasion, familiarity, full-time lobbying, a big-ass Rolodex, and the ability to say 'I will bring you people from both sides of the aisle,' that's pretty effective. It's even more effective when the other side doesn't lobby at all and doesn't show up . . . and doesn't raise a finger to defend themselves. . . . The good guys haven't really stepped up and started fighting." As Victor's remarks suggest, service providers need to do more to ensure that their voices and those of survivors are heard. At the same time, policy makers and bureaucrats overseeing implementer education need to acknowledge and harness the unique expertise of service providers to inform policy development and training. Their exclusive access to survivor experience is unparalleled in the constellation of antitrafficking decision makers.

Implementation has been a learning process for all parties involved. While many of my observations are critical of the sex trafficking focus of the criminal justice professionals whom I encountered, my goal is not to vilify law enforcement per se but rather to highlight the ways in which trafficking becomes imbued with tendentious and consequential meaning during the implementation process. Many strides have been made since the passage of the law and since the completion of my fieldwork. At the 2012 Freedom Network Conference (an annual meeting that brings together social service professionals, attorneys, law enforcement, and survivors), I was surprised to hear consistently from the high-level law enforcement representatives many of the same arguments being made by service providers, something that occurred with much less frequency during my fieldwork. In talking with a number of my former NGO contacts, it seems these changes have not filtered down to lower levels of law enforcement, but it is significant and positive that the higher-ups are recognizing the need for additional training of agents and local officers. Progress is being made, however slowly.

Trafficking is still a relatively new priority for the government, and because of the complexity of the implementation structure and the contested politics around it, what needs changing is not always obvious or easy to execute. If policies are to truly help those they are intended to protect, responses need to be evidence based and draw on the results of high-quality, empirical research, such as the present study highlighting the knowledge and experiences of professionals and survivors. To make the TVPA, and antitrafficking in general, more effective, more studies are needed that examine the details and particularities of antitrafficking laws (not only the TVPA but also laws in other locales, both at the national and local levels) and their implementation. What makes certain laws succeed, and what factors are preventing others laws from achieving all that they are intended to accomplish? Ethnographic studies, in particular, will capture the "nitty-gritty" dynamics that make trafficking and implementation so challenging to fully grasp.

Survivors remain an untapped research resource. While no one should be made to participate, investigation is needed on the full spectrum of survivors—young and old, U.S. citizens and nonnative victims, those coerced into commercial sex and other types of labor. What characteristics make people vulnerable to abuse, and are there any observable differences between those who are trafficked or otherwise exploited? Denise Brennan's detailed account of the lives of formerly trafficked persons stands out in this regard, and more similar work is needed.[10] Men, in particular, are so often excluded from trafficking research because they do not fit the typical victim profile. As we learn more about the characteristics, motivations, and experiences of survivors in their multiplicity, it will become easier to recognize abuse and to respond effectively.

The United States must address the realities of trafficking, not just an oversimplified caricature of it. Men, women, and children living under deplorable conditions are being overlooked every day and made invisible by the cultural myth that trafficking equals forced prostitution. No one deserves to be trafficked, but everyone who is deserves to be connected with the rights and protections to which they are entitled under the law. Identifying and protecting *all* victims requires a broad reenvisioning of trafficking in which *all* exploitation by force, fraud, and coercion is deemed equally problematic, both within the legal text and as a social issue in the eyes of policy makers, service providers, law enforcement, and engaged citizens.

Data Archiving Requirements and Threats to Confidentiality

In 2006 I was awarded a research grant from the National Institute of Justice, an agency that does not often fund ethnographic research. *After* receiving the grant, I learned of the condition that I must deposit my data at the National Archive of Criminal Justice Data (NACJD)[1] at the completion of my project. I panicked. How could I deposit thousands of pages of sensitive interviews, including those with federal crime victims, in a publicly accessible archive when people were already hesitant to even talk to me, much less have their thoughts archived for all time and accessible to researchers from around the world? The idea of data archiving was well meant—to enable other researchers to reproduce and verify results of studies funded by taxpayer dollars.

Aside from the obvious problems with trying to use someone else's ethnographic data, I was distraught that my study would not move forward and no one would agree to participate because of the threats to their confidentiality. Although all identifying information (name, address, phone number) would be stripped from the data, huge amounts of indirectly identifying information (country and city of origin, organization names, prosecution details, locations of trafficking, etc.) would remain,[2] to be used at the discretion of future researchers (who had never met my informants). Given the small number of trafficking victims in New York City (and the country), such details could easily be pieced together to identify victims and potentially put them at risk of retaliation by their traffickers. Further, NACJD officials told me they could not confirm the level of security that would be applied to my data until *after* I submitted it to the archive.[3] Human subjects officials at NACJD also assured me that I was not obligated to inform research subjects that my data would be archived; they told me it was no longer considered "data" once stripped of direct identifiers.

I had no intention of misleading my informants in this way. After a full year of negotiating with officials from Columbia University's Institutional Review Board, Office of Research, General Counsel's Office, and representatives from NIJ and NACJD,

I made the difficult decision to turn down the funding. Ironically, after refusing to budge for an entire year, NIJ agreed to lift the archiving requirement one day after I declined the funding, citing "inconsistencies" in application of the policy to previous grantees. As a result, I was not required to archive my data and was able to make a good-faith commitment to the confidentiality of my informants.

Appendix B

Interviewees Quoted in the Text

NGO Professionals

Audra—immigration attorney
Bridget—director of a trafficking services program
Charlotte—director of a trafficking services program
Ella—immigration attorney
Jarrah—immigration attorney
Maribel—case manager
Nancy—case manager
Nora—case manager
Radha—immigration attorney
Roxanne—former immigration attorney
Sadie—case manager
Sheila—director of a trafficking services program
Tess—case manager

Law Enforcement and Government Officials

Angela—former federal policy advisor
Annette—policy advisor on victim services
Dale—federal law enforcement administrator
Dean—federal prosecutor
Fran—director of a federal grant program
Gwen—federal victim witness coordinator
Jim—federal law enforcement agent and the head of a human trafficking unit
Katherine—federal prosecutor
Katrina—federal prosecutor

Kira—federal victim witness coordinator
Kyle—federal prosecutor
Larry—local law enforcement agent
Leila—federal victim witness coordinator
Lynn—federal prosecutor
Marina—federal victim witness coordinator
Mark—federal prosecutor
Max—congressional staffer
Megan—former congressional staffer
Molly—federal prosecutor
Paul—federal policy advisor
Pete—federal criminal justice administrator
Sara—grant monitor for a federal funding program
Victor—congressional staffer
Will—federal law enforcement agent

Trafficking Survivors

Camille—32 years old, from a southern African country
Nadia—early 30s, originally from one of the former Soviet republics
Simone—mid 20s, originally from Mexico
Victoria—26 years old, from a South American country
Rocio—late 20s, originally from Mexico
Silvia—early 30s, originally from Mexico
Malcolm—20 years old, from a southern African country, had been
    trafficked to the United States as a child

Notes

Introduction

1. Ian Fisher, "17th Arrest Made in Case of Deaf Mexican Peddlers," *New York Times*, August 2, 1997; Deborah Sontag, "Poor and Deaf from Mexico Betrayed in Their Dreams," *New York Times*, July 25, 1997.

2. Pub. L. No. 106-386, 22 U.S.C. 7101 et seq. The TVPA was amended and reauthorized in 2003, 2005, 2008, and 2013, and the amended version is referred to as the Trafficking Victims Protection Reauthorization Act (TVPRA). I use the acronym TVPA throughout the text to refer to the law as enacted and its subsequent reauthorizations.

3. All names are pseudonyms with the exception of those individuals speaking at public events.

4. The term *sex trafficking* has become shorthand for what the law defines as one of the arms of "severe forms of trafficking." The use of the term is somewhat confusing because legally it refers solely to movement into prostitution, while "sex trafficking by force, fraud, or coercion" refers to forced prostitution. Because of the clunky nature of the latter, most implementers use the shorthand of *sex trafficking* and *labor trafficking*, usually implying force. I also use the terms *forced prostitution* and *forced commercial sex* to avoid the confusion inherent in the term.

5. Alicia W. Peters, "'Things That Involve Sex Are Just Different': U.S. Anti-Trafficking Law and Policy on the Books, in Their Minds, and in Action," *Anthropological Quarterly* 86, no. 1 (2013): 223–57.

6. I use the terms *victim of trafficking* and *survivor of trafficking* somewhat interchangeably. The former is favored in legal discourse, while the latter is primarily used by service providers to assert that their clients are more than their victim status. The concept of a survivor will be further discussed in Chapter 5.

7. Liz Kelly, "'You Can Find Anything You Want': A Critical Reflection on Research on Trafficking in Persons Within and into Europe," *International Migration* 43, no. 1/2 (2005): 238.

8. Alicia Peters, "Broadening the Lens on Human Trafficking," *Huffington Post*, August 2, 2012, http://www.huffingtonpost.com/american-anthropological-association/broadening-the-lens-on-hu_b_1728820.html.

9. Kevin Bales, Laurel E. Fletcher, and Eric Stover, *Hidden Slaves: Forced Labor in the United States* (Berkeley, CA: Free the Slaves, 2004).

10. Peter Schuck, "Law and the Study of Migration," in *Migration Theory: Talking Across Disciplines*, ed. Caroline Brettell and James Hollifield (New York: Routledge, 2000).

11. Anna-Maria Marshall and Scott Barclay, "In Their Own Words: How Ordinary People Construct the Legal World," *Law & Social Inquiry* 28, no. 3 (2003); Elizabeth A. Hoffman, "Legal Consciousness and Dispute Resolution: Different Disputing Behavior at Two Similar Taxicab Companies," *Law & Social Inquiry* 28, no. 3 (2003).

12. George Marcus, *Ethnography Through Thick and Thin* (Princeton, NJ: Princeton University Press, 1988).

13. Jacqueline Berman, "The Left, the Right, and the Prostitute: The Making of U.S. Antitrafficking in Persons Policy," *Tulane Journal of International and Comparative Law* 14 (2006); Gretchen Soderlund, "Running from the Rescuers: New U.S. Crusades Against Sex Trafficking and the Rhetoric of Abolition," *NWSA Journal* 17, no. 3 (2005); Elizabeth Bernstein, "The Sexual Politics of the 'New Abolitionism,'" *differences* 18, no. 3 (2007).

14. Julia O'Connell Davidson, *Children in the Global Sex Trade* (Cambridge: Polity, 2005); Kamala Kempadoo, Jyoti Sanghera, and Brandana Pattanaik, eds., *Trafficking and Prostitution Reconsidered: New Perspectives on Migration, Sex Work, and Human Rights* (Boulder, CO: Paradigm, 2005); Janie A. Chuang, "Rescuing Trafficking from Ideological Capture: Prostitution Reform and Anti-Trafficking Law and Policy," *University of Pennsylvania Law Review* 158 (2010).

15. Jane Huckerby, "United States of America," in *Collateral Damage: The Impact of Anti-Trafficking Measures on Human Rights Around the World*, ed. Global Alliance Against Traffic in Women (Bangkok: Global Alliance Against Traffic in Women, 2007).

16. Dina Francesca Haynes, "Good Intentions Are Not Enough: Four Recommendations for Implementing the Trafficking Victims Protection Act," *University of St. Thomas Law Journal* 6, no. 1 (2009): 77–95.

17. Ronald Weitzer, "The Social Construction of Sex Trafficking: Ideology and Institutionalization of a Moral Crusade," *Politics and Society* 35 (2007); Soderlund, "Running from the Rescuers"; Julietta Hua, *Trafficking Women's Human Rights* (Minneapolis: University of Minnesota Press, 2011).

18. Barbara Ann Stolz, "Interpreting the U.S. Human Trafficking Debate Through the Lens of Symbolic Politics," *Law & Policy* 29, no. 3 (2007): 311–38.

19. Laura Maria Agustín, *Sex at the Margins: Migration, Labour Markets and the Rescue Industry* (New York: Zed Books, 2007); Denise Brennan, "Competing Claims of Victimhood? Foreign and Domestic Victims of Trafficking in the United States," *Sexuality Research & Social Policy* 5, no. 4 (2008): 45–61; Denise Brennan, *Life Interrupted: Trafficking into Forced Labor in the United States* (Durham, NC: Duke University Press, 2014); Sealing Cheng, *On the Move for Love: Migrant Entertainers and the U.S. Military in South Korea* (Philadelphia: University of Pennsylvania Press, 2010);

Sealing Cheng, "Muckraking and Stories Untold: Ethnography Meets Journalism on Trafficked Women and the U.S. Military," *Sexuality Research & Social Policy* 5, no. 4 (2008): 6–18; John Davies, *"My Name Is Not Natasha": How Albanian Women in France Use Trafficking to Overcome Social Exclusion* (Amsterdam: Amsterdam University Press, 2009); Susan Dewey, *Hollow Bodies: Institutional Responses to Sex Trafficking in Armenia, Bosnia, and India* (Sterling, VA: Kumarian Press, 2008); Jennifer Lynne Musto, "The NGO-Ification of the Anti-Trafficking Movement in the United States: A Case Study of the Coalition to Abolish Slavery and Trafficking," *Wagadu* 5 (2008): 6–20; Rhacel Salazar Parreñas, *Illicit Flirtations: Labor, Migration and Sex Trafficking in Tokyo* (Palo Alto, CA: Stanford University Press, 2011); Penelope Saunders, "Traffic Violations: Determining the Meaning of Violence in Sexual Trafficking Versus Sex Work," *Journal of Interpersonal Violence* 20, no. 3 (2005): 343–60; Svati P. Shah, *Street Corner Secrets: Sex, Work, and Migration in the City of Mumbai* (Durham, NC: Duke University Press, 2014); Edward Snajdr, "Beneath the Master Narrative: Human Trafficking, Myths of Sexual Slavery, and Ethnographic Realities," *Dialectical Anthropology* 37, no. 2 (2013): 229–56; Kay Warren, "The 2000 UN Protocol: Rights, Enforcement, Vulnerabilities," in *The Practice of Human Rights: Tracking Law Between the Global and the Local*, ed. Mark Goodale and Sally Engle Merry (Cambridge: Cambridge University Press, 2007).

20. Brennan, *Life Interrupted*, 5.

21. For example, Rayna Rapp's innovative ethnography of the social impact and cultural meaning of prenatal diagnosis influenced the way I have thought about the intersecting, overlapping, and juxtaposed perspectives on trafficking; her work informs my weaving together of an account drawing on that complexity of meaning. For Rapp, this meant attending medical lectures, interviewing women undergoing amniocentesis, observing genetic counselors, and learning the science of prenatal diagnosis. Although the sites of my fieldwork differ significantly, I nonetheless have striven to provide a similarly holistic account of antitrafficking policy. Rayna Rapp, *Testing Women, Testing the Fetus: The Social Impact of Amniocentesis in America* (New York: Routledge, 1999).

22. Alison Mountz, *Seeking Asylum: Human Smuggling and Bureaucracy at the Border* (Minneapolis: University of Minnesota Press, 2010).

23. Chris Shore and Susan Wright, *Anthropology of Policy: Critical Perspectives on Governance and Power* (New York: Routledge, 1997), 21.

24. Roscoe Pound, "Law in Books and Law in Action," *American Law Review* 44 (1910); Austin Sarat, "Legal Effectiveness and Social Studies of Law: On the Unfortunate Persistence of a Research Tradition," *Legal Studies Forum* 9, no. 1 (1985).

25. Patricia Ewick and Susan S. Silbey, "Conformity, Contestation, and Resistance: An Account of Legal Consciousness," *New England Law Review* 26 (Spring 1992): 731; David Engel, "How Does a Law Matter in the Constitution of Legal Consciousness?" in *How Does Law Matter*, ed. Bryant G. Garth and Austin Sarat (Evanston, IL: Northwestern University Press, 1998); Austin Sarat and Thomas R. Kearns, eds., *Law in*

Everyday Life (Ann Arbor: University of Michigan Press,1995); Sally Engle Merry, *Getting Justice and Getting Even: Legal Consciousness Among Working-Class Americans* (Chicago: Univeristy of Chicago Press, 1990).

26. Schuck, "Law and the Study of Migration"; Peter Schuck, "Rethinking Informed Consent," *Yale Law Journal* 103 (1994).

27. Schuck, "Law and the Study of Migration."

28. Kay Warren, notes a similar phenomenon occurring with the UN Protocol to Prevent, Suppress, and Punish Trafficking in Persons, Especially Women and Children. Kay Warren, "The 2000 UN Protocol: Rights, Enforcement, and Vulnerabilities," in *The Practice of Human Rights*, ed. Mark Goodale and Sally Engle Merry (Cambridge: Cambridge University Press, 2007), 507–44.

29. The TVPA differentiates severe forms of sex trafficking from other forms of forced labor. Throughout the book, I use the terms *labor trafficking* and *non-sex trafficking* interchangeably. Although many cases of labor trafficking involve an element of sexual abuse, the terms *sex trafficking* and *labor trafficking* are ingrained in the U.S. human trafficking response, and those are the terms most commonly used by law enforcement personnel and service providers.

30. R. W. Connell, "The State, Gender, and Sexual Politics: Theory and Appraisal," *Theory and Society* 19, no. 5 (1990).

31. David Valentine, *Imagining Transgender: An Ethnography of a Category* (Durham, NC: Duke University Press, 2007).

32. Ewick and Silbey, "Conformity, Contestation, and Resistance."

33. The vast majority of media depictions have focused on trafficking for forced prostitution. For example, television programs such as *Law and Order: SVU* and a number of journalistic exposés (see Peter Landesman, "Sex Slaves on Main Street," *New York Times Magazine*, January 25, 2004 and numerous pieces by Nicholas Kristof) and television dramas (such as the Lifetime movie *Human Trafficking*) have all contributed to the construction of the issue.

34. Jyoti Sanghera, "Unpacking the Trafficking Discourse," in *Trafficking and Prostitution Reconsidered: New Perspectives on Migration, Sex Work, and Human Rights*, ed. Kamala Kempadoo, Jyoti Sanghera, and Bandana Pattanaik (Boulder, CO: Paradigm, 2005), 3–24.

35. Elżbieta M. Goździak and Micah N. Bump, *Data and Research on Human Trafficking: Bibliography of Research-Based Literature* (Washington, DC: Institute for the Study of International Migration, Walsh School of Foreign Service, Georgetown University, 2008), 9.

36. Eithne Luibhéid, *Entry Denied: Controlling Sexuality at the Border* (Minneapolis: University of Minnesota Press, 2002).

37. See, for example, the Lifetime Television movie *Human Trafficking* (2005), which features an American teenager kidnapped off the street while visiting Manila with her parents.

38. Jo Doezema, "Loose Women or Lost Women? The Re-Emergence of the Myth of 'White Slavery' in Contemporary Discourses on 'Trafficking in Women,'" *Gender Issues* 18, no. 1 (2000): 24.

39. Nils Christie, "The Ideal Victim," in *From Crime Policy to Victim Policy: Reorienting the Justice System*, ed. Ezzat A. Fattah (London: Macmillan, 1986), 18.

40. Sandra Walklate, *Imagining the Victim of Crime* (Maidenhead, UK: Open University Press/McGraw-Hill, 2007).

41. Jayashri Srikantiah, "Perfect Victims and Real Survivors: The Iconic Victim in Domestic Human Trafficking Law," *Boston University Law Review* 87, no. 157 (2007): 160.

42. Chris Greer, "News Media, Victims, and Crime," in *Victims, Crime and Society*, ed. Pamela Davies, Peter Francis, and Chris Greer (London: Sage, 2008), 22.

43. Arthur Kleinman and Joan Kleinman, "The Appeal of Experience; the Dismay of Images: Cultural Appropriations of Suffering in Our Times," in *Social Suffering*, ed. Arthur Kleinman, Veena Das, and Margaret Lock (Berkeley: University of California Press, 1997), 10, emphasis in original.

44. Jennifer Terry and Jacqueline L. Urla, eds., *Deviant Bodies: Critical Perspectives on Difference in Science and Popular Culture* (Bloomington: Indiana University Press,1995).

45. Gayle S. Rubin, "Thinking Sex: Notes for a Radical Theory of the Politics of Sexuality," in *Pleasure and Danger: Exploring Female Sexuality*, ed. Carole Susan Vance (New York: Routledge & Kegan Paul, 1984).

46. Stanley Cohen, *Folk Devils and Moral Panics: The Creation of the Mods and Rockers* (London: MacGibbon & Kee, 1972), 9.

47. Ibid.

48. Rubin, "Thinking Sex," 267.

49. Ronald Weitzer, "New Directions in Research on Human Trafficking," *The Annals of the American Academy of Political and Social Science* 653 (May 2014).

50. David A. Feingold, "Trafficking in Numbers: The Social Construction of Human Traffficking Data," in *Sex, Drugs, and Body Counts: The Politics of Numbers in Global Crime and Conflict*, ed. Peter Andreas and Kelly M. Greenhill (Ithaca, NY: Cornell University Press, 2010), 47. See also Kay Warren, "The Illusiveness of Counting 'Victims,'" in *Sex, Drugs, and Body Counts: The Politics of Numbers in Global Crime and Conflict*, ed. Peter Andreas and Kelly M. Greenhill (Ithaca, NY: Cornell University Press, 2010).

51. Feingold, "Trafficking in Numbers"; United Nations Educational, Scientific and Cultural Organization, "UNESCO Trafficking Statistics Project," http://www.unescobkk.org/index.php?id=1022.

52. Amy O'Neill Richard, *International Trafficking in Women to the United States: A Contemporary Manifestation of Slavery and Organized Crime* (Washington, DC: Center for the Study of Intelligence, 1999).

53. U.S. Government Accountability Office, *Human Trafficking: Better Data, Strategy, and Reporting Needed to Enhance U.S. Antitrafficking Efforts* (Washington, DC: Government Accountability Office, 2006), 2.

54. As children are not required to be certified, this number includes 2,776 adult certifications and 405 children receiving letters of eligibility for federal victim benefits; U.S. Department of Justice, *Attorney General's Annual Report to Congress and Assessment of U.S. Government Activities to Combat Trafficking in Persons: Fiscal Year 2011* (Washington, DC: U.S. Government Printing Office, 2012).

55. Heather Clawson, *Estimating Human Trafficking into the United States: Development of a Methodology Final Phase Two Report* (Fairfax, VA: ICF International, 2007).

56. For a more thorough discussion, see Haynes, "Good Intentions Are Not Enough."

57. "Empower" is a pseudonym for my main NGO field site.

58. The HTPU is responsible for human trafficking crimes; however, CEOS oversees prosecution of cases involving sex trafficking of minors.

59. Marina Tzvetkova, "NGOs Response to Trafficking in Women," *Gender and Development* 10, no. 1 (2002): 61.

60. Dvora Yanow, *How Does a Policy Mean? Interpreting Policy and Organizational Actions* (Washington, DC: Georgetown University Press, 1997), 10.

61. Mountz, *Seeking Asylum*, 58.

62. Steve Herbert, *Policing Space: Territoriality and the Los Angeles Police Department* (Minneapolis: University of Minnesota Press, 1996), 11.

63. Clifford Geertz, *Interpretation of Cultures* (New York: Basic Books, 1973), 10.

64. Elżbieta M Goździak and Elizabeth A Collet, "Research on Human Trafficking in North America: A Review of Literature," *International Migration* 43, no. 1/2 (2005).

65. See supra, note 19, for some notable exceptions.

66. See, for example, Davies, *"My Name Is Not Natasha"*; Amy Farrell, Jack McDevitt, and Stephanie Fahy, *Understanding and Improving Law Enforcement Responses to Human Trafficking* (Boston: Northeastern University Institute on Race and Justice, 2008); Musto, "The NGO-Ification of the Anti-Trafficking Movement in the United States."

67. Laura Nader, "Up the Anthropologist: Perspectives Gained from Studying Up," in *Reinventing Anthropology*, ed. Dell H. Hymes (New York: Pantheon Books, 1972), 284–311.

68. Chris Shore, Susan Wright, and Davide Però, eds., *Policy Worlds: Anthropology and the Analysis of Contemporary Power* (New York: Berghahn Books, 2011).

69. Denise Brennan, "Methodological Challenges in Research with Trafficked Persons: Tales from the Field," *International Migration* 43, no. 1/2 (2005): 37.

70. James Clifford and George E. Marcus, eds., *Writing Culture: The Poetics and Politics of Ethnography* (Berkeley: University of California Press, 1986); Akhil Gupta and James Ferguson, eds., *Anthropological Locations: Boundaries and Grounds of a Field Science* (Berkeley: University of California Press, 1997).

71. Marcus, *Ethnography Through Thick and Thin*, 37.

72. Shore and Wright, *Anthropology of Policy*, 14.

73. NIJ ultimately lifted the requirement, and I accepted the grant.

74. Cathy Zimmerman, *WHO Ethical and Safety Reccomendations for Interviewing Trafficked Women* (Geneva: World Health Organization, 2003).

75. Brennan, "Methodological Challenges."

76. See, for example, Nancy Scheper-Hughes, "Ire in Ireland," *Ethnography* 1, no. 1 (2000).

77. Goździak and Collet, "Research on Human Trafficking in North America," 117

78. Anette Brunovskis and Rebecca Surtees, "Untold Stories: Biases and Selection Effects in Research with Victims of Trafficking for Sexual Exploitation," *International Migration* 48, no. 4 (2010).

79. Dewey, *Hollow Bodies*.

80. See Janie A. Chuang, "The United States as Global Sheriff: Using Unilateral Sanctions to Combat Human Trafficking," *Michigan Journal of International Law* 27, no. 2 (2006); Cheng, *On the Move for Love*; Anne T. Gallagher, "Improving the Effectiveness of the International Law of Human Trafficking: A Vision for the Future of the U.S. Trafficking in Persons Reports," *Human Rights Review* 12, no. 1 (2010).

81. Michael Lipsky, *Street-Level Bureaucracy: Dilemmas of the Individual in Public Services* (New York: Russell Sage Foundation, 1980).

82. John Marzulli, "4-Foot-10 Mexican 'Mini Madam' Facing Slave Trial," *New York Daily News*, July 20, 2008.

83. Eric Konigsberg, "Couple's Downfall Is Culminating in Sentencing in Long Island Slavery Case," *New York Times,* June 23, 2008.

Chapter 1

1. Laura Nader, "The Anthropological Study of Law," *American Anthropologist* 67, no. 6 (1965): 3–32.

2. I use quotations here to suggest that depending on who is using it, the term *trafficking* takes on different meanings that may or may not correlate to the federal definition.

3. Jeffrey Weeks, *Sex, Politics, and Society: The Regulation of Sexuality Since 1800* (New York: Longman, 1981), 20.

4. See, for example, the work of Catherine MacKinnon, Andrea Dworkin, and Kathleen Barry.

5. For a thorough discussion, see Birgit Locher, *Trafficking in Women in the European Union: Norms, Advocacy-Networks and Policy-Change* (Wiesbaden: VS Verlag für Sozialwissenschaften, 2007).

6. William Jefferson Clinton, "Executive Memorandum: Steps to Combat Violence Against Women and Trafficking in Women and Girls" 1 Pub. Papers 358 (March 11, 1998).

7. Ibid.

8. The term *slave-like conditions* was also used; U.S. Department of State, *Trafficking in Persons Report* (Washington, DC: U.S. Government Printing Office, 2003).

9. Barbara Stolz, "Educating Policymakers and Setting the Criminal Justice Policymaking Agenda: Interest Groups and the 'Victims of Trafficking and Violence Act of 2000,'" *Criminal Justice* 5, no. 4 (2005): 407–30.

10. 144 Cong. Rec. S1702 (March 10, 1998); Congresswoman Louise Slaughter (D-New York) introduced the same resolution in the House of Representatives (144 Cong. Rec. H1021 [March 10, 1998]).

11. 106th Congress, 1st Session, S. 600 (March 11, 1999); Congresswoman Louise Slaughter (D-New York) introduced the companion bill in the House (H.R. 1238).

12. H.R. 1356, 106th Cong. (1999).

13. Wendy Chapkis, "Trafficking, Migration, and the Law: Protecting Innocents, Punishing Immigrants," *Gender & Society* 17, no. 6 (2003): 923–37.

14. E. Benjamin Skinner, *A Crime So Monstrous: Face-to-Face with Modern-Day Slavery* (New York: Free Press, 2008).

15. S. 1842, 106th Cong. (1999).

16. H.R. 3154, 106th Cong. (1999).

17. H.R. 3244, 106th Cong. (1999).

18. S. 2449, 106th Cong. (2000); S. 2414, 106th Cong. (2000).

19. Stolz, "Educating Policymakers."

20. *Freedom from Sexual Trafficking Act of 1999, Markup of H.R.1356 by the Subcommittee on International Operations and Human Rights,* 106th Cong. (August 4, 1999), 5.

21. Ibid., 38.

22. *Trafficking of Women and Children in the International Sex Trade: Hearing Before the Subcommittee on International Operations and Human Rights,*106th Cong. (September 14, 1999), 3.

23. Republican Senator Sam Brownback (KS) was an exception and introduced legislation addressing trafficking into all sectors (International Trafficking Act of 2000, S. 2449, 106th Cong. [2000]).

24. Protocol to Prevent, Suppress, and Punish Trafficking in Persons, Especially Women and Children, Supplementing the United Nations Convention Against Transnational Organized Crime, November 15, 2000, 2237 U.N.T.S. 319.

25. Ann Jordan, *The Annotated Guide to the Complete UN Trafficking Protocol* (Washington, DC: Human Rights Law Group, 2002).

26. Stolz, "Educating Policymakers," 408.

27. *International Trafficking in Women and Children: Hearing Before the Subcommittee on Near Eastern and South Asian Affairs of the Committee on Foreign Relations,* 106th Cong. (February 22 and April 4, 2000).

28. Stolz, "Interpreting the U.S. Human Trafficking Debate," 322.

29. Ibid.

30. In Jo Doezema, "Who Gets to Choose? Coercion, Consent and the UN Trafficking Protocol," *Gender and Development* 10, no. 1 (2002): 21.

31. Ali Miller and Alison N. Stewart, "Report from the Roundtable on the Meaning of 'Trafficking in Persons': A Human Rights Perspective," *Women's Rights Law Reporter* 20, no. 1 (1998): 15, emphasis in original.

32. Jordan, "The Annotated Guide to the Complete UN Trafficking Protocol"; Stolz, "Interpreting the U.S. Human Trafficking Debate."

33. *International Trafficking in Women and Children*, 20–21.

34. Doezema, "Who Gets to Choose?"; Janice G. Raymond, *Guide to the New UN Trafficking Protocol* (North Amherst, MA: Coalition Against Trafficking in Women, 2001).

35. Kathleen Barry, *The Prostitution of Sexuality: The Global Exploitation of Women* (New York: New York University Press, 1995); Kathleen Barry, *Female Sexual Slavery* (Englewood Cliffs, NJ: Prentice-Hall, 1979); Dorchen Leidholdt, "Prostitution: A Modern Form of Slavery," in *Making the Harm Visible: Global Sexual Exploitation of Women and Girls,* ed. Donna M. Hughes and Claire M. Roche (North Amherst, MA: Coalition Against Trafficking in Women, 1999), http://www.uri.edu/artsci/wms/hughes/mhvslave .htm; Janice G. Raymond, "Prostitution as Violence Against Women: NGO Stonewalling in Beijing and Elsewhere," *Women's Studies International Forum* 21, no. 1 (1998): 1–9.

36. Barry, *The Prostitution of Sexuality*, 1.

37. Nina Shapiro, "The New Abolitionists," *Seattle Weekly,* August 25, 2004.

38. Jacqueline Berman, "The Left, the Right, and the Prostitute," 278.

39. William Bennett and Charles Colson, "The Clintons Shrug at Sex Trafficking," *Wall Street Journal,* January 10, 2000.

40. Berman, "The Left, the Right, and the Prostitute"; For further analysis of the evangelical engagement with the trafficking issue, see Elizabeth Bernstein, "Militarized Humanitarianism Meets Carceral Feminism: The Politics of Sex, Rights, and Freedom in Contemporary Anti-Trafficking Campaigns," *Signs* 35, no. 1 (2010): 45–71.

41. S. 600, 106th Cong. (1999).

42. Jessica Neuworth et al., "Letter to Senator Wellstone Regarding International Trafficking of Women and Children Victim Protection Act of 1999 (S.600)," Trafficking Policy Research Project, http://www.bayswan.org/traffick/antiwellstone.html.

43. Ibid.

44. Jo Doezema, "Loose Women or Lost Women?"; Gail Pheterson, ed., *A Vindication of the Rights of Whores* (Seattle: Seal Press, 1989).

45. Doezema, "Loose Women or Lost Women?" 25.

46. Ibid.

47. Rubin, "Thinking Sex."

48. Janie Chuang, "Redirecting the Debate over Trafficking in Women: Definitions, Paradigms, and Contexts," *Harvard Human Rights Journal* 11 (1998): 65–107; Katrin Corrigan, "Putting the Brakes on the Global Trafficking of Women for the Sex Trade: An Analysis of Existing Regulatory Schemes to Stop the Flow of Traffic," *Fordham International Law Journal* 25, no. 1 (2001): 151.

49. Chuang, "Redirecting the Debate over Trafficking in Women," 76; Nora V. Demleitner, "The Law at the Crossroads: The Construction of Migrant Women Trafficked into

Prostitution," in *Global Human Smuggling: Comparative Perspectives*, ed. David Kyle and Rey Koslowski (Baltimore, MD: The Johns Hopkins University Press, 2001), 257–93.

50. Chuang, "Redirecting the Debate over Trafficking in Women," 77.

51. Ch. 395, 36 Stat. 825. 18 U.S.C. §§ 2421–2424 (1910).

52. Chuang, "Redirecting the Debate over Trafficking in Women," 83.

53. Ibid., 76–77.

54. Miller and Stewart, "Report from the Roundtable."

55. See 18 U.S.C. 1581 and 18 U.S.C. 1584.

56. U.S. Department of Justice, "Ten Thai Nationals Indicted on New Charges of Slavery and Kidnapping," news release, November 9, 1995, http://www.usdoj.gov/opa/pr/Pre_96/November95/577.txt.html.

57. Coalition of Immokalee Workers, *Anti-Slavery Campaign,* last modified 2012, http://www.ciw-online.org/slavery.html.

58. U.S. Department of Justice, "Case Updates," *Anti-Trafficking News Bulletin* 3, no. 3 (2007): 7–9; Ian Fisher, "17th Arrest Made in Case of Deaf Mexican Peddlers."

59. U.S. Department of Justice, *Report on Activities to Combat Human Trafficking, Fiscal Years 2001–2005* (Washington, DC: Government Printing Office, 2006).

60. For a thorough analysis, see Jennifer M. Chacon, "Misery and Myopia: Understanding the Failures of U.S. Efforts to Stop Human Trafficking," *UC Davis Legal Studies Research Paper Series* 79 (August 2006).

61. United States v. Kozminski, 487 U.S. 931 (1988).

62. For a summary of the scandal, see Danny Hakim and William K. Rashbaum, "Spitzer Is Linked to Prostitution Ring," *New York Times,* March 10, 2008.

63. H.R. 3244, 106th Cong. (1999).

64. Victims of Trafficking and Violence Protection Act of 2000, Pub. L. No. 106–386, 22 U.S.C. 7101 et seq. (2000).

65. Ibid.

66. Ibid.

67. Lynn explained that she and other prosecutors initially charge defendants with a litany of offenses. During plea negotiations, one or more charges may be dropped.

68. The phrase "or maintains" was added to the 2008 reauthorization.

69. William Wilberforce Trafficking Victims Protection Reauthorization Act of 2008, Pub. L. No. 110–457, 122 Stat. 5044 (2008). The 2008 reauthorization of the TVPA also added a benefiting provision to the forced labor statute.

70. Patricia Ewick and Susan S. Silbey, *The Common Place of Law: Stories from Everyday Life* (Chicago: University of Chicago Press, 1998), 17.

Chapter 2

1. Schuck, "Law and the Study of Migration."

2. Force, fraud, or coercion is not required (but is implied) in cases of sex trafficking when the individual is under eighteen years of age.

3. I use the term *discretion* in two ways throughout the book. In most cases I am referring to the subjectivity and interpretive scope of the individual making a "discretionary" assessment of a trafficking case. The term also takes on legal significance in cases of "prosecutorial discretion." The *Encyclopedia of the American Constitution* describes prosecutorial discretion as follows: "The prosecutor may choose which crimes and which persons to prosecute. She is entitled to prosecute whenever she has probable cause to believe a certain person committed a certain crime. She need not be certain that she can prove guilt beyond a reasonable doubt. In the twentieth century, there have always been many more legitimately prosecutable people than resources allow for prosecution, in addition to laws that the public has not wanted prosecutors to rigorously enforce." Leonard W. Levy, Kenneth L. Karst, and Adam Winkler, *Encyclopedia of the American Constitution* (New York: Macmillan Reference USA, 2000), 2058.

4. Because these women chose to be repatriated to their home country, they were not formally documented and certified as trafficking victims.

5. Denise Brennan notes a similar phenomenon: "Just how much information individuals should reveal in order to make a legal case can be particularly difficult to gauge since doing so challenges their instincts for self-preservation. Trusting others—whether a police officer, social worker, bunkmate in a temporary shelter, or coworker—runs contrary to the techniques of concealment that may have helped them endure abusive conditions. In Tatiana's case, her abusers had deepened her anxieties by lying to her about the police: 'They told us not to trust the police—that they [the police] would take us to jail and then send us home with stamps in our passports that would make it impossible to come back here again. And they told us we would be sent home as prostitutes—that the stamp would say this!'" Brennan, *Life Interrupted*, 123.

6. See Agustín, *Sex at the Margins*; Soderlund, "Running from the Rescuers."

7. Chacon, "Misery and Myopia," 2.

8. The main defendant pleaded guilty to conspiracy to commit forced labor and document servitude, conspiracy to harbor aliens within the United States, extortionate extensions of credit, and possession of false alien registration cards.

Chapter 3

1. Dan Sperber, *Explaining Culture: A Naturalistic Approach* (Oxford: Blackwell, 1996).

2. Carole S. Vance, "Thinking Trafficking, Thinking Sex," *GLQ: A Journal of Lesbian and Gay Studies* 17, no. 1 (2010).

3. See also Davies, *"My Name Is Not Natasha"*; Ronald Weitzer, "Flawed Theory and Method in Studies of Prostitution," *Violence Against Women* 11, no. 7 (2005).

4. Alice M. Miller, "Sexuality, Violence Against Women, and Human Rights: Women Make Demands and Ladies Get Protection," *Health and Human Rights* 7, no. 2 (2004): 19.

5. Michel Foucault, *The History of Sexuality: An Introduction* (New York: Vintage Books, 1980).

6. Carole S. Vance, "Negotiating Sex and Gender in the Attorney General's Commission on Pornography," in *Uncertain Terms: Negotiating Gender in American Culture*, ed. Faye Ginsburg and Anna Lowenhaupt Tsing (Boston: Beacon Press, 1990), 119.

7. For an overview of the case, see Konigsberg, "Couple's Downfall."

8. Movement into commercial sex of anyone under the age of eighteen constitutes a severe form of trafficking; no force, fraud, or coercion is required. Because movement across borders is not necessary under the TVPA, a number of U.S. citizen youth involved in prostitution meet the definition of victims of trafficking.

9. For a discussion of the construction of iconic victims versus "illegal aliens," see Srikantiah, "Perfect Victims and Real Survivors."

10. Doezema, "Loose Women or Lost Women?"

11. Weitzer, "The Social Construction of Sex Trafficking."

12. For a detailed discussion, see Bernstein, "The Sexual Politics."

13. The one such individual I attempted to interview—because her work straddled the line between advocacy and service delivery—declined my request for an interview. I did interview a small number of service providers and other professionals who espoused abolitionist philosophies but were not part of this most vocal group of anti-prostitution *advocates*.

14. A small number of antiprostitution advocates provided legal services to victims but did not provide comprehensive services. Additionally, one organization provided services to girls and young women who experienced commercial sexual exploitation and domestic trafficking and advocated against youth prostitution in particular.

15. The term *sex trafficking* may also imply that the individual is under the age of eighteen, in which case force is still implied.

16. Dorchen A. Leidholdt, "A Call to Action: Joining the Fight Against Trafficking in Persons" (paper presented at the U.S. Embassy to the Holy See June 17, 2004).

17. The TVPA was scheduled to be reauthorized in 2007; however, it was not reauthorized until 2008.

18. "Sonia Ossorio, Now NYC, March 1, 2007," YouTube video, posted by NOW NewYorkCity, http://www.youtube.com/watch?v=Y3Lxf_rXHjU.

19. Victims of Trafficking and Violence Protection Act of 2000, Pub. L. No. 106–386, 22 U.S.C. 7101 et seq.

20. Denise Brennan, *What's Love Got to Do with It? Transnational Desire and Sex Tourism in the Dominican Republic* (Durham: Duke University Press, 2004).

21. The Obama administration has worked to broaden this focus, although sources tell me that the priority on the ground is still very much forced prostitution.

22. Consent *is* relevant in all cases except those involving minors. Although a person can initially consent to sex work and then be forced or coerced such that it becomes trafficking, these women consented throughout the entire process. The prosecutor's point was legally irrelevant.

23. Anne Schneider and Helen Ingram, "Social Construction of Target Populations: Implications for Politics and Policy," *American Political Science Review* 87, no. 2 (1993): 338.

24. "Human Trafficking: A Global Challenge in Our Own Backyard," NYU Center for Global Affairs Special Event, New York University, November 30, 2006.

25. "Trafficking in Persons National Security Presidential Directive," news release, February 25, 2003 (Washington, DC: Office of the Press Secretary, The White House).

26. U.S. Department of State, "The Link between Prostitution and Sex Trafficking."

27. Weitzer, "The Social Construction of Sex Trafficking"; Weitzer, "Flawed Theory and Method in Studies of Prostitution."

28. Schneider and Ingram, "Social Construction of Target Populations," 336.

29. Shore and Wright, *Anthropology of Policy*, 3.

30. Freedom Network USA 2008 Annual Conference, Atlanta, Georgia, April 23–24, 2008.

31. U.S. Department of Justice, *Attorney General's Annual Report to Congress and Assessment of U.S. Government Activities to Combat Trafficking in Persons: Fiscal Year 2009* (Washington, DC: U.S. Government Printing Office, 2010).

32. Weitzer, "The Social Construction of Sex Trafficking," 462.

33. Stepen Maynard-Moody and Michael Musheno, "State Agent or Citizen Agent: Two Narratives of Discretion," *Journal of Public Administration Research and Theory* 10, no. 2 (2000): 341.

34. During the 2007/2008 TVPA reauthorization, abolitionist advocates lobbied for—and the House passed—a bill that removed the force, fraud, and coercion requirements from the definition of (severe forms of) sex trafficking, relocated the crimes of trafficking that involve commercial sex acts into the Mann Act, and made all intrastate prostitution a subject for federal investigation. William Wilberforce Trafficking Victims Protection Reauthorization Act of 2007, H.R. 3887, 110th Cong. (2007). The changes were dropped from the final compromise bill with the Senate.

35. Vance, "Negotiating Sex and Gender," 129; Weitzer, "The Social Construction of Sex Trafficking."

36. Lipsky, *Street-Level Bureaucracy*.

37. Schuck observed this phenomenon during his research with INS agents, noting that power over day-to-day immigration decisions runs bottom up rather than top down. Schuck, "Law and the Study of Migration."

38. Prior to the 2008 reauthorization, the law covered fraud as a means of labor trafficking only when it rose to a level of "serious harm." The 2008 reauthorization added a new statute (18 U.S.C. 1351) that criminalized fraud in foreign labor contracting. William Wilberforce Trafficking Victims Protection Reauthorization Act of 2008, Pub. L. No. 110–457, 122 Stat. 5044 (2008). The discrepancy remains between 1589 and 1591, as 1351 is a separate statute and only applies to *foreign* labor *contracting*. It is unclear how this new statute will be applied and whether it will apply to cases without formal labor contracts.

39. Bales, Fletcher, and Stover, *Hidden Slaves.*

40. For examples, see Kirk Semple, "Housekeeper in New Jersey Accuses Peruvian Diplomat of Human Trafficking," *New York Times,* June 25, 2013; "Case Profile—Sabbithi, et al. v. Al Saleh, et al.," American Civil Liberties Union, last modified February 15, 2012, https://www.aclu.org/human-rights-womens-rights/case-profile-sabbithi-et-al-v-al-sale h-et-al.

Chapter 4

1. I have included profiles of five of the six survivors I interviewed. I chose these five survivors based on the length of time that I knew each of them, the unique features of their lives (there was quite a bit of overlap between the sixth survivor's story and those of the other women), and their abilities to provide a detailed articulation of their experiences. Although I do not include a complete narrative for the sixth survivor, I do draw on her interview to inform my discussion later in the book.

2. Brennan, "Methodological Challenges"; Brennan, *Life Interrupted.*

3. After eight years, DHS released regulations on T and U visa adjustment of status on December 12, 2008.

4. Victims of severe forms of trafficking may apply to bring certain relatives, including minor children, spouses, and parents and minor siblings (if the victim is a minor) to the United States under derivative T visas. Other relatives, such as grown children, do not qualify for the derivative T visa.

5. Jo Goodey, "Sex Trafficking in Women from Central and East European Countries: Promoting a 'Victim-Centered' and 'Woman-Centered' Approach to Criminal Justice Intervention," *Feminist Review* 76 (2004): 34.

6. Cathy Zimmerman, *The Health Risks and Consequences of Trafficking in Women and Adolescents: Findings from a European Study* (London: London School of Hygiene & Tropical Medicine, 2003).

7. See Chapter 5 for a lengthier discussion of the Carreto case.

Chapter 5

1. The federal government has successfully prosecuted some single-victim cases with strong evidence. See U.S. Department of Justice, "Wisconsin Couple Sentenced for Forcing a Woman to Work as Their Domestic Servant for 19 Years," news release, June 9, 2009.

2. These numbers refer only to cases in which a defendant was indicted in federal district court. Other defendants may have been identified but not charged, charged with a lesser offense, or charged at the state level. Additional cases were also identified in neighboring areas (i.e., Long Island, New Jersey).

3. Referrals were skewed even higher in favor of sex trafficking because of local law enforcement's referrals for domestic minor sex trafficking.

4. In their study of human trafficking in the United States, Bales and Lize found that in two-thirds of reviewed cases, trafficking victims were *not identified by law enforcement*. Rather, they escaped of their own volition or were assisted by Good Samaritans. The investigators discovered that although trafficking victims often had contact with police, law enforcement failed to notice victims or bring them to safety due to lack of sufficient training. Kevin Bales and Steven Lize, *Trafficking in Persons in the United States: A Report to the National Institute of Justice* (Oxford, MS: Croft Institute for International Studies, University of Mississippi, 2005).

5. Freedom Network USA 2008 Annual Conference, Atlanta, Georgia, April 23–24, 2008.

6. See also Amy Farrell and Rebecca Pfeffer, "Policing Human Trafficking: Cultural Blinders and Organizational Barriers," *Annals of the American Academy of Political and Social Science* 653 (May 2014).

7. For a full discussion of the impact of law enforcement raids as a tool for identifying trafficking victims, see Melissa Ditmore, *Kicking Down the Door: The Use of Raids to Fight Trafficking in Persons* (New York: Sex Workers Project, 2009).

8. § 102(b)(20).

9. Ibid., § 107(b)(1)(E)(i); The Department of Health and Human Services is responsible for certifying victims once the required documentation is submitted to USCIS.

10. There was some debate among various criminal justice authorities as to whether granting T visas to victims (discoverable information during a prosecution) could be used by the defense as evidence of the government exchanging benefits for victim testimony. Several prosecutors suggested that it did not matter whether the victim had CP or a T visa—an argument could be made by the defense on both counts, and it was more important to ensure that victims had access to benefits. Other prosecutors and agents would not complete an endorsement for the T visa until a prosecution was complete.

11. CP is not required to receive a T visa. Rather, CP fills the gap in benefits and immigration status for some victims while they wait to apply or receive approval for the visa.

12. During the period of my fieldwork, the government had not yet released regulations on the process for victims transitioning from T visa status to legal permanent residency (allowable after three years, according to the TVPA). As a result, immigration officials warned victims that they may not be allowed to reenter the United States should they leave the country temporarily to visit family.

13. *Combatting Modern Slavery: Reauthorization of Anti-Trafficking Programs Hearing Before the Committee on the Judiciary*, 110th Cong. 83 (October 31, 2007).

14. The Department of Justice runs a trafficking hotline that victims and service providers can call to report cases of trafficking. Generally a staff member conducts an intake by phone and then the case is referred to a prosecutor for assessment, determination of viability, need for further investigation, and so forth.

15. U.S. Department of State, *Trafficking in Persons Report* (Washington, DC: U.S. Government Printing Office, 2004).

16. U.S. Government Accountability Office, *Human Trafficking*.

Chapter 6

1. This coalition consisted of many of the same groups that lobbied during the 2000 drafting effort.

2. Pub. L. No. 110–457, 122 Stat. 5044 (2008).

3. For a more thorough discussion, see Brennan, "Competing Claims of Victimhood?"

4. Sara Ann Friedman, *Who Is There to Help Us? How the System Fails Sexually Exploited Girls in the United States: Examples from Four American Cities* (Brooklyn, NY: ECPAT-USA, 2005). The version of the report now posted online has eliminated the portion of the cartoon that included "foreign girls." An older version of the report with the original image is available at http://www.tejiendoredes.net/documentos/152_whois theretohelpus.pdf.

5. The 2008 TVPRA authorized funds for U.S. citizens.

6. Agustín, *Sex at the Margins.*

7. See, for example, Haynes, "Good Intentions Are Not Enough"; Hila Shamir, "A Labor Paradigm for Human Trafficking," *UCLA Law Review* 60, no. 1 (2012).

8. See, for example, Shamir, "A Labor Paradigm."

9. "Voices for Change," Coalition to Abolish Slavery & Trafficking, http://www .castla.org/caucus-of-survivors.

10. Brennan, *Life Interrupted*; see also Laura T. Murphy, *Survivors of Slavery: Modern-Day Slave Narratives* (New York: Columbia University Press, 2014).

Appendix A

1. NACJD is part of the Inter-University Consortium for Political and Social Research (ICPSR) at the University of Michigan.

2. NACJD now provides a guide to depositing qualitative data that notes, "If the item cannot be anonymized using pseudonyms or generalized text, the entire text should be removed and explicitly marked as such. For example, replace text with [MASKED] or ellipses ('. . .') as a general indicator." However, at the time of my field-work no such guidelines existed, and during discussions with NACJD no such specific allowances were mentioned.

3. NACJD offers three levels of security: restricted use (users must sign a "data use agreement" and may download data from the Web), restricted access (users sign a "re-stricted data use agreement" and submit a letter from their institution's IRB; data is mailed on a CD to the requestor), and enclave restricted access (data is accessible only onsite at NACJD's University of Michigan offices).

Bibliography

Agustín, Laura Maria. *Sex at the Margins: Migration, Labour Markets and the Rescue Industry.* New York: Zed Books, 2007.

American Civil Liberties Union. "Case Profile–Sabbithi, et al. v. Al Saleh, et al." Last modified February 15, 2012. https://www.aclu.org/human-rights-womens-rights /case-profile-sabbithi-et-al-v-al-saleh-et-al.

Bales, Kevin, Laurel E. Fletcher, and Eric Stover. *Hidden Slaves: Forced Labor in the United States.* Berkeley, CA: Free the Slaves, 2004.

Bales, Kevin, and Steven Lize. *Trafficking in Persons in the United States: A Report to the National Institute of Justice.* Oxford, MS: Croft Institute for International Studies, University of Mississippi, 2005.

Barry, Kathleen. *Female Sexual Slavery.* Englewood Cliffs, NJ: Prentice-Hall, 1979.

———. *The Prostitution of Sexuality: The Global Exploitation of Women.* New York: New York University Press, 1995.

Bennett, William, and Charles Colson. "The Clintons Shrug at Sex Trafficking." *Wall Street Journal,* January 10, 2000.

Berman, Jacqueline. "The Left, the Right, and the Prostitute: The Making of U.S. Antitrafficking in Persons Policy." *Tulane Journal of International and Comparative Law* 14 (2006): 269–93.

Bernstein, Elizabeth. "Militarized Humanitarianism Meets Carceral Feminism: The Politics of Sex, Rights, and Freedom in Contemporary Anti-Trafficking Campaigns." *Signs* 35, no. 1 (2010): 45–71.

———. "The Sexual Politics of the 'New Abolitionism.'" *differences* 18, no. 3 (2007): 128–51.

Bowe, John. *Nobodies: Modern American Slave Labor and the Dark Side of the New Global Economy.* New York: Random House, 2007.

Brennan, Denise. "Competing Claims of Victimhood? Foreign and Domestic Victims of Trafficking in the United States." *Sexuality Research & Social Policy* 5, no. 4 (2008): 45–61.

———. *Life Interrupted: Trafficking into Forced Labor in the United States.* Durham, NC: Duke University Press, 2014.

————. "Methodological Challenges in Research with Trafficked Persons: Tales from the Field." *International Migration* 43, no. 1/2 (2005): 35–54.

————. *What's Love Got to Do with It? Transnational Desires and Sex Tourism in the Dominican Republic.* Durham, NC: Duke University Press, 2004.

Brunovskis, Anette, and Rebecca Surtees. "Untold Stories: Biases and Selection Effects in Research with Victims of Trafficking for Sexual Exploitation." *International Migration* 48, no. 4 (2010): 1–37.

Chacon, Jennifer M. "Misery and Myopia: Understanding the Failures of U.S. Efforts to Stop Human Trafficking." *UC Davis Legal Studies Research Paper Series* 79 (August 2006).

Chapkis, Wendy. "Trafficking, Migration, and the Law: Protecting Innocents, Punishing Immigrants." *Gender & Society* 17, no. 6 (2003): 923–37.

Cheng, Sealing. "Muckraking and Stories Untold: Ethnography Meets Journalism on Trafficked Women and the U.S. Military." *Sexuality Research & Social Policy* 5, no. 4 (2008): 6–18.

————. *On the Move for Love: Migrant Entertainers and the U.S. Military in South Korea.* Philadelphia: University of Pennsylvania Press, 2010.

Christie, Nils. "The Ideal Victim." In *From Crime Policy to Victim Policy: Reorienting the Justice System,* ed. Ezzat A. Fattah, 17–30. London: Macmillan, 1986.

Chuang, Janie. "Redirecting the Debate over Trafficking in Women: Definitions, Paradigms, and Contexts." *Harvard Human Rights Journal* 11 (1998): 65–107.

————. "Rescuing Trafficking from Ideological Capture: Prostitution Reform and Anti-Trafficking Law and Policy." *University of Pennsylvania Law Review* 158 (2010): 1655–728.

————. "The United States as Global Sheriff: Using Unilateral Sanctions to Combat Human Trafficking." *Michigan Journal of International Law* 27, no. 2 (2006): 437–94.

Clawson, Heather. *Estimating Human Trafficking into the United States: Development of a Methodology. Final Phase Two Report.* Fairfax, VA: ICF International, 2007.

Clifford, James, and George E. Marcus, eds. *Writing Culture: The Poetics and Politics of Ethnography: A School of American Research Advanced Seminar.* Berkeley: University of California Press, 1986.

Clinton, William Jefferson. "Executive Memorandum: Steps to Combat Violence Against Women and Trafficking in Women and Girls." 1 Pub. Papers 358 (March 11, 1998).

Coalition of Immokalee Workers. "Anti-Slavery Campaign." Last modified 2012. http://www.ciw-online.org/slavery.html.

Coalition to Abolish Slavery & Trafficking. "Voices for Change." http://www.castla.org/caucus-of-survivors.

Cohen, Stanley. *Folk Devils and Moral Panics: The Creation of the Mods and Rockers.* London: MacGibbon & Kee, 1972.

Combatting Modern Slavery: Reauthorization of Anti-Trafficking Programs Hearing Before the Committee on the Judiciary, 110th Cong. 83 (October 31, 2007).

Commission on Security and Cooperation in Europe. *The Sex Trade: Trafficking of Women and Children in Europe and the United States*. Washington, DC: U.S. Government Printing Office, 1999.

Comprehensive Antitrafficking in Persons Act of 1999, H.R. 3154, 106th Cong. (1999).

Comprehensive Antitrafficking in Persons Act of 1999, S. 1842, 106th Cong. (1999).

Connell, R. W. "The State, Gender, and Sexual Politics: Theory and Appraisal." *Theory and Society* 19, no. 5 (1990): 507–44.

Corrigan, Katrin. "Putting the Brakes on the Global Trafficking of Women for the Sex Trade: An Analysis of Existing Regulatory Schemes to Stop the Flow of Traffic." *Fordham International Law Journal* 25, no. 1 (2001): 151–214.

Davies, John. *'My Name Is Not Natasha': How Albanian Women in France Use Trafficking to Overcome Social Exclusion*. Amsterdam: Amsterdam University Press, 2009.

Demleitner, Nora V. "The Law at the Crossroads: The Construction of Migrant Women Trafficked into Prostitution." In *Global Human Smuggling: Comparative Perspectives*, ed. David Kyle and Rey Koslowski, 257–93. Baltimore, MD: The Johns Hopkins University Press, 2001.

DeStefano, Anthony M. *The War on Human Trafficking: U.S. Policy Assessed*. New Brunswick, NJ: Rutgers University Press, 2007.

Dewey, Susan. *Hollow Bodies: Institutional Responses to Sex Trafficking in Armenia, Bosnia, and India*. Sterling, VA: Kumarian Press, 2008.

Ditmore, Melissa. *Kicking Down the Door: The Use of Raids to Fight Trafficking in Persons*. New York: Sex Workers Project, 2009.

Doezema, Jo. "Loose Women or Lost Women? The Re-Emergence of the Myth of 'White Slavery' in Contemporary Discourses on 'Trafficking in Women.'" *Gender Issues* 18, no. 1 (2000): 23–50.

———. "Who Gets to Choose? Coercion, Consent and the UN Trafficking Protocol." *Gender and Development* 10, no. 1 (2002): 20–27.

Duguay, Christian. "Human Trafficking." 176 min. Montreal: Lifetime TV, 2005.

Engel, David. "How Does Law Matter in the Constitution of Legal Consciousness?" In *How Does Law Matter?* ed. Bryant G. Garth and Austin Sarat, 109–44. Evanston, IL: Northwestern University Press, 1998.

Ewick, Patricia, and Susan S. Silbey. *The Common Place of Law: Stories from Everyday Life*. Chicago: University of Chicago Press, 1998.

———. "Conformity, Contestation, and Resistance: An Account of Legal Consciousness." *New England Law Review* 26 (Spring 1992): 731–49.

Farrell, Amy, Jack McDevitt, and Stephanie Fahy. *Understanding and Improving Law Enforcement Responses to Human Trafficking*. Boston: Northeastern University Institute on Race and Justice, 2008.

Farrell, Amy, Jack McDevitt, Noam Perry, Staphanie Fahy, Kate Chamberlain, William Adams, Colleen Owens, et al. *Review of Existing Estimates of Victims of Human Trafficking in the United States and Recommendations for Improving Research and*

Measurement of Human Trafficking. Washington, DC: The Alliance to End Slavery and Trafficking, 2010.

Farrell, Amy, and Rebecca Pfeffer. "Policing Human Trafficking: Cultural Blinders and Organizational Barriers." *Annals of the American Academy of Political and Social Science* 653 (May 2014): 46–64.

Feingold, David A. "Trafficking in Numbers: The Social Construction of Human Trafficking Data." In *Sex, Drugs, and Body Counts: The Politics of Numbers in Global Crime and Conflict,* ed. Peter Andreas and Kelly M. Greenhill, 46–74. Ithaca, NY: Cornell University Press, 2010.

Fisher, Ian. "17th Arrest Made in Case of Deaf Mexican Peddlers." *New York Times,* August 2, 1997.

Foucault, Michel. *The History of Sexuality: An Introduction.* New York: Vintage Books, 1980.

Freedom from Sexual Trafficking Act of 1999, H.R. 1356, 106th Cong. (1999).

Freedom from Sexual Trafficking Act of 1999, Markup of H.R.1356 by the Subcommittee on International Operations and Human Rights, 106th Cong. (August 4, 1999).

Friedman, Sara Ann. *Who Is There to Help Us? How the System Fails Sexually Exploited Girls in the United States: Examples from Four American Cities.* Brooklyn, NY: ECPAT-USA, 2005.

Gallagher, Anne T. "Improving the Effectiveness of the International Law of Human Trafficking: A Vision for the Future of the U.S. Trafficking in Persons Reports." *Human Rights Review* 12, no. 1 (2010): 381–402.

Geertz, Clifford. *Interpretation of Cultures.* New York: Basic Books, 1973.

Goodey, Jo. "Sex Trafficking in Women from Central and East European Countries: Promoting a 'Victim-Centered' and 'Woman-Centered' Approach to Criminal Justice Intervention." *Feminist Review* 76 (2004): 26–45.

Goździak, Elżbieta M., and Micah N. Bump. *Data and Research on Human Trafficking: Bibliography of Research-Based Literature.* Washington, DC: Institute for the Study of International Migration, Walsh School of Foreign Service, Georgetown University, 2008.

Goździak, Elżbieta M., and Elizabeth A Collet. "Research on Human Trafficking in North America: A Review of Literature." *International Migration* 43, no. 1/2 (2005): 99–127.

Greer, Chris. "News Media, Victims, and Crime." In *Victims, Crime and Society,* ed. Pamela Davies, Peter Francis, and Chris Greer, 20–49. London: Sage, 2008.

Gupta, Akhil, and James Ferguson, eds. *Anthropological Locations: Boundaries and Grounds of a Field Science.* Berkeley: University of California Press, 1997.

Hakim, Danny, and William K. Rashbaum. "Spitzer Is Linked to Prostitution Ring." *New York Times,* March 10, 2008.

Halley, Janet, Prabha Kotiswaran, Hila Shamir, and Chantal Thomas. "From the International to the Local in Feminist Legal Responses to Rape, Prostitution/Sex

Work, and Sex Trafficking: Four Studies in Contemporary Governance Feminism." *Harvard Journal of Law and Gender* 29, no. 2 (2006): 335–423.

Haynes, Dina Francesca. "The Celebritization of Human Trafficking." *Annals of the American Academy of Political and Social Science* 653 (May 2014): 25–45.

———. "Exploitation Nation: The Thin Grey Legal Lines Between Trafficked Persons and Abused Migrant Laborers." *Notre Dame Journal of Law, Ethics and Public Policy* 23, no. 1 (2009). Available at http://scholarship.law.nd.edu/ndjlepp/vol23/iss1/1.

———. "Good Intentions Are Not Enough: Four Recommendations for Implementing the Trafficking Victims Protection Act." *University of St. Thomas Law Journal* 6, no. 1 (2009): 77–95.

———. "Used, Abused, Arrested, and Deported: Extending Immigration Benefits to Protect the Victims of Trafficking and Secure the Prosecution of Traffickers." *Human Rights Quarterly* 26, no. 2 (2004): 221–72.

Herbert, Steve. *Policing Space: Territoriality and the Los Angeles Police Department*. Minneapolis: University of Minnesota Press, 1996.

Hoang, Kimberly Kay, and Rhacel Salazar Parreñas, eds. *Human Trafficking Reconsidered: Rethinking the Problem, Envisioning New Solutions*. New York: IDEBATE Press, 2014.

Hoffman, Elizabeth A. "Legal Consciousness and Dispute Resolution: Different Disputing Behavior at Two Similar Taxicab Companies." *Law & Social Inquiry* 28, no. 3 (2003): 691–716.

Holmes, Seth M. *Fresh Fruit, Broken Bodies: Migrant Farmworkers in the United States*. Berkeley: University of California Press, 2013.

House Concurrent Resolution 82—Relative to a Violation of Fundamental Human Rights, 144 Cong. Rec. H1021 (March 10, 1998).

Hua, Julietta. *Trafficking Women's Human Rights*. Minneapolis: University of Minnesota Press, 2011.

Huckerby, Jane. "United States of America." In *Collateral Damage: The Impact of Anti-Trafficking Measures on Human Rights Around the World*, ed. Global Alliance Against Traffic in Women, 230–53. Bangkok: Global Alliance Against Traffic in Women, 2007.

Hyland, Kelly E. "Protecting Human Victims of Trafficking: An American Framework." *Berkeley Women's Law Journal* 16 (2001): 29–71.

International Trafficking Act of 2000, S. 2449, 106th Cong. (2000).

International Trafficking in Women and Children: Hearing Before the Subcommittee on Near Eastern and South Asian Affairs of the Committee on Foreign Relations, 106th Cong. (February 22 and April 4, 2000).

International Trafficking of Women and Children Victim Protection Act of 1999, H.R. 1238, 106th Cong. (1999).

International Trafficking of Women and Children Victim Protection Act of 1999, S. 600, 106th Cong. (1999).

Jordan, Ann. *The Annotated Guide to the Complete UN Trafficking Protocol*. Washington, DC: Human Rights Law Group, 2002.

———. "Human Rights or Wrongs? The Struggle for a Rights-Based Response to Trafficking in Human Beings." *Gender & Development* 10, no. 1 (2002): 28–37.

Kelly, Liz. "'You Can Find Anything You Want': A Critical Reflection on Research on Trafficking in Persons Within and into Europe." *International Migration* 43, no. 1/2 (2005): 235–65.

Kempadoo, Kamala, Jyoti Sanghera, and Brandana Pattanaik, eds. *Trafficking and Prostitution Reconsidered: New Perspectives on Migration, Sex Work, and Human Rights*. Boulder, CO: Paradigm, 2005.

Kim, Kathleen. "Psychological Coercion in the Context of Modern-Day Involuntary Labor: Revisiting *United States v. Kozminski* and Understanding Human Trafficking." *Toledo Law Review* 38 (2007): 941–72.

Kleinman, Arthur, and Joan Kleinman. "The Appeal of Experience; the Dismay of Images: Cultural Appropriations of Suffering in Our Times." In *Social Suffering*, ed. Arthur Kleinman, Veena Das, and Margaret Lock, 1–24. Berkeley: University of California Press, 1997.

Konigsberg, Eric. "Couple's Downfall Is Culminating in Sentencing in Long Island Slavery Case." *New York Times*, June 23, 2008.

Kristof, Nicholas. "Leaving the Brothel Behind." *New York Times*, January 19, 2005.

Landesman, Peter. "Sex Slaves on Main Street." *New York Times Magazine*, January 25, 2004.

Leidholdt, Dorchen A. "A Call to Action: Joining the Fight Against Trafficking in Persons." Paper presented at the U.S. Embassy to the Holy See, June 17, 2004.

———. "Demand and the Debate." Coaltion Against Trafficking in Women. Last modified October, 2013. http://www.catwlac.org/en/wp-content/uploads/2013/10/Demand_and_the_Debate.pdf.

———. "Prostitution: A Modern Form of Slavery." In *Making the Harm Visible: Global Sexual Exploitation of Women and Girls*, ed. Donna M. Hughes and Claire M. Roche (North Amherst, MA: Coalition Against Trafficking in Women, 1999). Available at http://www.uri.edu/artsci/wms/hughes/mhvslave.htm.

Levy, Leonard W., Kenneth L. Karst, and Adam Winkler. *Encyclopedia of the Amercan Constitution*. New York: Macmillan Reference USA, 2000.

Lipsky, Michael. *Street-Level Bureaucracy: Dilemmas of the Individual in Public Services*. New York: Russell Sage Foundation, 1980.

Locher, Birgit. *Trafficking in Women in the European Union: Norms, Advocacy Networks and Policy Change*. Wiesbaden: VS Verlag für Sozialwissenschaften, 2007.

Luibhéid, Eithne. *Entry Denied: Controlling Sexuality at the Border*. Minneapolis: University of Minnesota Press, 2002.

Mahdavi, Pardis. *Gridlock: Labor, Migration, and Human Trafficking in Dubai*. Palo Alto, CA: Stanford University Press, 2011.

Marcus, George. *Ethnography Through Thick and Thin*. Princeton, NJ: Princeton University Press, 1988.

Marshall, Anna-Maria, and Scott Barclay. "In Their Own Words: How Ordinary People Construct the Legal World." *Law & Social Inquiry* 28, no. 3 (2003): 617–28.

Marzulli, John. "4-Foot-10 Mexican 'Mini Madam' Facing Slave Trial." *New York Daily News*, July 20, 2008.

Maynard-Moody, Stepen, and Michael Musheno. "State Agent or Citizen Agent: Two Narratives of Discretion." *Journal of Public Administration Research and Theory* 10, no. 2 (2000): 329–58.

Merry, Sally Engle. *Getting Justice and Getting Even: Legal Consciousness Among Working-Class Americans*. Chicago: Univeristy of Chicago Press, 1990.

Miller, Ali, and Alison N. Stewart. "Report from the Roundtable on the Meaning of 'Trafficking in Persons': A Human Rights Perspective." *Women's Rights Law Reporter* 20, no. 1 (1998): 11–19.

Miller, Alice M. "Sexuality, Violence Against Women, and Human Rights: Women Make Demands and Ladies Get Protection." *Health and Human Rights* 7, no. 2 (2004): 16–47.

Mountz, Alison. *Seeking Asylum: Human Smuggling and Bureaucracy at the Border*. Minneapolis: University of Minnesota Press, 2010.

Murphy, Laura T. *Survivors of Slavery: Modern-Day Slave Narratives*. New York: Columbia University Press, 2014.

Musto, Jennifer Lynne. "The NGO-Ification of the Anti-Trafficking Movement in the United States: A Case Study of the Coalition to Abolish Slavery and Trafficking." *Wagadu* 5 (2008): 6–20.

Nader, Laura. "The Anthropological Study of Law." *American Anthropologist* 67, no. 6 (1965): 3–32.

———. "Up the Anthropologist: Perspectives Gained from Studying Up." In *Reinventing Anthropology*, ed. Dell H. Hymes, 284–311. New York: Pantheon Books, 1972.

Nathan, Debbie. "Oversexed: Anti-Trafficking Efforts Place Undue Emphasis on Commercial Sex Work and Downplay Other Forms of Forced Labor." *The Nation*, April 29, 2005.

Neuworth, Jessica, Gloria Feldt, Adrienne Germain, Patricia Ireland, Mim Kelber, Frances Kissling, Laura Lederer, et al. "Letter to Senator Wellstone Regarding International Trafficking of Women and Children Victim Protection Act of 1999 (S.600)." Trafficking Policy Research Project. http://www.bayswan.org/traffick/antiwellstone.html.

O'Connell Davidson, Julia. *Children in the Global Sex Trade*. Cambridge: Polity, 2005.

O'Neill Richard, Amy. "International Trafficking in Women to the United States: A Contemporary Manifestation of Slavery and Organized Crime." Washington, DC: Center for the Study of Intelligence, 1999.

Parreñas, Rhacel Salazar. *Illicit Flirtations: Labor, Migration, and Sex Trafficking in Tokyo*. Palo Alto, CA: Stanford University Press, 2011.

Peters, Alicia. "Broadening the Lens on Human Trafficking." *Huffington Post*, August 2, 2012. http://www.huffingtonpost.com/american-anthropological-association /broadening-the-lens-on-hu_b_1728820.html.

———. "Challenging the Sex/Labor Trafficking Dichotomy with Victim Experience." In *Human Trafficking Reconsidered: Rethinking the Problem, Envisioning New Solutions*, ed. Kimberly Kay Hoang and Rhacel Salazar Parreñas, 30–40. New York: IDEBATE Press, 2014.

———. " 'Things That Involve Sex Are Just Different': U.S. Anti-Trafficking Law and Policy on the Books, in Their Minds, and in Action." *Anthropological Quarterly* 86, no. 1 (2013): 223–57.

Pheterson, Gail, ed. *A Vindication of the Rights of Whores*. Seattle: Seal Press, 1989.

Pound, Roscoe. "Law in Books and Law in Action." *American Law Review* 44 (1910): 12–25.

Protocol to Prevent, Suppress, and Punish Trafficking in Persons, Especially Women and Children, Supplementing the United Nations Convention Against Transnational Organized Crime. November 15, 2000, 2237 U.N.T.S. 319.

Rapp, R. *Testing Women, Testing the Fetus: The Social Impact of Amniocentesis in America*. New York: Routledge, 1999.

Raymond, Janice G. *Guide to the New UN Trafficking Protocol*. North Amherst, MA: Coalition Against Trafficking in Women, 2001.

———. "Prostitution as Violence Against Women: NGO Stonewalling in Beijing and Elsewhere." *Women's Studies International Forum* 21, no. 1 (1998): 1–9.

Rubin, Gayle S. "Thinking Sex: Notes for a Radical Theory of the Politics of Sexuality." In *Pleasure and Danger: Exploring Female Sexuality*, ed. Carole Susan Vance, 267–319. New York: Routledge & Kegan Paul, 1984.

Sanghera, Jyoti. "Unpacking the Trafficking Discourse." In *Trafficking and Prostitution Reconsidered: New Perspectives on Migration, Sex Work, and Human Rights*, ed. Kamala Kempadoo, Jyoti Sanghera, and Bandana Pattanaik, 3–24. Boulder, CO: Paradigm, 2005.

Sarat, Austin. "Legal Effectiveness and Social Studies of Law: On the Unfortunate Persistence of a Research Tradition." *Legal Studies Forum* 9, no. 1 (1985): 23–32.

Sarat, Austin, and Thomas R. Kearns, eds. *Law in Everyday Life*. Ann Arbor: University of Michigan Press, 1995.

Saunders, Penelope. "Traffic Violations: Determining the Meaning of Violence in Sexual Trafficking Versus Sex Work." *Journal of Interpersonal Violence* 20, no. 3 (2005): 343–60.

Scheper-Hughes, Nancy. "Ire in Ireland." *Ethnography* 1, no. 1 (2000): 117–40.

Schneider, Anne, and Helen Ingram. "Social Construction of Target Populations: Implications for Politics and Policy." *American Political Science Review* 87, no. 2 (1993): 334–47.

Schuck, Peter. "Law and the Study of Migration." In *Migration Theory: Talking Across Disciplines*, ed. Caroline Brettell and James Hollifield, 239–58. New York: Routledge, 2000.

———. "Rethinking Informed Consent." *Yale Law Journal* 103 (1994): 899–959.

Semple, Kirk. "Housekeeper in New Jersey Accuses Peruvian Diplomat of Human Trafficking." *New York Times,* June 25, 2013.

Senate Concurrent Resolution 82—Relative to a Violation of Fundamental Human Rights. 144 Cong. Rec. S1702 (March 10, 1998).

Shah, Svati P. *Street Corner Secrets: Sex, Work, and Migration in the City of Mumbai.* Durham, NC: Duke University Press, 2014.

Shamir, Hila. "A Labor Paradigm for Human Trafficking." *UCLA Law Review* 60, no. 1 (2012): 76–136.

Shapiro, Nina. "The New Abolitionists." *Seattle Weekly,* August 25, 2004.

Shore, Chris, and Susan Wright. *Anthropology of Policy: Critical Perspectives on Governance and Power.* New York: Routledge, 1997.

Shore, Chris, Susan Wright, and Davide Però, eds. *Policy Worlds: Anthropology and the Analysis of Contemporary Power.* New York: Berghahn Books, 2011.

Skinner, E. Benjamin. *A Crime So Monstrous: Face-to-Face with Modern-Day Slavery.* New York: Free Press, 2008.

Snajdr, Edward. "Beneath the Master Narrative: Human Trafficking, Myths of Sexual Slavery, and Ethnographic Realities." *Dialectical Anthropology* 37, no. 2 (2013): 229–56.

Soderlund, Gretchen. "Running from the Rescuers: New U.S. Crusades Against Sex Trafficking and the Rhetoric of Abolition." *NWSA Journal* 17, no. 3 (2005): 64–87.

"Sonia Ossorio, NOW-NYC, March 1, 2007." YouTube video, posted by NOWNewYork-City. http://www.youtube.com/watch?v=Y3Lxf_rXHjU.

Sontag, Deborah. "Poor and Deaf from Mexico Betrayed in Their Dreams." *New York Times,* July 25, 1997.

Sperber, Dan. *Explaining Culture: A Naturalistic Approach.* Oxford: Blackwell, 1996.

Srikantiah, Jayashri. "Perfect Victims and Real Survivors: The Iconic Victim in Domestic Human Trafficking Law." *Boston University Law Review* 87, no. 157 (2007): 157–86.

Stolz, Barbara. "Educating Policymakers and Setting the Criminal Justice Policymaking Agenda: Interest Groups and the Victims of Trafficking and Violence Act of 2000." *Criminal Justice* 5, no. 4 (2005): 407–30.

———. "Interpreting the U.S. Human Trafficking Debate Through the Lens of Symbolic Politics." *Law & Policy* 29, no. 3 (2007): 311–38.

Terry, Jennifer, and Jacqueline L. Urla, eds. *Deviant Bodies: Critical Perspectives on Difference in Science and Popular Culture.* Bloomington: Indiana University Press, 1995.

"Trafficking in Persons National Security Presidential Directive." News release, February 25, 2003. Washington, DC: Office of the Press Secretary.

*Trafficking of Women and Children in the International Sex Trade: Hearing Before the Subcommittee on International Operations and Human Rights,*106th Cong. (September 14, 1999).

Trafficking Victims Protection Act of 1999, H.R. 3244, 106th Cong. (1999).

Trafficking Victims Protection Act of 2000, S. 2414, 106th Cong. (2000).

Trafficking Victims Protection Reauthorization Act of 2003, Pub. L. No. 108-193 (2003).

Trafficking Victims Protection Reauthorization Act of 2005, Pub. L. No. 109-164 (2005).

Tzvetkova, Marina. "NGOs Response to Trafficking in Women." *Gender and Development* 10, no. 1 (2002): 60–68.

United Nations Educational, Scientific, and Cultural Organization. "UNESCO Trafficking Statistics Project." Last modified February 2011. http://www.unescobkk.org /index.php?id=1022.

United States v. Kozminski, 487 U.S. 931 (1988).

U.S. Department of Homeland Security, Immigration and Customs Enforcement. "ICE Mounts Outdoor Ad Campaign to Raise Awareness About Human Trafficking." News release, July 9, 2008. https://www.ice.gov/news/releases/0807/080709sandiego .htm.

U.S. Department of Justice. *Attorney General's Annual Report to Congress and Assessment of U.S. Government Activities to Combat Trafficking in Persons: Fiscal Year 2009.* Washington, DC: U.S. Government Printing Office, 2010.

———. *Attorney General's Annual Report to Congress and Assessment of U.S. Government Activities to Combat Trafficking in Persons: Fiscal Year 2011.* Washington, DC: U.S. Government Printing Office, 2012.

———. "Case Updates." *Anti-Trafficking News Bulletin* 3, no. 3 (2007): 7–9.

———. *Report on Activities to Combat Human Trafficking: Fiscal Years 2001–2005.* Washington, DC: U.S. Government Printing Office, 2006.

———. "Ten Thai Nationals Indicted on New Charges of Slavery and Kidnapping." News release, November 9, 1995. http://www.usdoj.gov/opa/pr/Pre_96/November95 /577.txt.html.

———. "Wisconsin Couple Sentenced for Forcing a Woman to Work as Their Domestic Servant for 19 Years." News release, June 9, 2009.

U.S. Department of State. "The Link Between Prostitution and Sex Trafficking." News release, November 24, 2004.

———. *Trafficking in Persons Report.* Washington, DC: U.S. Government Printing Office, 2003.

———. *Trafficking in Persons Report.* Washington, DC: U.S. Government Printing Office, 2004.

———. *Trafficking in Persons Report.* Washington, DC: U.S. Government Printing Office, 2005.

———. *Trafficking in Persons Report.* Washington, DC: U.S. Government Printing Office, 2006.

———. *Trafficking in Persons Report.* Washington, DC: U.S. Government Printing Office, 2007.

———. *Trafficking in Persons Report.* Washington, DC: U.S. Government Printing Office, 2008.

———. *Trafficking in Persons Report.* Washington, DC: U.S. Government Printing Office, 2009.

———. *Trafficking in Persons Report.* Washington, DC: U.S. Government Printing Office, 2010.

———. *Trafficking in Persons Report.* Washington, DC: U.S. Government Printing Office, 2011.

———. *Trafficking in Persons Report.* Washington, DC: U.S. Government Printing Office, 2012.

———.*Trafficking in Persons Report.* Washington, DC: U.S. Government Printing Office, 2013.

———. *Trafficking in Persons Report.* Washington, DC: U.S. Government Printing Office, 2014.

U.S. Government Accountability Office. *Human Trafficking: Better Data, Strategy, and Reporting Needed to Enhance U.S. Antitrafficking Efforts Abroad.* Washington, DC: Government Accountability Office, 2006.

Valentine, David. *Imagining Transgender: An Ethnography of a Category.* Durham, NC: Duke University Press, 2007.

Valverde, Mariana. *Law's Dream of a Common Knowledge.* Princeton, NJ: Princeton University Press, 2003.

Vance, Carole. "Innocence and Experience: Melodramatic Narratives of Sex Trafficking and Their Consequences for Law and Policy." *History of the Present* 2, no. 2 (2012): 200–218.

———. "Negotiating Sex and Gender in the Attorney General's Commission on Pornography." In *Uncertain Terms: Negotiating Gender in American Culture*, ed. Faye Ginsburg and Anna Lowenhaupt Tsing, 118–51. Boston: Beacon Press, 1990.

———. "States of Contradiction: Twelve Ways to Do Nothing About Trafficking While Pretending To." *Social Research* 78, no. 3 (2011): 933–48.

———. "Thinking Trafficking, Thinking Sex." *GLQ: A Journal of Lesbian and Gay Studies* 17, no. 1 (2010): 135–43.

Victims of Trafficking and Violence Protection Act of 2000, Pub. L. No. 106-386, 22 U.S.C. 7101 et seq. (2000).

Walklate, Sandra. *Imagining the Victim of Crime.* Maidenhead, UK: Open University Press/McGraw-Hill, 2007.

Warren, Kay. "The 2000 UN Protocol: Rights, Enforcement, Vulnerabilities." In *The Practice of Human Rights: Tracking Law Between the Global and the Local*, ed. Mark Goodale and Sally Engle Merry, 242–69. Cambridge: Cambridge University Press, 2007.

———. "The Illusiveness of Counting 'Victims.'" In *Sex, Drugs, and Body Counts: The Politics of Numbers in Global Crime and Conflict*, ed. Peter Andreas and Kelly M. Greenhill, 110–26. Ithaca, NY: Cornell University Press, 2010.

Weeks, Jeffrey. *Sex, Politics, and Society: The Regulation of Sexuality Since 1800.* New York: Longman, 1981.

Weitzer, Ronald. "Flawed Theory and Method in Studies of Prostitution." *Violence Against Women* 11, no. 7 (2005): 934–40.

——. "New Directions in Research on Human Trafficking." *Annals of the American Academy of Political and Social Science* 653 (May 2014): 6–24.

——. "The Social Construction of Sex Trafficking: Ideology and Institutionalization of a Moral Crusade." *Politics and Society* 35 (2007): 447–75.

White Slave Traffic Act of 1910, 36 Stat. 825, 18 U.S.C. §§ 2421–2424 (1910).

William Wilberforce Trafficking Victims Protection Reauthorization Act of 2007, H.R. 3887, 110th Cong. (2007).

William Wilberforce Trafficking Victims Protection Reauthorization Act of 2008, Pub. L. No. 110-457, 122 Stat. 5044 (2008).

Yanow, Dvora. *How Does a Policy Mean? Interpreting Policy and Organizational Actions.* Washington, DC: Georgetown University Press, 1997.

Zhang, Sheldon. "Beyond the 'Natasha' Story: A Review and Critique of Current Research on Sex Trafficking." *Global Crime* 10, no. 3 (2009): 178–95.

Zimmerman, Cathy. *The Health Risks and Consequences of Trafficking in Women and Adolescents: Findings from a European Study.* London: London School of Hygiene & Tropical Medicine, 2003.

——. *WHO Ethical and Safety Recommendations for Interviewing Trafficked Women.* Geneva: World Health Organization, 2003.

Index

abolitionists and abolitionism, 50–51, 54–56, 60–65, 94–121, 143–44, 195–97, 201–2

advocacy and advocates, 1, 4, 14–15, 17, 30, 49–54, 76, 87; antiprostitution, 44, 50, 62, 87, 95–119, 195–96, 201; antitrafficking, 14, 24–30, 33–36, 75, 86–87, 98–101, 116–17, 151–54, 160, 191–204

agency, personal, 37, 45, 51, 53, 109, 112, 144

Agustín, Laura, 86

anthropology, 7–9, 26–27

antiprostitution: advocates, 44, 50, 62, 87, 95–119, 195–96, 201; and Bush administration, 115–19, 160; and Clinton administration, 45, 51–53, 57–58, 62–64

antitrafficking apparatus, 18–35

antitrafficking community, 27–30, 33

Assistant United States Attorney (AUSA), 19, 175–76

attorneys, immigration, 18–19, 29, 36; Audra, 1, 11, 78, 86, 123, 143–44, 151, 160, 172, 176, 182–83, 188–89; Ella, 103–4, 111–12, 122, 125–26, 144, 159, 162, 170, 178, 186–87, 196, 202; Jarrah, 77, 103–6, 118–19, 123, 164–65, 170–73, 175–76, 184, 186, 187, 201; Radha, 156–58, 164, 178, 182, 184; Roxanne, 78–79, 104–5, 160, 169; Vanessa, 19

benefits for survivors: access to, 3, 5–6, 9, 18–19, 23, 32–33, 37–38, 58, 132, 154, 166–76; endorsement by law enforcement, 5, 167, 171–72, 174–78, 181–86, 193

Bennett, William, 52–53

Berman, Jacqueline, 52–53

Brennan, Denise, 8, 112, 203, 219 n.5

brothels, 83, 93, 102, 107–8, 110–11, 113, 115, 158, 162–64

Brownback, Sam, 46–47

Bump, Micah, 13

Bureau of Justice Assistance (BJA), 21, 23

Bureau of Population, Refugees, and Migration (PRM), 21

bureaucracy, 20, 23–24, 26, 29, 147

Bush, George W., administration, 33, 115–19, 160

Cadena case (United States v. Cadena), 58

Canada, 8, 24

Carreto case (United States v. Carreto), 146, 188, 191–93

case management, 18, 24, 26, 29–32, 34, 76, 84, 145, 197

case managers, 22–23, 29–32, 34, 130, 132, 135, 141, 155, 192; Laura, 18–19; Maribel, 168, 196; Nancy, 76, 126, 158, 165–66, 179, 188; Nora, 88–89, 120–24, 127, 147, 153, 160, 163, 173–74, 178, 182–83, 186, 191, 193; Sadie, 131, 176, 178; Tess, 192–93

certification as a victim of a severe form of trafficking, 19, 26, 136, 157, 196; and continued presence, 180–82; obstacles, 166–78, 180–82, 186; pre-certification, 18, 22, 173, 174; statistics, 17

Chacon, Jennifer, 87

Child Exploitation and Obscenity Section (CEOS), 21, 23, 214 n.58

children of survivors held as collateral, 192

Christie, Nils, 14

Chuang, Janie, 36, 55

Clinton, Bill, administration, 45–46, 51–53, 57–59, 62–65
Clinton, Hillary, 62
Coalition Against Trafficking in Women, 53
Coalition to Abolish Slavery and Trafficking (CAST), 200
coercion, 48–49, 53–54, 109–12, 125, 143, 157, 167, 178, 192, 203–4; psychological, 2, 46, 58–59, 77, 134, 138. *See also* force, fraud, and coercion
Cohen, Stanley, 15
Colson, Chuck, 47, 52–53
Comprehensive Antitrafficking in Persons Act (1999), 47
conflation of prostitution and trafficking, 100–105
consent, 48, 50–55, 220 n.21
continued presence (CP), *22*, 68, 76, 167, 171–75, 177–83, 185–86, 193; T visa comparison, *168*, 223 nn. 10–11
crime: "new," 50; organized, 45; trafficking as, 55–64, 67–70, 73–79, 87; victims, 14–15, 31, 83, 85, 168, 187. *See also* trafficking survivors
criminal justice response, 156–82, 191–95
criminalization, 2, 55, 61, 66–68, 102, 195
cultural beliefs and values, 3, 5–6, 12–15, 36, 39, 91, 115, 124, 193–94, 197, 199, 203
cultural text, 9–12, 27, 36, 70

Department of Homeland Security (DHS), 19, *22*, 200
Department of Justice (DOJ), *21*, 23, 47, 58, 146, 156, 161, 176; Human Trafficking Prosecution Unit (HTPU), 19, *21*, 34, 113, 158–59, 214 n.58; Office for Victims of Crime (OVC), 18, *22*, 23–24
Department of Labor (DOL), *22*
Department of State (DOS), *21*, 35, 118, 152
deportation, 46, 85, 140, 169–70, 174, 187–89, 201
deserving and undeserving victims, 14, 194
discretion, 37, 79–82, 118, 120, 159, 183, 189; use of the term, 219 n.3
diversity of trafficking survivors, 37, 92, 125–26, 142–43
Doezema, Jo, 54
domestic minor sex trafficking, *21–22*, 196–97

domestic violence, 45, 187
domestic work, trafficking for, 48–49, 65, 92, 95, 97–99, 121–29, 142–43, 157–63

Employment Authorization Document (EAD), 19, 179
Empower (pseudonymous NGO), 18–19, 29–32, 34, 128–30, 132, 135, 139, 141, 173, 214 n.57
English as a Second Language (ESL) education, 19, 155
Equality Now, 64
ethnography, 8–9, 211 n.21; ethnographic fieldwork, 2–4, 24–27; limits of, 34–36; as instrument of institutional change, 38, 191, 197–204
evangelicals, 10, 52, 54, 60, 62, 106–7, 116, 202
Ewick, Patricia, 11, 69
exploitation, continuum of, 86–89

fear, climate of, 59, 77–78, 95, 123, 163, 187
Federal Bureau of Investigation (FBI), *22*, 23, 82, 139, 153, 158, 169, 175, 181
federal prosecutors, 23, 29, 34, 113, 139, 158–59; Dean, 67–68, 74–75, 115, 152, 156–58, 166, 182–83; Katherine, 73–74, 152–53; Katrina, 146, 158; Kyle, 77, 84–85, 107–8, 144, 157–58; Lynn, 66, 80–81, 84, 87–88, 110, 113–14, 157, 159, 161–62, 180–81, 186, 218 n.67; Mark, 56–57, 60, 65, 69–70, 106–7; Molly, 79, 81, 85, 90, 92–94, 99, 146, 153, 155, 188, 199
Feingold, David, 16
Feldt, Gloria, 53
Feminist Majority, 53
feminists, 8, 10, 45; antipornography, 100–101, 119; antiprostitution, 50–56, 60, 62, 64, 100–103, 106, 111, 113, 117, 119, 143, 195, 201–2
Flores case (*United States v. Flores*), 57–58
force, fraud, and coercion, 10, 43, 47, 50–54, 63–67, 76–79, 100–107, 113–15, 195–96, 198, 204
Forman, Marcy, 171
Foucault, Michel, 91
Fourth World Conference on Women, 45
Freedom from Sexual Trafficking Act (1999), 47–48
Freedom Network Conference, 202

Geertz, Clifford, 25
Gejdenson, Sam, 47–48, 60, 62
gender: gender-neutral definition of
    trafficking, 10, 47, 65, 70; "gender regime,"
    10–11; gendered lens focused on commer-
    cial sex, 7, 98; normative conceptions of,
    3, 7–8, 13
General Equivalency Diploma (GED), 104, 155
Gomez, Sebastian, 57. See also Flores case
Good Samaritans, 140, 159, 223 n.4
Goodey, Jo, 144
Goździak, Elżbieta, 13

harm, 14, 48–49, 77–78, 81, 90–91, 98–99, 111,
    157, 198–99, 221 n.37; psychological, 120;
    sexual, 3, 90, 96
health issues, 24, 174, 179; mental, 18, 24, 120,
    124, 155
Homeland Security. See Department of
    Homeland Security
Horowitz, Michael, 47
human rights, 36, 45, 60–61, 111, 126, 156;
    practitioners/advocates, 10, 50–52, 91, 99
Human Rights Caucus, 51
Human Rights Watch (HRW), 50
Human Trafficking Prosecution Unit
    (HTPU), 19, 21, 34, 113, 158–59, 214 n.58

immigrants and immigration, 1–2, 24, 29,
    38–39, 57–58, 127, 169, 182, 190; immigra-
    tion policy, 87, 166–78; immigration relief,
    58, 68, 84–85, 156, 166–67, 171, 183, 187.
    See also attorneys, immigration
Immigration and Customs Enforcement
    (ICE), 18–19, 22, 23, 82–83, 134, 153, 171,
    173, 175, 178, 181, 188–90, 192; "Hidden in
    Plain Sight" campaign, 189, 189
implementation and implementers of the
    TVPA: collaboration between implement-
    ers, 57, 152–53, 191, 193–94; consequences
    for survivors, 180–90, 193–200; stratified
    response, 6; struggles between imple-
    menters, 156–78, 185–90, 199; uneven, 37,
    44, 194; varying roles of implementers,
    152–56
Ingram, Helen, 117
innocence, 14
International Convention for the Suppres-
    sion of the White Slave Traffic (1910), 55
International Justice Mission (IJM), 50

International Trafficking of Women and
    Children Victim Protection Act (1999),
    46–47
interpretation of the TVPA, 7, 10, 20, 78–82,
    99, 152, 159–60, 195
interviewees: Angela (former federal policy
    advisor), 43, 46, 69, 78; Annette (policy
    advisor on victim services), 164; Audra
    (immigration attorney), 1, 11, 78, 86, 123,
    143–44, 151, 160, 172, 176, 182–83, 188–89;
    Bridget (director of a trafficking services
    program), 82, 119–21, 124–25, 145, 147,
    164–66, 172, 179–80, 183–84; Camille
    (trafficking survivor, southern Africa),
    129–31, 138, 142, 176, 178–79, 200;
    Charlotte (director of a trafficking
    services program), 92, 95–99, 118, 145, 154,
    188, 201; Dale (federal law enforcement
    administrator), 168, 196; Dean (federal
    prosecutor), 67–68, 74–75, 115, 152,
    156–58, 166, 182–83; Ella (immigration
    attorney), 103–4, 111–12, 122, 125–26, 144,
    159, 162, 170, 178, 186–87, 196, 202; Gwen
    (federal victim witness coordinator), 76,
    125, 165, 172, 177; Jarrah (immigration
    attorney), 77, 103–6, 118–19, 123, 164–65,
    170–73, 175–76, 184, 186, 187, 201; Jim
    (federal law enforcement agent, head of a
    human trafficking unit), 2, 6, 11, 84–85,
    92, 98–99, 158, 166, 172, 185, 188;
    Katherine (federal prosecutor), 73–74, 152;
    Katrina (federal prosecutor), 146, 158;
    Kira (federal victim witness coordinator),
    123–24; Kyle (federal prosecutor), 77,
    84–85, 107–8, 144, 157–58; Larry (local law
    enforcement agent), 107, 121, 154–55,
    162–63; Leila (federal victim witness
    coordinator), 156; Lynn (federal
    prosecutor), 66, 80–81, 84, 87–88, 110,
    113–14, 157, 159, 161–62, 180–81, 186,
    218 n.67; Maribel (case manager), 168, 196;
    Mark (federal prosecutor), 56–57, 60, 65,
    69–70, 106–7; Max (congressional staffer),
    64–67, 77, 156; Megan (former congres-
    sional staffer), 60, 62; Molly (federal
    prosecutor), 79, 81, 85, 90, 92–94, 99, 146,
    153, 155, 188, 199; Nancy (case manager),
    76, 126, 158, 165–66, 179, 188; Nora (case
    manager), 88–89, 120–24, 127, 147, 153,
    160, 163, 173–74, 178, 182–83, 186, 191, 193;

interviewees (*Continued*)
Paul (federal policy advisor), 57–59, 61–62;
Pete (federal criminal justice administrator), 161, 182; Radha (immigration attorney), 156–58, 164, 178, 182, 184; Roxanne (former immigration attorney), 78–79, 104–5, 160, 169; Sadie (case manager), 131, 176, 178; Sara (grant monitor for a federal funding program), 76–77; Sheila (director of a trafficking services program), 92, 94–95, 99, 108–9, 118, 145, 161, 169, 173, 187–89, 196; Tess (case manager), 192–93; Victor (congressional staffer), 1, 60, 202; Victoria (trafficking survivor, South America), 133–36, 138, 142–43, 200; Will (federal law enforcement agent), 89, 120, 163, 182, 185
investigation, 19–20, *22*, 23–26, 81–84, 88, 118–21, 153–67, 170–84, 199, 201, 203
Ireland, Patricia, 53
isolation, 97, 124–25, 128–30, 134, 138, 192, 200

Kelly, Liz, 4
Kleinman, Arthur, 14
Kleinman, Joan, 14
Koh, Harold, 51
Kozminski case (*United States v. Kozminski*), 59–60

labor trafficking, 11, 53, 66–67, 90–92, 94–99, 104–5, 113, 116–17, 121–25, 159–63; forced labor, 38–39, 56–68, 86–88, 90–100, 120–23, 158–63, 193–94; non-sex trafficking, 10, 37, 68, 82, 195, 199; use of the term, 10, 102, 195, 212 n.29
law: in action, 7, 9–11, 36, 153–56, 176, 185, 194; on the books, 7, 9–10, 36, 44, 70, 74, 151, 185, 194; in their minds, 7, 9–10, 36, 151, 185, 194
law enforcement: agents, 1–2, 36–37, 75–76, 119–22, 141, 151–55, 159–62, 175–80, 199; discretion, 37, 79–82, 118, 120, 159, 183, 189, 219 n.3; fear/mistrust of, 24, 134–35, 139, 142, 163–70, 174; hesitancy to pursue cases, 5; raids by, 18, 84, 93, 107, 113, 115, 162–65, 188–89; rescue, 14, 125, 134, 165, 197; training, 4, *22*, 29, 100, 122, 152–53, 155–56, 161, 79, 187–88, 201–3
legal consciousness, 9–10
Leidholdt, Dorchen, 53

Lize, Steven, 223 n.4
Luibhéid, Eithne, 13

Mann Act (White-Slave Traffic Act), 55, 57, 60, 106–7, 221 n.33
Marcus, George, 7, 27
Maynard-Moody, Steven, 118, 151
McKinney, Cynthia, 48
media, 27–28, 45, 73; focus on trafficking into forced commercial sex, 6, 12–13, 96, 99–101, 104, 110; portrayals of trafficking, 212 n.33; repercussions of, 13–15; sensationalism, 6, 13, 26, 91, 120, 122, 144
mental health, 18, 24, 120, 124, 155
methodology of book, 26–36
migrant rights, 29, 86, 198
migrant workers, 26, 87, 99–100
migration, 17, 45, 50, 54, 59, 61, 86–87, 112. *See also* immigrants and immigration
Miller, Alice, 91
Miller, John, 116
modern day slavery, 1, 46, 77, 190
moral crusades, 91, 117, 119
moral panic, 15, 91, 120
Mountz, Alison, 8, 24
Musheno, Michael, 118, 151
Mussry case (*United States v. Mussry*), 59–60
mythology of trafficking, 8, 13, 54, 203

Nader, Laura, 26
narratives of trafficking, 129–47
National Organization for Women (NOW), 103
Neuwirth, Jessica, 53
New York City, 1–3, 19, 26–30, 33–35, 97, 101–2, 113, 155, 159, 161–62, 172, 191–92
non-sex trafficking. *See* labor trafficking
nongovernmental organizations (NGOs), 3–5, *23*, 23–38, 57, 61, 76, 82–88, 153–61, 164–65, 191, 193, 199, 201

Obama, Barack, administration of, 159, 220 n.20
Office for Victims of Crime (OVC), 18, *22*, 23–24
Office of Refugee Resettlement (ORR), 19, *22*
Office to Monitor and Combat Trafficking in Persons (G/TIP), *21*, 116
Ossorio, Sonia, 103

Paoletti case (*United States v. Adriana Paoletti-Lemus*), 1–3, 6, 38–39, 58, 191
participant observation, 4, 26–27, 29–30, 32
Planned Parenthood Federation of America, 53
President's Interagency Task Force to Monitor and Combat Trafficking in Persons (PITF), *21*
President's Interagency Council on Women (PICW), 45, 62
prevention of trafficking, 17–18, 35, 45–46, 64–66, 116, 198
prosecution, 18–19, *21–22*, 32, 35–39, 44, 57–70, 156–57, 165–77; focus on, 18; and Three Ps framework, 25, 45; worthy cases, 11, 156–85. *See also* federal prosecutors
prostitution and commercial sex, 90–99, 196–97; role in defining trafficking, 47, 100–126, 221 n.33; youth, 220 n.8. *See also* antiprostitution
protection, 5–7, 8–11, 25, 37–39, 45–48, 166, 169, 173, *174*, 174–83, 198–99
psychological coercion, 2, 46, 58–59, 77, 134, 138

Rapp, Rayna, 211 n.21
rescue industry, 86
rescue model/framework, 13–14, 52, 99, 108, 120, 125, 145, 179, 197
research on trafficking (methodology), 4–12, 25–35
resiliency of trafficking survivors, 124, 144–45
Rubin, Gayle, 15, 54

Sabhnani case (*United States v. Sabhnani*), 92, 162–63
Sanghera, Jyoti, 13
Schneider, Anne, 117
Schuck, Peter, 9–10, 221 n.36
Senior Policy Operating Group (SPOG), *21*
sensationalism, 26, 122
sex and sexuality, anxieties about, 12, 15, 54, 70, 95
sex trafficking: disproportionate focus on, 33, 94–95, 157–65, 193–200; privileging of, 5, 10–11, 13, 37, 62, 115–26, 143, 159, 200–202; use of the term, 209 n.4
sex work, 2, 8, 11, 29, 33, 48, 51–52, 93, 100, 103, 121–24, 132, 180, 194–98; spectrum of, 105–15. *See also* prostitution

sexual abuse, 45, 49, 78, 95, 123–24, 140, 145, 212 n.29
sexual harm, 3, 14, 90, 96
sexual slavery, 2–3
Shore, Chris, 9, 27, 117
Silbey, Susan, 11, 69
slavery, 12, 38, 46, 48, 51, 54–67, 77, 106, 124–25, 129, 142–43, 190
Smeal, Eleanor, 53
Smith, Chris, 46–49, 60, 64–67
Smith-Gejdenson bill. *See* Trafficking Victims Protection Act (TVPA)
Social Security, 19, 132, 155, 179
social service providers, 114, 118, 121, 156, 183, 202, 204. *See also* nongovernmental organizations (NGOs)
Special Immigrant Juvenile Status (SIJS), 187
spectrum of exploitation, 17, 86–89; and sex work, 105–15
Steinem, Gloria, 53, 202
Stolz, Barbara, 50
strength of survivors, 141, 144–45
subjectivity, 5, 80–82, *83*, 85, 93, 124–25, 144, 151, 160, 181, 194, 219 n.3
survivors: diversity of, 37, 92, 125–26, 142–43; experiences/narratives of, 129–47, 222 n.1; missing out on protections, 7, 186, resilience of, 124, 144–45; strength of, 141, 144–45. *See also* trafficking survivors
symbolic frameworks of sex, gender, and victimization, 6, 82, 86–87, 99, 108, 152

T visa, 19, *22*, 76, 136, 139, 142, 144, 147, 157, 167, *168*, 169–78, 180–88, 193, 200–201, 222 n.3
Terry, Jennifer, 14
Thirteenth Amendment, 55, 60
"Three P's" framework, 25, 45
trafficking: as a category, 17; conditions of, 107, 128, 193; debates, 4–5; definitions of, 44–60; discourses on, 4, 6, 8–9, 14–15, 117–18; estimates, 15–17, 185; and force, fraud, and coercion, 10, 43, 47, 50–54, 63–67, 76–79, 100–107, 113–15, 195–96, 198, 204; for forced commercial sex, 2–3, 5–9, 11, 13, 24; for forced labor, 38–39, 56–68, 86–88, 90–100, 120–23, 158–63, 193–94; meanings of, 3, 9, 11–12, 24–27, 35, 37, 56, 128; of men, 7, 11, 33, 45–46, 49, 58–59, 98, 117, 194, 203; operational and nonoperational

trafficking (*Continued*)
definitions, 62–65, 70, 74–76, 99, 101–2, 110, 114, 143; perceptions of, 6, 200; what counts as, 81, 84, 193; use of the term, 6, 11
Trafficking in Persons Report (TIP Report), 16, *21*, 35
trafficking survivors: Camille (southern Africa), 129–31, 138, 142, 176, 178–79, 200; interviewing process, 30–33; Malcolm (southern Africa), 147; Miriam (Mexico), 18–20; Nadia (former Soviet republic), 136–39, 142, 145, 169, 200; Rocio (Mexico), 170; Silvia (Mexico), 131–33, 142, 200; Simone (South America), 139–43, 200; Victoria (South America), 133–36, 138, 142–43, 200
Trafficking Victims Protection Act (TVPA): bifurcation of definitions, 44, 62, 65, 68, 70, 74, 92, 94–95, 120–21, 127, 174, 198–99; complexity of, 8–11, 19–21, 24–27, 44, 70, 74–79, 89, 92, 203; and compromise, 61–70; criminal statutes, 57, 62–64, 66–68, 76, 82, 122, 154, 199; drafting of, 5, 7, 9–10, 12–13, 36, 43–46, 49–50, 55–66, 69–70, 173, 195, 198–99; history of, 2; incorporation of cultural beliefs, 9–12; interpretation of, 7, 10, 20, 78–82, 99, 152, 159–60, 195; symbolism in, 5, 8, 11, 63, 68, 73, 101, 159, 194, 198–99. *See also* implementation and implementers of the TVPA
Trafficking Victims Protection Reauthorization Act (TVPRA), 209 n.2
trauma, 81, 85, 93, 97, 123–25, 131, 135, 141, 145, 152, 167–68, 170
trust, 24–25, 28, 31, 85, 133, 137, 139–40, 169, 179, 219 n.5

U visa, 187, 222 n.3
United Nations: Convention for the Suppression of the Traffic in Persons and of the Exploitation of the Prostitution of Others (1949 Convention), 54–55; Protocol to Prevent, Suppress, and Punish Trafficking in Persons, Especially Women and Children, 49–52, 55, 212 n.28
Unzueta, Miguel, 190
Urla, Jacqueline, 14
undocumented migrants, 2, 17, 24, 46, 58–59, 86–87, 113–14, 127, 155, 169–71, 173, 176, 188–90

United States Congress, *21*, 46, 48–49, 55, 58, 60, 181, 193, 202
United States Citizenship and Immigration Services (USCIS), *22*, 186, 223 n.9; Vermont Service Center, 19, 186–87, 201

Valentine, David, 11
Valverde, Mariana, 90
Vance, Carole, 91
Vermont Service Center, 19, 186
victim definition vs. criminal definitions, 11, 67–68, *69*, 73, 76, 156, 164, 193, 198–99
victim of a severe form of trafficking (VSFT), 76, 82–84, 87, 122, 154, 158, 177, 185, 188
victim services, 37
victimhood, 8, 85, 98
victimization, 3–5, 13–15, 36, 45, 52, 70, 82, 91, 99, 124–25, 133, 144, 188, 197
victims: categories of, 14; definitions, 67–68, *69*, 73, 76, 156, 164, 193, 199; ideal, 14; stereotypes, 9, 14, 197
violence, 3, 57, 59, 75, 99, 157, 187; domestic, 18, 45, 187; sexual, 52, 143, 187; against women, 24, 102–3, 110–11
Violence Against Women Act (VAWA) self-petition, 187
vulnerability, 2–3, 14, 17, 28, 31, 39, 85–86, 92, 103, 144, 169, 197, 203

waiting by trafficking survivors for benefits, 136, *168*, 172–73, 176, 179–80, 183–84
Walklate, Sandra, 14
Washington, D.C., 2, 4, 18–19, 23, 29, 34–35, 83, 113
Weeks, Jeffrey, 45
Weitzer, Ronald, 117
Wellstone, Paul, 46–48, 51, 53, 60
White-Slave Traffic Act (Mann Act), 55, 57, 60, 106–7, 221 n.33
white slavery, 12, 54–55, 91, 143
William Wilberforce Reauthorization Act, 67
witnesses, trafficking survivors as, 139, 146, 154–55, 160, 169, 179, 182, 192
women. *See* gender; violence, against women
Wright, Susan, 9, 27, 117

Yanow, Dvora, 24, 43, 73

Acknowledgments

I am immensely grateful to all of the service providers, law enforcement agents, prosecutors, congressional staffers, survivors, and others who shared their experiences, time, and expertise with me. Although confidentiality prevents me from naming the organizations and individuals I observed and interviewed, my most sincere gratitude goes out to them for their openness and honesty. In particular, I wish to acknowledge the members of Empower, whose offices I called home for more than a year, for their generosity and accommodation. I owe extra-special thanks to the survivors who shared their stories with me in the hope of broadening knowledge on the subject. I cannot thank them enough for their honesty and openness.

I owe utmost thanks to Carole Vance, who has been my sponsor, mentor, advocate, and friend over the past fifteen years. Carole has provided thoughtful and critical feedback since the inception of the project, and I am forever grateful for the time and consideration she has devoted to it (as well as for her companionship on many culinary adventures!). I am also indebted to Lesley Sharp, Elizabeth Bernstein, and Sealing Cheng for their valuable commentary, as well as to Alice Miller, whose legal expertise on the inter-workings of the antitrafficking world was critical to the development and execution of this project. I owe thanks to Pardis Mahdavi, Ernesto Vasquez, Brian Johnson, and Beth Filiano for their encouragement, camaraderie, and feedback as this project evolved. Thank you also to Kim Hopper, Peter Messeri, Connie Nathanson, Rebecca Young, and Rosalie Acinapura.

During the initial stages of this project, Ann Jordan, Martina Vandenberg, and Janie Chuang were incredibly generous in sharing their expertise on the drafting and implementation process in D.C. They made invaluable suggestions regarding the key players involved as well as on how to broach the subject of research with an otherwise skeptical group of individuals. I am also grateful to Nina Siulc and Anjie Rosga for their insights on fieldwork with law enforcement.

At the University of New England, my colleagues in the Department of Society, Culture, and Languages—Sam McReynolds, Alex Campbell, Ayala Cnaan, Steven Byrd, and Camille Vande Berg—have provided a warm and supportive community in which to work. Alex Campbell, Ayala Cnaan, Jenny Denbow, Ali Ahmeida, Brian Duff, and Beth

DeWolfe have also provided thoughtful and detailed suggestions at various stages of this project. I am grateful to the members of the SEEDS writing group and the entire affiliated faculty in the Program in Women's and Gender Studies for creating spaces to share my work. Julie Peterson, Jennifer Stiegler-Balfour, Amanda Hare, Rob Alegre, Julia Garrett, and Jennifer Tuttle have provided support and camaraderie in many forms.

It has been a pleasure working with Peter Agree at the University of Pennsylvania Press. I am appreciative for his enduring encouragement since our first encounter at the American Anthropological Association Meetings in New Orleans in 2010 and his thoughtful guidance throughout the publication process. Erica Ginsburg has been a most patient and supportive guide through the production process. Thank you to Amanda Ruffner for her assistance with preproduction preparations. I am also grateful to the two anonymous reviewers, one of whom I came to know as Rhacel Parreñas following the review stage, for their astute comments, which pushed me in new directions and have shaped this book for the better. Thank you also to Katie Van Heest for her sharp and skillful editing.

I am grateful for the generous financial assistance of the Training Program in Gender, Sexuality, and Health at Columbia's Mailman School of Public Health; the Institute for Social and Economic Research and Policy; the Wenner-Gren Foundation for Anthropological Research (grant #7572); the National Science Foundation (award #SES-0617259); and the National Institute of Justice (award #2006-IJ-CX-0003). Thank you to my grant monitors at NIJ for the large time commitments they made to a relatively small research grant: Jennifer Hanley, Cornelia Sorensen Sigworth, and Karen Bachar. The opinions, findings, conclusions, and recommendations expressed in this publication are those of the author and do not necessarily reflect the views of the Department of Justice or any other funding agency. I am also grateful to John Picarelli at NIJ and Kreg Purcell at the National Criminal Justice Research Service for their assistance in moving this publication forward. A different version of Chapter 3 appeared in *Anthropological Quarterly* as "'Things That Involve Sex Are Just Different': U.S. Antitrafficking Law and Policy on the Books, in Their Minds, and in Action" (86, no. 1 [2013]: 223-57).

My family has been more invested in this project than I ever could have hoped. I am grateful to my parents, Jim and Janet Peters, and my brother, Geoff Peters, for their love and support, and a special thank you to my father for reading and editing an early draft of the manuscript. My grandmother, Mamie Wood, has been inquiring gently about the status of this book since its earliest inception. Thanks for continuing to care! Thank you to the entire Cacciola family for their enthusiastic cheerleading. Holly Danzeisen, Dawn Mechanic-Hamilton, Emily Krell, Meredith Gunlicks-Stoessel, and Rachel Wadsworth have provided more than twenty years of friendship and are part of my extended family. My deepest gratitude of all goes to my partner, Tara Cacciola, for her constant encouragement, good humor, good cooking, and endless understanding. Over the course of writing this book, we welcomed our daughter, Kleio, whose spirited and inquisitive nature fills me with joy.